BIRTHS, DEATHS AND SPONSORS
1717-1778

FR

ALBEMARLE

SURRY AND SUSSEX COUNTIES,
VIRGINIA

By

John Bennett Boddie

CLEARFIELD

Originally published
1958

Reprinted for
Clearfield Company, Inc. by
Genealogical Publishing Co., Inc.
Baltimore, Maryland
1992, 1998

Library of Congress Catalogue Card Number 64-22294
International Standard Book Number: 0-8063-0024-8

Made in the United States of America

BIRTHS AND DEATHS 1717-1778
FROM
THE ALBEMARLE PARISH REGISTER
OF
SURRY AND SUSSEX COUNTIES, VIRGINIA

Albemarle Parish was created by an Act of the General Assembly
in 1738. (5 Hening, 75-76.) The Act provided that the parishes of
Southwark and Lawne's Creek shall be divided by the Blackwater
River; and those parts situated on the north side of said River are
to be called the Parish of Southwark and those on the south side of
the River are to be called Albemarle.

The earliest entries in the parish register were made in 1738, but
many families upon entering the birth of a child in 1738 or there-
after also registered the birth dates of children born prior to 1738.

The Register was kept by the Reverend William Willie, who began
his services in the parish at least as early as 1739 as entries in
his handwriting began in that year. He died April 3, 1776, and left
a will dated May 18, 1773, which was probated May 15, 1777. (Sus-
sex W.B. C-pp. 242-244.) He was succeeded by the Reverend William Andrews.

A few entries seemed to have been made by the Reverend Mr. Andrews. The last entry in the register is that of the death of William
Avery, "July, 1778".

This register is important and unique in that it is the only existing
complete register in that section of Virginia south of the James
River extending from Brunswick to Princess Anne.

The entries were kept under alphabetical system according to the
first letter of the GIVEN name and not the family name. Thus the
first name in the records of births was "Amy, daughter of Robert
and Mary Hicks, born March 7th; 1742." These abstracts of births
and deaths have been in my possession for nearly twenty-five
years. The order has been changed alphabetically from GIVEN
names to FAMILY names.

The names of all sponsors at christenings are shown. These names
are very important as Grandparents, Uncles, Aunts and Cousins
were usually Godparents. This aid may be of assistance in other
research.

ADKINS

Richard and Hannah Adkins
Lewis, 2/9/41; John Adkins, Lewis Adkins, Lucy Main.
Pattie, 4/21/43; Thos. Cotton, Mary Adkins, Lucy Peters.
Thos, 11/11/44; John Dunn, Richard Scroggin, Lucy Dunn.
Thos Adkins, a child, died 10/1/45

Lewis and Eliz. Adkins
Thomas, 10/30/43, Thos. Adkins, Thos. Cotton, Mary Bailey.
Lewis, 8/22/45; Nath'l. Felts, Nath'l. Felts Jr., Sarah Woodland.
Mary, 2/22/48; Richard Felts, Jane Seat, Frances Williams.
William, 8/17/54; Robert Seat, John Felts, Eliz. Felts.

John and Mary Adkins
John, 1/17/38; John Painter, Anne Hight.
Joyce, 1/5/40; John Wilkerson, Lucretia Mannery.
William, 1/7/43; Richard Adkins, John Adkins Jr., Mary Adkins.
Mary, 12/10/45; Francis Niblet, Eliz. Partridge, Mary Adkins.
Eliz. Adkins, the wife of John Adkins, died, 9/5/67, reported by John Meacum.

John and Eliz. Adkins
Amey, 5/1/48; Nic'h. Partridge Jr., Eliz. Partridge, Amy Dunn.
Mary, 1/23/49; Richard Tomlinson, Mary Tomlinson, Eliz.Adkins.
Eliz., 9/22/51; Thos. Adkins, Sarah Barker, Mary Weaver.
Thomas, 1/25/53; Thos. Adkins, Wells Partridge, Susanna Moore.
John, 4/17/56; Henry Moss, Clement Hancock, Sarah Hobbs.
Howell, 2/18/59; Nath'l. Duncan, John Moss, Frances Moss.
Nicholis, 9/6/61; Henry Weaver, Henry Porch Jr., Mary Weaver.
William, 10/18/63; Boyce Parker, Jas. Tomlinson, Amy Adkins.
Willis, 1/18/66; Henry Moss, Jr., Eph. Moss, Mary Adkins.

Amos and Jane Adkins
Margaret, 3/1/53; James Bell, Fanny Judkins, Jane Parham.

Thomas and Lucy Adkins
Martha, 6/4/62; Wm. Willie, Susanna Harrisson, Mary Hancock.
John, 2/14/64, John and Wm. Harrison, Betty Harrison.

John and Lucy Adkins
John, 6/18/63, Wm. Hewett, Edw. Slate, Sarah Slate.

Thomas Adkins Jr. and Mary
Rebecca, 12/8/60, John Underhill, Mary Tomlinson, Mildred Davidson.
Jesse, 8/6/56; Thos. Stafford, Henry Underhill, Joyce Adkins.
Sarah, 1/7/59; John Mason Jr., Mary Jenkins, Lucy Adkins.
Mary, 9/25/63; Thos. Moss, Mary Chappell, Salley Jones.
Salley, 3/16/66; Isam Underhill, Sarah Jones, Sarah Cotton.
Thomas, 4/25/68; James Jones, Giles Underhill, Joyce Adkins.
Nancy, 6/21/70; Wm. Thompson, Sarah Underhill, Katy Hobbs.
John, 3/21/75; Richard Cook, Abraham Jones, Salley Underhill.

ADKINS (Continued)

Thomas Adkins died, 3/17/65, reported by Wells Partridge.
Grace Adkins died, 7/8/60; reported by John Adkins.
Thomas Adkins died, 4/11/51; reported by John Adkins, Jr.

ALDRIDGE
William and Anne Aldridge.
John, 2/2/53; Thos. Ezell Jr., Nath'l. Bedingfield, Mary Adkins.
John, 12/12/57;   "
NOTE: the first must have died.

Francis and Henrette Aldridge
Elijah, 6/9/55; Edwd. Prince, Joseph Ivy, Betty Prince.
Deliah, baptized, 4/27/60 - no sponsors.

Thomas Alsobrook died Jan. ------? 1773 - reported by Cap't.
Howell Briggs.

AMBROSE
Thomas and Amy Ambrose
Salley, 10/5/68; Thos. Young, Eliz. and Amy Shands
John, 12/18/72; Donald McIntosh, Reaps Mitchell, Amy Gee.

ANDERSON
James and Mary Anderson
Martha, 10/29/50; Drury Stokes, Phoebe Bell, Jane Judkins.
Katie, 3/25/53; Danial Knight, Angelica Cain, Mary Kellerman.

Charles and Sarah Anderson
Thomas, 7/18/62; Wm. Parsons, John Crossland, Mary Epps.
Frances, 6/24/64; Nath'l. Bedingfield, Eliz. and Mary Wynne.
Clairbourne, 11/5/66; Joseph Stacy, Edwd. Weaver Jr., Patty
Garland.

George and Mary Anderson
George, 9/15/64; John Barker Jr., John Petway, Amy Sledge.
Gray, 9/16'69; Thos. Parham, Edwd. Petway Jr., Anne Parham.

William and Jane Anderson
Susanna, 4/12/69; Thos. Young, Eliz. Mitchell, Eliz. Shands.

James Anderson, (Southwalk) died, 11/20/51, reported by Thos.
Bedingfield.
George Anderson, a child, died 7/6/69 - reported by Geo. Anderson.
George Anderson died 9/27/75; (consumption) - reported by John
Petway.
William Anderson died 12/3/73 - reported by Wm. Dunn Jr.

ANDREWS

William and Anne Andrews

John, 9/30/39; John Andrews Jr., Fred Bryan, Sarah Andrews
Bryan, 12/17/41, Fred Bryan, Hannah Andrews, Eliz. Simmons
Henry, 5/15/70; Henry Andrews, Dryry McGee, Lucy Andrews
Lewis, 2/6/69 - no sponsors given
Sally, 12/25/71; John Land Jr., Anne McGee, Anne Gilliam.
Steven, 4/9/72, Richard Andrews, Ben'g. Ellis, Susanna Andrews.
Jesse, 8/16/73, Rob't. Land Jr., Wm. Willie, Lucy McLamore

John and Sarah Andrews

Frederick, 8/18/40; Frederick Bryan, Wm. Carroll, Eliz. Bryan
Steven, 2/26/42, David Hunter, Thos. Andrews, Sarah Andrews
Elizabeth, 3/27/44; Jonathan Ellis, Mary Proctor, Eliz. Richardson
Sarah, 4/30/47; Wm. Bell, Mary Andrews, Mary Proctor
Mary, 8/15/49, Richard Andrews, Mary Richardson, Eliz. Pepper.
Richard, 4/5/56; Jonathan Ellis, Rob't. Andrews, Hannah Ellis.

Richard Andrews Jr. and Mary

Mary, 10/19/46, John Andrews, Sarah Andrews, Mary Richardson
Anne, 10/3/48, Arthur Smith, Sarah Carlisle, Eliz. Bane
Rebecca, 7/6/52; Thos. Tomlinson, Sarah Judkins, Mildred Hill

Wm. and Mary Andrews

William, 8/25/40, Jas. Sanensick, John Tamerlaine, Mary Rodgers

William Andrews died Jan. ------? 1769, reported by Col. Massenburg.

Steven and Mary Andrews

Joseph, 8/8/68, Joseph Ellis, Fred Andrews, Janet Rodgers
Ellis, 12/1/69, John Nicholson, Henry Underhill, Eliz. Nicholson
William, 10/1/71, John Summerville, Wm. Lamb, Sarah Summerville
Sarah, 10/7/74, Wm. Irby, Mildred Gray, Lucy Pride.

Frederick and Lydia Andrews

Elizabeth, 1/1/63, Steven Andrews, Eliz. Andrews, Eliz. Ellis
Fanny, 7/9/64, John Nicholson, Sarah Andrews, Lucy Proctor
John, 9/17/65, Richard Partridge, Wm. Ellis, Mary Andrews
Johannah, 2/16/67, Thos. Richardson, Sarah Andrews, Sarah Ogburn.
Drury, 10/10/68, Wm. Bird, Henry Underhill, Mary Tomlinson

William and Elizabeth Andrews

Wm. Conner, 5/7/77, Henry John Burgess, Hugh Belches, Patsy Belches

Henry and Lucy Andrews

Elizabeth, 10/19/54, John Clanton, Amy Clanton, Anne Andrews
Ben'g., 12/23/66, Ben'g. Wyche, Richard Rose, Anne Andrews
Robert, 6/1/68, Nath'l. Holt, Gray Dunn, Patty Clanton
George, 2/19/70, Wm. Andrews, Wm. Rose, Anne Andrews

ANDREWS (Continued)

Hannah Andrews died, 10/14/43, reported by Thos. Andrews.

ARMSTRONG
Joseph and Elizabeth Armstrong
Mary, 1/25/47, Robert Bulloch, Sarah and Elizabeth Harwood

Robert and Molly Armstrong
Patty, 8/14/60, Geo. Hogwood, Aggy Newsom, Sally Freeman
John, 1/19/62, Henry Gee, Thos. Holt, Anne Holt
Betsy, 1/15/70, Wm. Longbottom, Polly and Milly Newsom

ARRINGTON
Ben'g. and Hannah Arrington
John, 1/15/61, Thos. Holt, Jesse Newsom, Amy Moss
Ben'g., 11/25/69, Cornelius Mabrey, John Fort, Sarah Rawlings

ATKINSON
Winefred and William Atkinson
Ester, 3/13/40, Wm. Tatum, Hannah Felts, Eliz. Rose
Winefred, 7/13/42, Thos. Weathers, Sophia Stokes, Mary Dickens.

Thomas and Elizabeth Atkinson
Eliz., 2/4/40, Wm. Woodland, Lucy Atkinson, Eliz. Rose
Absolum, 1/8/44, John Bell, Thos. Weathers, Hannah Bell
Joel, 12/27/43, Alex. Dickens, Joseph Prince, Amy Dickens
Mary, 1/27/46, Edwd. Powell, Mary Powell, Frances Atkinson
Patty, 9/10/54, Jas. Bell, Amy Freeman, Tabitha Rolland.
Lydia, 5/13/57, Peter Rives, Mary Rachael, Rebecca Prince

Eliz. Atkinson died 1/16/40, reported by Thos. Atkinson.
Frances Atkinson died 10/23/40, reported by Thos. Atkinson.
Wm. Atkinson reported the death of Mary Burton 1/23/43.

Eliz. Creed and ------------?
John, 3/29/48, Richard King, Abra. Brown, Frances Atkinson

Wm. and Lettice Atkinson
Salley, 3/27/61, Thos. Atkinson, Sarah Slate, Betty Atkinson

Wm. and Martha Atkinson
Dolly. 10/5/64, Richard Harewell, Lucy Vaughn, Lucy Butler

John and Anne Atkinson
Frederick, 2/1/61, John Weathers, Eliz. Atkinson

Thos. and Anne Atkinson
Betsy, 6/22/68, Isam Whitehead, Wynefred Atkinson, Eliz. Spane

ATKINSON (Continued)
John and Lucy Atkinson
Selah, 7/8/49, Richard Northcross, Francis Atkinson, Tabitha
   Northcross
Amos, Edwd. Powell, John Eaton, Hannah North
Arthur, 11/14/57, Wm. Oliver, Wm. Atkinson, Sarah Slate.
Henry, 2/1/61, Ben'g. Adams, Wm. Hill, Winefred Atkinson

ATHERTON
Chas. and Anne Atherton
Charles, 11/14/47, Morris and Henry Prichard, Lucy Prithard

Geo. and Mary Atherton
Mary, 8/8/67, Arthur Turner, Eliz. Rives, Sarah Wallace

AVERY
Cap't. Richard Avery and Sarah
Sarah, 12/13/40, Chas. Judkins, Sarah Judkins, Eliz. Shelton
Martha, 3/13/43, Drury Parker, Lucy Judkins, Eliz. Rolland
Cyrill, 8/17/45, Thos. Bridges, John Rachael, Martha Bridges
Judieth, 2/22/47, James Jones, Phlis Northington, Sarah Avery

John and Anne Avery (she was dead in 1767)
Richard Avery Jr. died 10/29/59, reported by Richard Avery
Wm. Avery died 7/-/78, reported by Cyrill Avery

Sarah Avery, the wife of Richard Avery, died Nov. ----/66, she
   was the mother of Elizabeth Harrison and Sarah Cargill
Wm. Avery died July 1778, reported by Cyrill Avery

Judieth Avery, b. 2/22/47, dgh. of Cap't. Richard Avery, married
Thos. Driver 12/1/70, he died 2/2/71.

AVENT
John and Mary Avent
Eliz., 3/13/39, Thos. Avent, Mary Avent, Hannah Underwood
Peter, 2/4/49, Sam'l. Peete, Chas. Judkins, Mary Coleman

Peter and Amy Avent
Eliz., 10/12/52, John Avent, Margarett Avent, Eliz. Shelton

John and Margarett Avent
Thomas, 1/12/43, Thos. Avent, Mathew Hubbard, Mary Avent
John, 3/16/45, Thos. and Mathew Hubbard, Mary Avent
William, 4/15/48, Beadles Underwood, Wm. Thompson, Eliz. Lee
James, 11/19/52, Peter Avent, Edwd. Shelton, Amy Avent

AVENT (Continued)

Thomas and Rebecca Avent

Jonnie, 3/19/68, Moses McKenny, Avery Wilkerson, Eliz. Woodland

Eliz., 12/30/69, John Avent, Eliz. Massie, Jemimma Jones.

William, 4/5/72, David Mason, Peter Avent, Margarett Solomon, Laurana Jones

Col. Thos. Avent died 10/3/57, reported by Wm. Avent

BACKHURST

James and Eliz. Backhurst

Thomas, 6/29/67, Her'b. and Aghus't. Clairborne, Anne and Susanna Clairborne

BAILEY

Peter and Lucy Bailey

Miles, 12/8/45; Benj. Hill, Lucy Oliver, Mary Grizzard

Mary, 12/8/45, Terrance Myham, Wm. Hix, Martha Roberts

Mary Bailey died 1/2/40, reported by Wm. Evans.

John and Lucy Bayley

Pamelia, 8/5/52, Jas. Hern, Mary Hern, Jane Land

Thos. and Lucy Bailey

Mary Anne, 4/23/50, Jas. Carter, Tabitha Ezell, Eliz. Stokes

Philip and Mary Bailey

John, 3/5/32, No sponsors given

Richard, 3/2/34, No sponsors given

Lucy, 5/8/39, No sponsors given

Amy, 6/19/41, Alex. Dickens, Lydia Dickens, Mary Shelton

William and Dianah Bayley

Sarah, 9/18/51, Sam'l. Tatum, Mary Cotton, Jane Bane

Humphrey and Anne Bayles (Bailey?)

Mary, 7/20/52, John Lamb, Mary Lamb, Eliz. Clary

BAIRD

Wm. and Mary Baird

Partridge, 12/27/72, Jesse and Wm. Partridge, Eliz. Partridge

Rubin and Mary Baird

Ben'g., 3/24/56, Richard Partridge, Wm. Tomlinson, Mary Baird

Barbara, 2/14/62, Richard Jones Jr., Mason Baird

Steven and Lucy Baird

Hamlin, 11/16/68, Wm. Baird, Fred Andrews, Eliz. Geary

BAIRD (Continued)

Steven and Lucy Baird (Continued)

Mary, 4/9/70, Richard Ogburn, Martha Massengale, Rebecca Cotton

Martha, 4/20/72, Fred Hines, Mary Baird, Eliz. Barker

John Rookings, 8/29/75, Thos. Moss, Thos. Adkins, Eliz. Partridge.

BANE

James Bane Jr. and -----------?

Littleberry, 6/13/75, John and Jesse Bane, Lucy Blaton

John and Sarah Bane

Howell, 3/3/36, no sponsors given

Eliz., 11/24/35, no sponsors given

James and Eliz. Bane

Eliz., 10/30/45, John Rollins, Mary and Rebecca Barlow

Jesse, 3/25/47, Thos. Bane, John Smith, Jr., Martha Smith

James, 9/9/48, Ben'g. Smith, Wm. Pynes, Eliz. Sawry

John, 1/1/52, Richard Andrews, John Mangrove, Susanna Bane

Mely, 11/1/53, John Burgess, Mary Sawry, Sarah Smith

BANKS

James and Martha Banks

Susanna, 1/7/39, Chas. Gilliam, Catherine Mitchell, James Mathews

James Banks died 3/3/58, Martha Banks died 3/20/58, reported by Amos Love. They were husband and wife.

Susanna Banks died 3/27/58, reported by Cap't. Gibbons.

William and Sarah Banks

Charles, 11/1/51, Ben'g. Adams, Jesse Rowland, Hannah Seat

James, 3/26/54, John Atkinson, Burwell Banks

Burwell and Mary Banks

James, 1/16/63, Timothy Ezell, Wm. Gilbert, Sarah Tomlinson, Sarah Mason

Martha, 3/2/68, Wm. Parham, Dorothy Hunt, Martha Harewell

BARHAM

Thomas and Sarah Barham

Patty, 1/4/63, Chas. Knight, Eliz. Knight, Anne Wrenn

Lucy, 5/2/68, Nath'l. Newsom, Lucy Fort, Eliz. Adams

Ben'g. and Sarah Barham

John, 2/13/71, Fred Fort, Wm. Knight, Mary Hix, Jr.

BARHAM (Continued)
Charles and Mary Barham
Eliz., 1/23/63, Ben'g. Adams, Rebbecca Longbottom, Frances
   Adams
Rebbecca, 4/16/64, Chas. Knight, Sarah Knight, Amy Harwood
Charlotte, 6/14/68, Sam'l. Harwood, Alice and Mildred Newsom
Mary Harwood, 1/19/71, Dan'l. Harwood, Rebbecca Moore, Eliz.
   Richardson
Damial, 12/2/73, Thos. Barham, Nath'l. Newsom, Mary Hix

Thomas and Betty Barham
Polly, 10/29/74, Wm. Moss, Anne Harwood, Lucy Battle

BARKER
John and Mary Barker
Jehu, 12/11/39, Richard Partridge, Eliz. Partridge, Sarah Barker
Mary, 1/12/46, Richard Partridge, John Tomlinson, Sr., Mary
   Partridge

Joel and Sarah Barker
Sally, 3/10/41, Drury Parker, Judieth and Phylis Edmunds

Ben'g. and Mary Barker
Katherine, 1/26/45, John Irby, Kath. Barker, Jane Barker
Wm., 10/22/47, Wm. Cook, Wm. Brown, Frances Chamberlis
Nathanial, 3/21/66, Donald McInnish, Thos. Johnson, Eliz. Wil-
   kerson
Nathan, 1/13/49, Chas. Barker, John Baird, Eliz. Cook
Aniass, 4/20/71, John Underhill, Nathan Barker, Frances Barker

Ben'g. Barker Jr. died 1/30/72, reported by John Adkins.
Katherine Hobbs died 1/30/72, reported by John Adkins.

Henry and Catherine Barker
Mary, 9/12/39, Robert Long, Mary Figures, Martha Long.
Anne, 2/11/33, no sponsors given
Henry Barker died 3/21/59, reported by Henry Barker.
William Barker died 10/13/40, reported by Henry Barker.

Thomas and Mary Barker
Jesse, 3/13/44, John Warburton, John Smith, Anne Warburton
William, 11/10/47, Joel Barker, Thos. Bane, Lucy Briggs.
James Barker died 2/10/72, reported by John Bane

James Barker Jr. and Johannah
Jesse, 3/14/58, no sponsors given
James, 6/11/60, no sponsors given
Eliz., 7/17/62, no sponsors given
Anne, 7/18/71, Robert Winfield, Mildred Wynne, Martha Rainy
Nathanial, 5/11/69 Wm. Harrisson, Joel Davis, Sarah Sheffield

Joshua and Lucy Barker
Eliz., 9/15/73, Jesse Partridge, Prissilla Wallace, Cherry Jarrett

BARKER (Continued)
Henry and Eliz. Barker
Susanna, 4/30/62, no sponsors given
Eliz., 10/5/64, no sponsors given
John Henry, 12/26/66, no sponsors given
Charles, 2/15/69, no sponsors given
Jerimiah, 12/27/71, John Gilbert, Richard Cook, Lucy Gilbert
Katherine, 3/17/74, Frederick Andrews, Lucy Johnson, Johannah
    Hight

John Barker Jr. and Lucy
Nich., 5/28/65, Nich. Partridge, Mary Jarrett, Selah Wallace
Mary, 11/23/67, Nich Jarrett, Jesse Wallace, Sarah Barker

John and Eliz. Barker
Susanna, 2/12/45, Williard Roberts, Sarah Carlisle, Mourning
    Thomas
Rebbecca, 6/24/47, Ben'g. Barker, Mary and Amy Gilliam

Nathanial and Sarah Barker
Lucy, 12/10/55, Jas. Barker, Anne Barker, Anne Stacey
Rebecca, 2/23/57, Henry Barker, Jr., Mary Cook, Mary Parker

Jehu Barker and Lucy
Sarah, 11/9/69, Petway Johnson, Sarah Jones, Eliz. Jarrett

Grace Barker died Nov. 3rd 1749, reported by Richard Barker

BARLOW
Wm. and Mary Barlow
Mildred, 12/2/41, Richard Barlow, Mary Avent, Margaret Avent

Richard and Eliz. Barlow
Mary, 9/20/52, Math. Hubbard, Anne Barlow, Mary Hubbard

Samuel and Alice Barlow
Mely, 4/26/52, Wyatt Harper, Eliz. Kelly, Mary Parker

BARNES
Abra. and Eliz. Barns
Amy, 6/19/41, Josh. Rolland, Hannah Bell, Eliz. Rolland

James and Eliz. Barns
Myrick, 3/5/64, Wm. Myrick, Owen Myrick, Anna Myrick
Martha, 7/10/67, Chas. Judkins, Jr., Mrs. Myrick, ---------.
John, 4/29/69, David Mason, Wm. Richardson, Mary Fort.
Eliz. Barnes, the wife of James died Apr. 1770, reported by Jas. Barnes

BARR
Walter and Anne Barr
Gabrial, 10/14/55, Wm. Stewart, Richard Knight, Mary Stewart.

BARR (Continued)

Gabrial and Anne Barr

James, 7/17/74, James and Timothy Ezell, Anne Archwell
William, 1/3/76, Wm. Diggs, Eph. King, Anne Barr

BARROW

Edmund and Mary Barrow

Eliz., 6/13/52, Thos. Cooper, Eliz. and Lucy Warren

BASS

Waller and Anne Bass

Margarett, 2/21/52, John Painter, -------? Moore, Mary Nunn

James and Eliz. Bass

Eliz., 9/30/45, John Rollings, Mary and Rebecca Barlow

John and Mary Bass

Lydia, 5/20/40, Beagles Underwood, Unity Bass, Anne Pate

BATTLE

John and Sarah Battle

Hartwell, 6/5/50, Susanna Newsom, Samuel Long Cotton, Mary
Capel
John, 7/25/53, James Carter, Wm. Horn, Jane Seat
Nanny, 12/27/54, Thos. Capel, Anne Evans, Eliz. Felts
William, 1/2/57, Wm. Richardson, James Carter Jr., Sucky Jud-
kins.
Angelica, 2/15/59, Thos. Battle, Mary Battle, Angelica Ezell

John and Mary Battle

Amy, 6/1/40, Simon Gale, Mary Sammons, Mary Battle

Thomas and Mary Battle

Frederick, 11/1/44, Burwell Gilliam, John King, Eliz. Mabrey
Phoebe, 7/8/46, Richard Knight, Martha Bridges, Rebbecca Mabrey
Lucy, 7/2/48, Wm. Richardson, Mary Stokes, Agnes Battle

John Battle Jr. and Anne

Hollsman, 11/8/72, Isaac Rawlings, Hartwell Battle, Mary Battle
Mary Battle died of cancer 9/18/54, reported by John Battle

BATTS

Bartholomew and Tabitha Batts

Drury, 1/1/63, Wm. Felts, Petway Johnson, Mary Johnson
Johannah, 9/22/65, Henry Cradle, Lucy Cradle, Sarah Arnold
Frankey, 2/19/67, John Creadle, Sarah Presson, Lucy Gilbert

BAUGH

John and Margaret Baugh

Richard, 1/18/50, John Eaton.James Northcross, Hannah Northcross

BEDINGFIELD
                    Nath'l. and Eliz. Bedingfield
Isabel, 9/12/47, Agu's. Clairbourne, Sarah Jones, Eliz. Willie
Eliz., 12/22/50, Isaac Mason, Eliz. Dobie, Mary Edwards
Henry, 10/25/52, Rob't. Glover, Nath'l. Tomlinson, Elenor Dobie
Wm., 7/29/55, John Mason, John Bradley, Frances Rives
Sarah, 2/10/60, Geo. Rives, Eliz. Dunn, Frances Rives, Jr.
John, 9/2/62, Epps Moore, Thos. Young Jr., Eliz. Weeks
Nath'l. Bedingfield died 3/1/67, "A good kind neighbor."
Henry Bedingfield died 5/4/47, reported by Nath'l. Bedingfield.

BELCHES
                    Hugh and Martha Belches
Sarah, 11/4/70, Cryill Avery, Lucy Cargil, Mary Belches
Robert, 7/2/73, Wm. Petway, Wm. Willie, Jacobina Willie
Eliz. Story, 9/4/74, Wm. Willie, Eliz. Willie, Judieth Burgess
Margarett, 5/11/79, no sponsors.
Nancy Avery, 10/1/81, Henry Harrison
Wm. Belches, a child, died 3/7/70.

BELL

                    William and Faith Bell
Lucy, 7/18/48, Robert Carrell, Sarah Carlisle, Sarah Andrews
Lettice, 9/6/50, Wm. Brown, Mary Hyde, Mildred Belamy
Richard, 4/24/54, Wm. Carlisle, Wm. Smith, Mary Proctor
Cherry, 6/15/60, Geo. Clarke, Eliz. Bradley

                    Baalam and Mary Bell
Phoebe, 11/8/55, Abraham Brown, Lucy Johnson, Phoebe Lofting

                    Wm. and Sarah Bell
Lucy, 10/4/53, Beuford Pleasant, Jr., Mary Pleasant, Sarah Hol-
    loway

                    Thomas and Mary Bell
John, 5/10/43, Wm. Coans, Nath'l. Willaford, Martha Willaford
Jesse, 9/25/45, Chas. Holt, Edwd. Farrington, Mary Gray
Lucy, 3/25/48, Mary Pleasant, Sarah Bell, Beuford Pleasant

                    John and Phoebe Bell
Sylvanus, 1/1/46, Cam'l. Northington, Sylvanus Stokes, Cecillia
    Stokes
John, 1/9/48, Burwell Bell, Ben'g. Bell, Tabitha Ezell
John Bell died 5/25/48, reported by Gregory Rawlings.

                    Sylvanus and Mary Bell
Eliz., 7/13/72, Sterling Northington, Anne Moore, Sarah Hood
John, 12/24/70, Lewis Johnson, John Bell, Jemima Johnson
James, 2/11/74, no sponsors given.

BELL (Continued)

Ben'g. and Martha Bell
Martha Jefferson, 11/16/51, Jos. Tucker, Prissilla Parham,
  Eliz. Nunn
Hannah, 12/3/53, Jas. Bell, Eliz. Vines, Martha Pepper
Jefferson Davis, 7/27/55, Thos. Huson, John Jones, Eliz. Pepper

Joseph and Margarett Bell
Martha, 3/1/60, Wm. Willie, Judieth Hay, Eliz. Willie
Graham Bird, 3/19/62, Wm. Willie, Edwd. Walker, Jacobina
  Willie

Richard and Mildred Bell
Ben'g., 12/10/53, Wm. Bellamy, Wm. Brown, Anne Moore

James and Mildred Bell
George, 3/1/55, Geo. Robertson, Wm. Gilliam Jr., Susanna
  Banks
Anne, 1/6/56, Rob't. Seat, Hannah Bell, Phylis Northington
Hannah, 6/2/58, Rob't. Powell, Mary Green, Eliz. Adams
Mary, 1/14/61, Burwell Banks, Mary Bell, Susanna Moss
Rebbecca, 12/14/62, Jas. Barns, Eliz. Myrick, Lucy Stokes
Baalam, 1/4/65, Cornelius Lofting, William Richardson, Amy
  Richardson
Mildred Lee, 1/4/68, Isam Gilliam, Prissilla Gilliam, Abby Holt
Betty Sawbridge, 7/28/69, twin, no sponsor
Salley Wilkes, 7/28/69, twin, no sponsor

John and Letty Bell
Salley Nelms, 5/3/75, Geo. Bell, Lucy Wellborn, Eliz. Hewitt

BENDALL
Isacc and Sarah Bendall
Eliz., 6/5/66, Joseph Pennington, Eliz. and Lucy Pennington
John, 4/28/68, Math. Wynne, Chas. Sturdivant, Anne Wrenn
Sarah, 6/6/70, Sam'l. Seaward, Hulda Owen, Anne Gee
Isaac, 6/26/72, Steth Wynne, Wm. Sturdivant Jr., Mary Wrenn

BERRYMAN
John and Prissilla Berryman
John, 1/11/60, no sponsors
Baalam, 6/27/63, Eph. Parham, Henry Jackson, Mary Hill
Josiah, 5/21/65, John Avery, Rob't. Owen, Hannah Parham
Mary Anne, 9/11/69, Joel Tucker, Judieth Tucker, Eliz. Powell

BIGBIE
John and Judieth Bigbie
George, 1/8/70, John Avent, Martha Newsom, Eliz. Northington
Nathan, 10/26/72, Nathan Northington, Wm. Longbottom, Mary
  Barham
Randall, 10/6/73, Ben'g. Wellborn, Math. Parham, Betty Hewett

BIRD
Richard and Sarah Bird
James, 2/27/40, Thos. Cate, Wm. Jones, Eliz. Peebles
John, 2/4/42, John Painter, Peter Hawthorn, Sarah Sykes
Mary, 1/16/46, Wm. and Mary Stewart, Lucy Dunn
Richard, 3/16/48, Edwd. Lee, Nath'l. and Eliz. Bedingfield
Richard, 11/3/50, Martha Gibbs, Josh. Hawthorn, Amy Dunn
Phoebe, 3/25/45, Thos. Thrower, Phoebe Thrower, Eliz. Wil-
  liams
Jane Bird died 4/13/50, reported by Richard Bird

William and Sarah Bird
John, 12/23/43, Josh. Hawthorn, John Bird, Eliz. Denton
Eliz., 3/23/45, Peter Hawthorn, Eliz. Weaver, Frances Denton
Amy, 5/5/52, John Painter, Rachael and Rebbecca Hawthorn
Nath'l., 5/11/55, Peter Hawthorn, Nath'l. Duncan

John and Mary Bird
Howell, 2/25/49, Wm. Tomlinson, Ben'g. Barker, Sarah Hamlin
Rubin and Mary Bird
Roberts, 7/9/54, Jas. and Ben'g. Tomlinson, Sarah Tomlinson
Rock, 1/9/60, Nich. Partridge, Jas. Bosseau Jones, ----? Bird.
Rebecca Bird died 2/12/58, reported by Math. Whitehead.

BIRDSONG
Miles and Mary Birdsong
Rebecca, 7/6/75, John Tomlinson, Mary White, Eliz. Tomlinson

BISHOP
Wm. Bishop and -------------?
Wm., 7/21/70, a young man baptized, presented by Thos. Wreen

Mason and Anne Bishop
Henry, 4/26/68, Chas. Sturdivant, Steth Wynne, Mary Moore

BLANKS
Joseph and Anne Blanks
Martha, 3/15/40, Thos. Booth, Prudence Jones, Susanna Lilly

BLATON
Joseph and Anne Blaton
Wm., 12/8/51, Richard Bird, Ben'g. Moss, Sarah Bird

Joseph and Elizabeth Blaton
Amy, 10/3/48, Francis Niblet, Eliz. Rix, Mary Davis

BLIZZARD
Charles and Anne Blizzard
Chas., 7/24/56, Phil. Harwood, Jas. Williams Jr., Eliz. Williams

Charles and Anne Blizzard (Continued)
Hannah, 5/19/59, Edwd. Shelton, Cecillia Stokes, Phylis Northington

Samuel and Sarah Blizzard
Randolph, 2/24/60, Aaron Peters, ------ Blizzard, Lucy Peters
Lucy, 1/21/61, Aaron Peters, Lydia Blizzard, Lucy Peters
Wm., 1/23/62, Timothy Santeen, Edwad. Blizzard, Barbary Bliz-
  zard

BLOW
Samuel and Martha Blow
Mary, 3/13/39, Cap't. Richard Blow, Mary Thomas, Jean Blow

John and Prissilla Blow
Rebbecca, 3/23/43, John Andrews Jr., Mary Figures, Eliz. Rich-
  ardson
Mely. 5/12/74, Ben'g. Ellis, Eliz. Blow, Eliz. Ellis

John and Lucy Blow
Betsy Margarett, 1/16/75, John Cargil, Anne Cargil, Mildred Wynne
Salley, twin, 1/16/75, Wm. Wynne, Anne and Anne Wynne

BLUNT
Richard and Anne Blunt
Mary, b. 3/25/27, Eliz., b. 11/16/31, Lucy, b. 8/19/36, Rich-
  ard, b. 8/19/36. No sponsors given for any of the above.
Lucy Blunt died 2/7/49, reported by Anne Blunt
Richard Blunt died 4/17/47

Richard and Jane Blunt
Colin, 11/30/60, John Edmunds, Wm. Nicholson
Robert, 7/10/63, John Nicholson, Edmunds Jones, Mary Irby.
Col. Richard Blunt died 4/13/74, in his ----- year, he was born
  Jan. 4, 1738

William and Frances Blunt
Martha, 3/11/77, Peter Jones, Lucretia Jones, Jane Briggs

Judkins and Martha Blunt
Wm., 1/9/72, Wm. and Thomas Batte, Eliz. Blunt

Wm. and Martha Blunt
Samuel, 12/5/65, Richard Blunt, Harris Nicholson, Mary Peete
Wm., 1/7/68, Robert and John Nicholson, Rebbecca Lucas
Mary, 3/2/70, John Irby, Eliz. Wyche, Mary Baylis
Eliz., 8/18/72, Steven Andrews, Susanna Andrews, Anne Rookings
  Bryan
Martha Blunt the wife of Wm. died 9/2/74

Henry and Sarah Blunt
Mary, 3/8/40, Henry Blow, Jean Blow, Mary Bell

BOLTON
Joshua and Mary Bolton
Abener, born 8/2/38, no sponsor given

BONNER
John and Sarah Bonner
Ben'g., 11/11/48, Peter Green, Wm. Mitchell, Mary Farrington
Mary, 10/30/59, Wm. Banks, Martha Bell, Martha Nants
Patty, 3/2/53, Lewis Tyus, Lucy Curtis, Mary Malone
Phoebe, 2/23/55, Wm. Richardson, Amy Williamson, Eliz. Nuns
Selah, 12/15/56, John Malone, Patty Richardson, Sucky Curtis
Salley, 7/6/60, Burwell Banks, Drusilla Bonner, Lucy Mahaney
Jane, 7/2/62, David Tucker, Mary Norris, Patty Kelly
John, 8/20/64, Wm. Yarborough, Mary Kelly
Thomas, 1/19/69, Thos. Love, Michael Malone, Mary Malone
Young, 12/18/70, Ro., Wynne Raines, Peter Green, Mary Ingram

Henry and Rebbecca Bonner
Wm., 1/3/70, Rob't. Wilkerson, Thos. Smith, Eliz. Adams

Mary Bonner died 5/3/70, reported by Howell Chappell
James Bonner married Mary, the daughter of Capt. Jas. Jones,
    4/22/73.
He died 2/18/74, reported by Susanna Cureton.

BOOTH
John and Hollum Booth
Molly, 9/12/64, Thos. Booth, Patience and Lucy Booth

Geo. and Anne Booth
Rob't., 3/9/70, Wood Tucker, Gilliam Booth, Mary Booth
Thos., 10/24/73, Thos. Vaughn, Richard Hill Jr., Judy Tucker

Mary Booth died 2/3/52, reported by Danial Nuns
Geo. Booth died 8/14/63, reported by his grandson, Geo. Booth,
    he was 84.

BRADLEY
John and Eliz. Bradley
Richard, 10/8/49, Henry Bradley, Anne Hargrave, Sarah Carlisle
Sarah, 11/24/51, Joseph Bell, Ben'g. Smith, Sarah Bell
Lucy, 11/13/55, John Bane, Eliz. Jarrett, Eliz. Ellis
Rebbecca, 6/15/60, Wm. Bell, Rebecca Hyde, Sarah Clark

John and Sarah Bradley
James, 2/29/52, Edwd. Petway, Henry Gee, Mary Gee
Gee, 2/14/54, John Mason, Thos. Barba, Eliz. Gee
Isam, 1/31/55, Wm. Bradley, Ben'g. Weathers, Susanna Hill
John, 5/18/59, Wm. Weathers, Nath'l. Bedingfield, Phoebe Petway
Sarah, 1/18/56, Jas. Gee, Mary Weathers, Mary Dunn

BRADLEY (Continued)
Henry and Eliz. Bradley
Hinchae, 6/27/59, none given
Michael, 3/6/63, Arnold Bradley, Wm. Willie, Mary Huson

Henry and Jane Bradley
Edmund, 8/24/61, none given.

BRIGGS
William and Mary Briggs
Wm., 10/3/36, Marmaduke Grussett, Simon Murphey, Anne Grussett, Sarah Felts
Rebbecca, 4/9/42, Josh. Proctor, Mary Briggs, Eliz. Winkle
Henry, 8/22/39, Wm. and Nath'l. Briggs, Joyce Washington
Lucy, 3/44, John Irby, Brainley Maggett, Anne Briggs
Wm., 10/22/63, Joseph Cook, Wm. Griffith, Sarah Cook
Henry Briggs died 10/25/39, reported by Jas. Chappell

Nath'l. and Mary Briggs
Sarah, 9/24/37, William Roberts, Mary Briggs, Anne Guthridge
Geo., 3/8/41, Steven Hamlin, Wm. Brown, Eliz. Davis
Nath'l., 1/6/43, John Brittle, Wm. Hix, Anne Brittle

Thomas and Frances Briggs
Joel, 3/28/41, Henry Tatum, Chas. Smith, Mary Raines
Jean, 2/11/42, Drury Parker, Eliz. Halley, Jean Woodruff
Sarah, 1/18/47, Richard Woodruff, Mary Stewart, Eliz. Oliver
Rebbecca, 1/7/49, Jas. Carter, Jane Andrews, Phoebe Bell

Wm. and Frances Briggs
Frederick, 2/14/44, Nath'l. Raines, Richard Jones Jr., Anne
Raines
John, 3/24/50, John and Richard Rives, Eliz. Rives

Chas. and Eliz. Briggs
Martha, 3/22/61, Sam'l. Blow, Wm. Briggs, Martha Blow, Eliz.
Briggs.

Geo. and Sarah Briggs
Francis, 12/4/43, Thos. Bryan, Eliz. Hern, Mary Briggs
Susanna, 4/22/51, Joseph Ellis, Eliz. Briggs, Eliz. Sawry

Henry Briggs died 10/25/39, reported by Jas. Chappell
Cap't. Howell Briggs died 4/21/75, reported by Gray Briggs
Frances Briggs died 9/2/51

BRITTLE
John and Eliz. Brittle
Wm., 10/25/38, Rob't. Warren, Arthur Smith, Sarah Long

18

BRITTLE (Continued)
John and Eliz. Brittle (Continued)
Jean, 6/16/40, Jas. Barrow, Jean Sawry, Jean Davis
Eliz., 6/16/42, Arthur Long, John Brittle, Mary Briggs

Wm. and Mary Brittle
Jas., 12/14/67, John Blow, Arthur Smith, Lucy Faison
Thos. Washington, 1/17/71, Michael and Abner James, Mary
Birdson

BROADNAX
Henry and Anne Broadnax
Wm., 3/3/62, none given
Eliz. Powell, 3/2/65, James Walker, Sarah Powell, Catherine
Walker

Wm. and Mary Broadnax
Ben'g., 11/18/72, Rob't. Skipwith, Wood Tucker, Rebbecca Jones
Salley, 3/24/74, Rob't. Blling, Wm. Willie, Anne Ward, Jacobina
Willie

BROADRIB
Thos. and Eliz. Broadrib
Thos., 1/31/48, David Hunter, John Andrews, Jane Pepper
Mely, 11/12/53, Wm. Carlisle, Mary Proctor
Ben'g., 3/24/58, Jesse Jones, Arthur Richardson, Rebbecca Pepper
Eliz., 11/2/60, Fred. Andrews, Eliz. Stacey, Eliz. Andrews

BROWDER
Isam Browder and Agnes Tatum
Isam Browder, 3/17/59, Edwd. Walker, Henry Tatum, Susanna Ray

BROWN
James and Mary Brown
Lucy, 10/30/40, Thos. Tadlock, Eliz. Titmash, Rebbecca Hawthorn

Wm. and Sarah Brown
Lucy, 2/22/40, Nath'l. Briggs, Eliz. Brittle, Anne Grussett
Mary, 11/18'42, Ben'g. Brown, Martha Long, Anne Brittle
John, 3/1/45, Jas. Turner, Wm. Carlisle, Mary Briggs
Sarah, 12/30/48, Wm. Bell, Sarah Carlisle, Hannah Carlisle

Lewis and Martha Brown
Thos., 11/18/60, Thos. Wade, Fred. Green, Lydia Hill
Lewis, 1/10/62, John Wynne, Edwd. Harper, Anne Harper
Nancy, 1/19/64, Rob't. Winfield, Betty Bonner, Betty Wynne

Wm. and Eliz. Brown
Susanna, 1/20/45, none given

BROWN (Continued)

Burwell and Amy Brown
Wm., 5/26/68, Nath'l. Parham, Wm. Meanley, Jane Raines
Epps, 1/17/67, Francis Epps, John Mangum, Jr., Lucy Freeman

Lewis and Eliz. Brown
Mary, 3/26/55, Thos. Wynne, Mary and Eliz. Rowland
Eliz., 1/12/56, John Rowland, Eliz. Rowland, Amy Randall
Aaron, 2/28/57, Jas. Jones, Wm. Richardson, Eliz. Jones.

Lewis and Martha Brown
Thos., 1/18/60, Thos. Wade, Fred. Green, Eliz. Hill

Abraham and Eliz. Brown
Henry, 3/14/56, Nath'l. Parham, Edwd. Clanton, Mary Battle
Mary Brown, the second wife of Abraham Brown died 2/15/55.
Lucy, 10/6/48, John Stokes, Lucretia Stokes, Eliz. Grantham

BRYAN

Thos. and Mary Bryan
Thomas, 10/30/41, John Ogburn, John Hargrave, Eliz. Richardson

Thomas and Margaret Bryan
Eliz., 4/21/44, Wm. Bailey, Eliz. Smith, Martha Smith
Edwd., 6/5/46, Willett Roberts, John Edwards, Mary Turne

Eliz. Bryan, a child, died 10/26/41, reported by Frederick Bryan

Frederick and Eliz. Bryan
Edwd., 8/16/41, born no sponsors given

BULLOCH

Richard and Martha Bulloch
Mary, 4/1/37, none given
Eliz., 12/8/40, Danial Roberts, Sarah Roberts, Amy Bulloch

John and Sarah Bulloch
Winny, 10/28/48, Thos. Felts, Agnes Bulloch, Agnes Felts
Drury, 1/15/51, Jerimiah Bulloch, Rob't. Seat, Kesiah Bulloch
Baalam, 4/6/54, Thos. Felts, Sam'l. Bulloch, Anne Seat
John, 7/6/56, Nath'l. Felts, Wm. Hicks, Mary Bulloch
Chas., 10/17/61, Jones Glover, Wm. Hill, Phoebe Seat

Wm. and Frances Bulloch
Moses, 8/15/64, Richard Hay, Richard Hay Jr., Lucy Hay
Richard, 1/5/69, Robert and Curtis Lynne, Margaret Hay

Robert and Martha Bulloch
Mary, 5/1/37
Eliz., 12/8/40, Danial Roberts, Sarah Roberts, Amy Bulloch
Joel, 12/11/43, Francis Felts, John Adams, Eliz. Roberts
Isacc, 5/6/48, Joseph Armstrong, John Wiggens, Agnes Bulloch

BULLOCH (Continued)
Jerimiah and Amy Bulloch
Chas., 12/25/40, twin Geo. Ezell, John Bulloch, Martha Bulloch
Richard, 12/25/40, twin, Robert Hix, Joseph Sasensick, Mary
   Sasensick

Lemuel and Agnes Bulloch
Eliz., 10/25/51, Nath'l. Felts, Mary Felts, Mary Bulloch
Molly, 10/23/53, Jerimiah Bulloch, Kesiah Bulloch, Betty Felts
Phoebe, 9/3/57, Wm. Harris, Lucy and Mary Phelps
Chas., 4/11/69, Nath'l. Newsom, Fred Fort, Agnes Phelps (Felts)
Nath'l., 10/1/61, John Bulloch, Thos. Pate Jr., Rebbecca Seat

BURGESS
Thos. and Sarah Burgess
Eliz., 9/12/36, none given
William, 10/28/39, none
Christian (dgh), 5/21/42, Isacc Winkler, Peter Winkle, Eliz. Hill
Robert, 5/10/49, Wm. and Robert Carrell, Mary Burgess

BURNELL
Wm. and Anne Burnell
Selah, 9/5/47, Wm. Johnson, Jr., Amy Crosswit, Lucretia Bradley

BURROWS
Thos. and Eliz. Burrow
Baalam, 9/18/55, Churchill Curtis, Joel Freeman, Eliz. Stokes
Anne, 3/2/53, Henry Burrows, Mary Jones, Jane Green
Mary, 4/26/58, John Stevens, Eliz. and Patty Roe.

Gerald and Elenor Burrows
Jemimma, 11/20/62, Nath'l. Rainey, Mary Hill, Mary ------?
Eliz., 10/30/65, Wm. Wade, Anne Wilkerson, Susanna Woodward
Mary, 3/22/68, Jas. Cain Jr., Patty and Angelica Cain
Frances, 6/8/72, John Petway, Rebbecca and Selah Parham
Philipp, 2/20/74, John Moss, Israel Powch, Sally Winfield

Philip and Patty Burrow
Eph., 4/30/68, Thos. Hunt, Peter Randall, Sarah ------?

Henry and Lucy Burrow
Patty, 5/11/60, none given
Jones, 6/6/62, none given

BUTLER
Thomas and Anne Butler
Martha, 11/8/41, Wm. Raines, Angelica Raines, Phoebe Wynne
Mary, 3/21/42, none given
Martha Butler, a child, died 10/19/42, reported by Maj. Wynne

BUTLER (Continued)

Thomas and Amy Butler
Eliz., born 1743, no sponsors given
Lucy, born 11/25/45.

Thomas and Eliz. Butler
Thomas, 11/1/52, Thos. Vaughn, Rob't. Mitchell, Dorothy Vaughn
Amy, 5/17/57, Thos. Vines Jr., Mary Jones, Mary Butler
Anne, 4/20/50, none given
Willie, 2/7/62, David Tucker, Anne Wilkerson, Eliz. Butler

Thomas Butler and Mary (nee Norris)
Sterling, 4/11/66, Thos. Hunt, Evans Mabrey, Mary Kelly
Vines, 5/30/67, Hinchey Petway, Lewis Maybrey, Judieth Green

NOTE: Mary Norris was sponsor for John and Sarah Bonner,
7/2/62, and for David and Athalia Tucker, 10/7/64.

Geo. and Sarah Butler
Micajah, 12/26/43, Joseph Rolland, Eliz. Pate, Anne Pate
Sarah, 7/14/45, Wm. Willie, Eliz. Oliver, Mary Clifton

NOTE: Thomas Butler, Chas. Collier, Susanna Collier were sponsors for Josiah and Eliz. Smith. 9/20/62.

BYRNHAM
John and Mary Byrnham
Arthur, 6/14/40, Wm. Willie, Arthur Smith, Jean Bennett

CAIN
James Cain Jr., and Lucretia
Allen, 12/8/58, Peter Cain, Jas. Richardson, Mildred Hill
Micajah, 1/9/48, none given
James, 4/9/56, John Mangum, Nath'l. Freeman, Martha Freeman
Mary, 12/22/52, Nath'l. Rainey, Winefred and Angelica Cain
Betsy, 9/16/64, Joseph Ingram, Sarah and Eliz. Delahay
Peter, 8/18/62, Wm. Hewett, John Crow Robertson, Angelica
   Cain
Lucretia, 7/20/67, Thos. Wynne, Jr., Martha and Mary Cain
Geo., 3/7/70, Geo. Randall, Micajah Cain, Susanna Delahay

Isam and Martha Cain
Geo., 3/24/61, Geo. Robertson, Philip Burrow, Kesiah Cain
Ruffin, 4/17/65, Seymour Robertson, Thos. Wade, Mary Abernethy
John, 4/6/65, Peter Cain, Wm. Burrow, Martha Cain
Rebbecca, 4/20/59, Jarrell Burrow, Tabitha Burrow, Angelica
   Cain

CAIN (Continued)

Isam and Martha Cain (Continued)
Jordan, 10/30/71, Wm. Cain, John Washer, Rebbecca Roberts
Susanna, 9/15/69, Micajah Cain, Olive Randall, Amy Underwood
Thomas, 1/8/68, James Mangum Jr., Joel Wilkerson, Bathia
    Burrow
Isam, 4/14/75, Lovel Barrison, Jesse Smith, Eliz. and Martha
    Powell

Elenor Cain died 9/3/58, reported by James Cain

Peter and Martha Cain
Anne, 8/9/59, Thos. Wade, Susanna Wade, Lucy Cain
Rebbecca, 12/29/63, Isam Cain, Martha and Kesiah Cain
Martha, 3/30/66, Geo. Randall, Bathia Burrow, Charlotte Freeman
Mary, 1/7/69, Miles Collier, Amy Cain, Dorothy Mitchell
Math. Hill, 11/14/71, Jarrett Burrow, Seymour Powell, Amy
    Woodward

Peter and Mary Cain
Clairbourne, 12/20/61, Jas. Cain, Jr., John Mangum, Angelica
    Cain

Micajah and Bathia Cain
Sally, 10/2/73, John Winfield, Mary Abernethy, Mary Hewett

CAMP

Wm. and Mary Camp
Wm., 7/14/69, Edwd. Weaver Jr., Howell Hight, Lucy Richardson

CAPEL

Thos. and Anne Capel
Charles, 1/31/41, Geo. Long, Chas. Webb, Frances Robertson
Ransom, 10/7/48, Wm. Hutchens, Jones Longbottom, Sarah Battle
Sterling, 10/2/51, John and Wm. Battle, Eliz. Harwood

John and Joyce Capel
Nanny, 11/19/63, Thos. Adkins, Mary Adkins, Eliz. Wilkerson

Sterling and Patty Capel
Robinson, 8/6/74, Curtis Land, Jas. Sisson, Anne Capel

Sarah Capel, aged 102, died 9/19/73, reported by Moses Johnson.

CARGIL

John and Lucy Cargil
Lucy Binns, 1/29/69, Nich. Massenburg, Lucy Massenburg,
    Martha Belches
Judieth, 12/13/73, Timothy Rives, Lucy Massenburg, Margarett
    Hay

CARGIL (Continued)

Lucy Cargil, the wife of John, died 12/13/73
Judieth Cargil, a child, died 12/17/73

John and Anne Cargil
John, 9/31/75, Rev. M. Burgess, John Massenburg, Lucy Mooring

CARLISLE
Wm. and Sarah Carlisle
Wm., 7/10/39, Andrew Lister, Eliz. Maggett, Eliz. Gilliam
Molly, 1/2/43, John Owen, Wm. Rodgers, Hannah Carrell

Chas. and Eliz. Cassell (or Capell)
Eldridge, 11/2/74, Howell Rawlings, Jas. Sisson, Mary Barham

CARRELL
Robert and Hannah Carrell
John, 12/13/44, Arthur Smith, Jonathan Ellis, Sarah Alsobrook
Sarah, 10/5/46, John Alsobrook, Sarah Carlisle, Mary Figures
Steven, 12/30/48, Wm. Brown, Arthur Richardson, Sarah Brown

Wm. Carrell Jr. and Anne
Lucy, 11/11/58, none given
Micajah, 4/2/62, John Carrell, Prissilla Carrell, Selah Wallace
Ede, 4/2/62, John Carrell, Prissilla Carrell, Selah Wallace
Ede, 6/7/63, Thos. Griffin, Thos. Richardson, Olive Griffin
Micajah, 6/7/63, Thos. Griffin, Thos. Richardson, Olive Griffin
Rebbecca, 3/21/65, Steven Andrews, Mary Andrews, Lucy Proctor
Wm., 1/19/72, Anderson Ramsey, Steven Pepper, Eliz. Ramsey
Hannah, 2/27/7, Ben'g. Dolen, Hannah Carrell, Hannah Owen
Peggy, 7/26/74, John Broadrib, Mary Carrell, Mary White

Wm. and Hannah Carrell
Jesse, 3/20/40, John Price, Danial Price, Eliz. Hay
Nathan, 8/22/42, Wm. Carlisle, Joseph Ellis, Jean Bane
Eliz., 4/30/44, Williard Roberts, Eliz. Vassar, Eliz. Meggs
Arthur, 7/16/46, Arthur Smith, Rob't. Carrell, Hannah Owen
Mark, 6/23/51, Robert Nicholson, Simon Stacey, Selah Huson

Thos. and Prissilla Carrell
Lucy, 11/30/58, none
Samuel, 9/12/60, Frederick and Nath'l. Andrews, Rebbecca Andrews
Cherry, 4/18/63, Edwd. Wright, Rebbecca and Sarah Carrell

Nathan and Mary Carrell
Dread, 9/5/70, John Smith, Joseph Glover, Rebbecca Smith
Patience, Wm. Atkinson, Lucy Atkinson, Eliz. Carrell

Richard and Sarah Carter
Mary, 6/27/39, none given
Eliz., 9/24/41, Edwd. Epps, Eliz. Willie, Amy Tomlinson
Amy, 11/26/43, John Rosser, Mary Epps, Anne Wren
Lucy, 10/16/48, Chas. Gee, Francis Rives, Mary Dansey
Rebbecca, 3/17/50, Joseph Carter, Eliz. Chappell, Amy Briggs
Patty, 9/5/53, Ben'g. Tomlinson, Jane Tomlinson, Sarah Moss

John and Amy Carter
Wm., 5/28/43, Joseph Tucker, Thomas Butler, Martha Williams
Chas., 10/24/62, Wm. Yarbrough, Wm. Carter, Mary Harris

Richard and Anne Carter
Anne, 7/12/45, Dan'l. Carter, Anne Cook, Rebbecca Heath

Danial and Rebbecca Carter
Angelica, 8/29/62, Wm. Carter, Fanny Carter, Mary Tucker

John and Sarah Carter
Robert, 12/31/72, none given
Rebbecca, 12/23/73, none given

Richard and Eliz. Carter
Eliz., 12/2/70, Willis Hall, Eliz. Hall, Amy Rives
(She, the above Eliz. Carter, had first married ------ Alsobrook
 and had one child, namely, Thomas Alsobrook, who died
 7/14/72. See page 2)

Edward and Agnes Carter
Robert, 8/27/54, John and David Stokes, Sarah Stokes
Cynthia, 1/29/52, John Wellborn Jr., Mary and Sucky Stokes
Molly, 7/18/59, none given
Molly, 6/16/60, Wm. Woodland, Betty Gilliam, Mary Ezell

James and Eliz. Carter
Eliz., 11/2/44, John Bell Jr., Cecillia Stokes, Sarah Judkins
Emanuel, 2/24/53, Thos. Dunn, John Battle, Jr., Hannah Phillips

CHAMBLESS
John and Sarah Chambless
John Edwards, 9/1/63, Wm. Weathers, Rob't. Anderson, Mary
 Epps

Wm. and Eliz. Chambless
Mary, 3/27/64, John Underhill, Eliz. Weeks, Frances Jones
Frances, 5/15/66, John Lessenbury, Mary Lessenbury, Susanna
 Hamilton
Eliz., 10/3/68, Timothy Rives, Martha Williams, Anne Parham
Sarah, 12/19/70, Nath'l. Barker, Martha Peebles, Sarah Lessen-
 bury

CHAMBLESS (Continued)
James and Sarah Chambless
John, 7/16/75, Isam Smith, Hartwell Marriable, Eliz. Mason

Amy, the wife of James Chambless, died 12/17/72, reported by
Wm. Dunn, her father.

CHAPPELL
James and Eliz. Chappell
Ann, 12/22/39, John Mason Jr., Nath'l. Duncan, Hannah Andrews,
Eliz. Mason
Lucretia, 2/10/41, James Chappell Jr., Amy Epps, Mary Chappell
Howell, 8/26/44, Jas. Chappell Jr., Robert Jones Jr., Sarah Jones
Eliz., 7/6/45, James Chappell, Sarah Chappell, Mary Turner

Samuel Chappell Jr. and Mary
Christopher, 10/24/44, John Tatum, John Steagul, Mary Adkins
Mary, 10/2/46, Wm. Rachael, Hannah Grantham, Lucretia Stokes

Samuel and Eliz. Chappell
Robert, 9/24/52, Chenay Tatum, Wm. Moss Jr., Mary Moss

Samuel Chappell died 1/2/65, reported by Richard Wilkerson

James Chappell Jr. and Eliz.

James, 3/5/46, Thos. Wallace, Thos. Tomlinson, Amy Briggs
John, 3/8/55, Thos. Chappell, Henry Jarrett, Anne Chappell
Amy, 4/19/58, Wm. Briggs, Rebbecca Briggs, Sarah Peebles
Rebbecca, 5/21/60, Wm. Briggs, ----- Cook, ----- Chappell
Wm., 6/10/62, Wm. Briggs, Howell Chappell, Eliz. Chappell
Kinchen, 11/30/66, none given
James Chappell died 2/12/69, reported by James Chappell Jr.
Eliz. Chappell died 6/11/62, reported by Jas. Chappell Jr.

John and Nanny Chappell
Eliz., 12/2/59, Henry Peebles, Anne Chappell, Mary Underhill
Thomas, 1/23/61, Robert Chappell, John Underhill Jr.

James Chappell Jr. and Judieth
Martha, 1/22/66, none given
Ben'g., 8/20/65, none given, wife's name not given

Thomas and Mary Chappell
Sarah Briggs, 5/17/61, Henry Briggs, Eliz. Briggs, ----- Chappell

Howell and Rebbecca Chappell
Henry, 9/16/64, Wm. Rodgers, Simon Stacey, Lucy Proctor
James, 2/12/67, Jas. Chappell Jr., Wm. Evans, Salley Andrews
Wm., 8/30/69, Henry and Robert Nicholson, Amy Cock
Zilpah Coker, 10/24/71, Henry Chappell, Mary Jarrett, Mary
Chappell

CHAPPELL (Continued)
                    Howell and Rebbecca Chappell (Continued)
Frances, 7/27/74, Lawrence Smith, Anne Williams, Rebecca
    Chappell

                    John and Mary Chappell
Howell, 2/27/59, Samuel Chappell, Wm. Hines Jr., Lucy Chappell
Martha, 7/17/61, Howell Chappell, Fanny Barham
John, 8/19/63, Wm. Seaborn, Drury Clanton, Eliz. Hines
Wm., 8/1/65, Fred Hines, Wm. Barham, Judieth Chappell
Eliz., 7/27/67, Anne Hines, Sarah Hines, Henry Hines
Thomas, 1/17/72, Hartwell Hines, Nic'h. Jarrett, Sarah Jones
Mary, 9/21/69, John Peters, Martha Peters, Olive Hines
Henry, 9/30/74, Thos. Tomlinson, Wm. Rives, Olive Tomlinson

                    Wm. and Mary Chappell
John, 10/27/73, Seymour Powell, John Malone, Susanna Oliver

                    James Chappell Jr. and Salley
Rebbecca Parham, 4/23/75, Henry Cock, Rebbecca and Frances
    Jones
Littleberry, 1/10/73, Nich. Jarrett, Wm. Lamb, Mary Jones

                    Anne Chappell and -----------?
Becky, 9/13/54, Wm. Willie, Eliz. Jones, Eliz. Partridge

CHAUNCEY. also spelled.CHANCEY
                    John and Eliz. Chauncey
John, 11/10/65, John Walker, Richard Parker, Mary Walker
Betsy, 7/14/67, Lawrence Gibbons Jr., Mary Williams, Frances
    Oliver
Thomas, 10/25/68, Drury and Wm. Oliver, Jane Land
Mary, 10/8/71, Joel Tucker, Judieth Tucker, Temperence Hill

CLAIRBOURNE
                    Augustine and Mary Clairbourne
Mary, 1/19/44, Chas. Fisher, Jas. Clairbourne, Mary Fisher,
    Mary Kennedy
Herbert, 4/7/46, Leonard Clairbourne, Wm. Willie, Susanna
    Steth, Eliz. Willie
Aug., 2/2/47, Rob't. Jones, Jr., Billy Clairbourne, Susanna
    Fisher
Billy, 11/2/54, Thos. Steth, Wm. Willie, Katherine Steth
Anne, 12/30/49, Peter Potheress, Susanna Potheress, Martha
    Kennon
Susanna, 11/29/57, John Jones, Mary and Eliz. Fisher

CLAIRBOURNE (Continued)
Augustine and Mary Clairbourne (Cont.)
Lucy Herbert, 8/22/60, John Mash, Jacobina Willie
John Herbert, 5/30/63, Wm. Eldridge, Chas. Harrison, Jacobina
  Willie, Anne Clairbourne
Bathurst, 4/6/74, Richard Yarbrough, Fred Jones, Susanna Clair-
  bourne

Wm. and Mary Clairbourne
Fernando, 3/9/72, Thos. West, John Ruffin, Jr., Mary Clairbourne
Wm. Cole, 8/13'73, Fernando Leigh, Thos. Moore, Eliz. West
Nath'l., 2/1/75, John Holmes, Buller Clairbourne, Eliz. Clair-
  bourne
Thos. Aughustine, 2/10/77, Aug. Clairbourne, Wm. Leigh, Mary
  Clairbourne

CLANTON
John and Mary Clanton
Rubin, 9/26/41, John Gilliam, Chas. Gilliam, Eliz. Shelton
Mely, 11/27/43, Thos. Holt, Eliz. Gilliam, Mary Lilly
Micajah, 7/21/48, Henry Prichard, Jas. Mangum, Tapenus Huson
Phoebe, 11/12/52, Isam Gilliam, Phoebe Lofting, Lucy Huson
Wm., 4/10/57, Hinchey Gilliam, Edwd. Shelton, Agnes Battel
Nath'l., 1/20/55, Chas. Wood, Baalam Bell, Prissilla Lofting'
Holt, 5/5/59, Lewis Dunn, Wm. Lofting, Anne Moore

John and Amy Clanton
Eliz., 5/23/40, John Dunn, Mary Webb, Mary King
Patty, 4/14/47, Henry Prichard, Lucy Prichard, Jane Hutchens
Mary, 12/2/50, David Clanton, Anne McGee, Mary Lilly
Amy, 12/2/50 (twin), David Clanton, Anne McGee, Mary Lilly
John, 12/31/58 Ben'g. Harrison, Drury Clanton, Anne Harrison

Drury and Sarah Clanton
Amy Wyche, 6/16/71, Nath'l. Newsom, Lucy Ezell, Lydia Rawlings

CLARKE
Joseph and Mary Clarke
Anne, 7/11/41, Wm. Willie, Eliz. Willie, Mary Berry
Joseph Clarke, a very old man, died 10/12/72, reported by David
  Mason

Ben'g. and Mary Clarke
Wm., 10/25/48, Buford Pleasant, Ben'g. Rodgers, Mary Pleasant

Geo. and Sarah Clarke
Eliz., 12/13/59, Rob't. Carlisle, Sarah Carlisle, Eliz. Broadrib

John and Eve Clarke
Wm., 5/19/75, Lawrence Smith, Mary Smith

CLARY
Burdis and Eliz. Clary
Anne, ---------, Humphrey Bayley, Anne Bailey, Mary Harrison

CLIFTON
Wm. and Charity Clifton
Eliz., 5/30/33; none given; John, 3/22/40, none given
Susanna, 12/22/41, John Lilly, Eliz. Morgan, Susanna Freeman
John and Miantifris Clifton
Absolum, 2/24/44, John Bell, Thos. Weather, Hannah Bell.
John and Mary Clifton
Wm., 3/15/64, Wm. Pare, Wm. Clifton, Betty Wynne
John, 8/26/65, Rob't. Wynne, Chas. Sturdivant, Susanna Lilly
Mary, 1/22/67, Ben'g. Weathers, Lucy Wynne, Anne Sturdivant
Eliz., 8/17/68, Matt. Wynne, Eliz. Pennington, Anne Lilly
Hazel, 2/23/70, Matt. Wynne, John Pare, Susanna Pare
Joseph, 11/17/71, Wm. Stewart, John Wynne, Jr., Mary Partan

Wm. and Sarah Clifton
David, 2/9/64, Peter Jennings, John Clifton, Susanna Clifton
Eliz., 2/26/67, John Pare, Mary Parham, Martha Pennington
Tabitha, 4/16/68, none given
James, 4/6/69, John and Amos Sledge, Eliz. Wilcox

COCKE
Wm. and Hannah Cocke
John, 6/1/70, Jas. Cocke, Josh. King, Amy King
Danial, 5/8/62, Jas. Cocke, Moses Williams, Judieth Knight
Wm., 5/26/66, John and James Cockes, Susanna Hern
Thomas, 5/18/64, Abner Sturdivant, Thos.Sturdivant, Bird Land,
    Wincy Hutchens
James, 5/18/64, Abner Sturdivant, Thos. Adkinson, Anne Stevens
Anna, 9/11/70, David Graves, Eliz. Owen, Anna Wrenn
Richard, 10/11/72, Wm. Wynne, Fred Lilly, Eliz. Wynne
Joel, 2/11/75, Wm. and Moses Knight, Drusilla King

Jas. and Amy Cocke
Edmund, 12/28/64, Wm. and John Cocke, Hannah Cocke
Nanny, 10/30/67, Bird Land, Rebbecca Land, Sally Hood
David, 5/14/70, Wm. Sturdivant, Absolum Spain, Frances Sturdi-
    vant
Polly, 4/17/75, Moses Knight, Drussilla King, Mary Sturdivant

Col. Thos. Cocke of S. walk Parish died 12/2/50, reported by
    Cocke.

COLE
John and Mary Cole
Joshua, 11/26/52, Wm. Mann, Joseph Cole, Mary Cole
Susanna, 3/14/57, John Bradley, Mary Nunn, Eliz. Gee

COLE (Continued)
John and Jane Coles
Selah, 3/3/54, Wm. Weathers, Mary Weathers, Sarah Bradley

COLEMAN
James and Eliz. Coleman
John, 6/11/63, Sloman Wynne, Jas. Williams Jr., Anne Stevens

COLLIER
Charles and Susanna Collier
Susanna, 2/27/61, John Edmunds, Gray Edmunds, Eliz. Edmunds
Lucy, 11/13/59, Josiah Smith, Lucy Davis, Eliz. Smith.
Wm. Smith, 4/26/62, Wm. Parham, Burwell Banks, Anne Gibbons

Charles and Lucretia Collier
Eliz., 12/19/39, Arthur Smith, Joyce Washington, Sarah Turner

Jesse and Rebbecca Collier
John, 2/21/72, David Lessenbury, Henry Underhill, Mary Lessenbury

CONLEY
Wm. and Sarah Conley
Conelly, 6/15/57, John Adkins, Phoebe Epps, Lucy Adkins
Salley, 2/27/60, none given

COOK - COOKE
Rubin and Anne Cook
----ish, 11/21/41, John Stokes, Joseph Carter, Amy Carter
Richard, 8/1/44, Joseph Mason, Wm. Moss Jr., Eliz. Cook
Sarah, 6/24/46, Chris. Mason, Sarah Carter, Mary Dempsey
Henry, 8/22/50. Jas. Chappell Jr.. Wm. Tomlinson, Amy Briggs
Chris. Mason, Sarah Carter

Rubin and Mary Cook
Wm., 12/3/55, Wm. Wilkinson, Amos Sledge, Mary Wallace
John, 1/2/58, John Weathers, Edwd. Weaver, Agnes Mangum
Sarah, 4/6/60, none given

Wm. and Eliz. Cook
Thomas, 12/4/41, John Peebles, Wm. Brown, Mary Richardson
Sarah, 10/6/44, David Jones, Anne Cook, Eliz. Shands
Forster, 6/14/47, Beng. and John Rives, Frances Rives
Henry, 2/26/49, Joseph Goodwynne, Jas. Bosseau Jones, Phoebe
Mason

Wm. and Naomi Cook
Mercurius, 3/12/42, Richard Knight, Wm. Clifton, Eliz. Knight
Lazarus, 4/30/44, John King, Richard Woodruff, Eliz. King
Eph., 1/30/51, John Ezell, John Sandefour, Sarah Sandefour

COOK-COOKE (Continued)
Richard and Mary Cook
Rebbecca, 12/16/70, Lawrence Smith, Rebbecca Cook, Mary Wilcox
Mary, 3/18/73, Wm. Wilcox, Mary Smith, Eliz. Holt
Salley, 12/13/74, Wm. Weaver, Anne Lucas, Rebbecca Underhill

Richard and Anne Cook
Richard Herbert, 9/5/69, Aug. Clairbourne, Nath'l. Cook, Mary Fisher, Jacobina Willie
Aug. Clairbourne, Aug. and Billy Clairbourne, Susanna Clairbourne

John and Lucretia Cook
Jeansey, 9/18/70, Moses Knight, Anne Pennington, Thany Pare

Henry and Rebbecca Cook
John, 10/14/71, Ben'g. Hill, Richard Cook, Mary Cook
Henry, 12/30/73, Lawrence Smith, John Salter, Eliz. Hill

James and Eliz. Cook
Sarah, 4/5/71, Jas. Barker, Mary and Anne Tomlinson
Forster, 4/19/73, Richard Cook, Dan'l. Ivy, Eliz. Barker

COOKE
John and Lucy Cooke
Lemenia, 11/9/56, Jas. Sturdivant, Eliz. Rodgers, Hannah Pennington
Lucretia, 2/10/58, Jas. Cox, Mary Harwood, Anne Woodland
Chany, 9/15/59, Joseph Prince, Amy Threewitt, Sarah Williams
Wm., 2/15/65, Chas. Williams, Frances Woodruff, Eliz. Williams
Judy, 2/15/65, Wm. and Jas. Cockes, Thany Williams
Patty, 6/13/68, Bird Land, Prissilla Gilliam, Eliz. Spane
Salley, twin, Wm. Spane, Mary Hill, Eliz. Williams

COOPER
James and Mary Cooper
Richard, 1/15/72, Josh. and Jesse Johnson, Mary Johnson
Margarett, 1/11/75, James Johnson, Eliz. Cooper, Milly Johnson

James and Eliz. Cooper
Bunyee, 11/12/40, Geo. Long, Mary Cooper, Eliz. Cooper

Wm. and Eliz. Cooper
James, 12/?/51, Nath'l. Johnson, Israel Cullom, Susanna Johnson
Eliz., 9/7/55, Anne Gilbert, Susanna Johnson, David Wiggens
Wm., 6/15/52, Petway Johnson, Howell Chappell, Richard Johnson

Wm. and Eliz. Cooper
Maerina, 11/8/42, David Wiggins, Anne Pate, Eliz. Cooper

CORNET

Geo. and Martha Cornet
Joel, 9/17/41, Rob't. Bulloch, Thos. Barlow, Mary Morgan
Jones, 1/9/43, Wm. and Mary Jones, John Jones
Selah, 3/11/45, Richard Barlow, Mary Hix, Elenor Evans
Jonas, 12/24/47, John Davis, Wallace Johnson, Judieth Hill
Josiah, 2/11/52, John Eaton, Ben'g. Hale, Mary Jelks

Jones and Edieth Cornet
Martha, 9/30/71, John Hagood, Patience Hay, Selah Ma----?
  (Martin)
George, 12/28/73, John Pate, Chas. Long, Mary Hagood

COTTON

Thomas and Jean Cotton
Isam, 9/23/39, John Underhill, John Wilkerson, Amelia Underhill
Mary, 9/23/43, Joseph Mason, Agnes Wilkerson, Eliz. Atkins

John and Lucy Cotton
Amelia, 12/1/39, Nath'l. Duncan, Eliz. Weaver, Eliz. Hall
Sarah, 9/24/41, Henry Prichard, Lucy Prichard, Sarah Hay
Jane, 12/9/44, Wm. Hutchens, Lucy Cain, Susanna Crossland
Eph., 12/13/46, Joseph Prince, Samuel Tatum, Eliz. Copeland

Richard and Betty Cotton
Salley, 1/12/48, Thos. Cotton, Jane Weaver, Eliz. Cotton
Seth, 11/1/40, Jas. Tomlinson, Nath'l. Cotton, Mary Weaver
Harris, 8/25/53, Richard Jarrett, Wm. Cotton, Eliz. Moss
Beckey, 3/29/56, Josh. Cotton, Susanna Weaver, Joyce Adkins
Archibald, 2/28/59, John Adams, Mary Weaver, Tany Cotton
Jane, 4/14/62, Travis Weaver, Mary Weaver, Mary Cotton
Cary, 3/12/65, Edwd. Weaver Jr., John Moss, Salley Cotton
Weaver, 7/2/68, John Ogburn Jr., Seth Cotton, Selah Cotton
Wm., 7/2/68, (twin), John Ogburn Jr., Seth Cotton, Selah Cotton

Joshua and Susanna Cotton
Jesse, 12/18/57, Richard Cotton, Jones Crossland, Anne Hight
Frederick, 6/11/60, Henry Cotton, Drury Cotton, Eliz. Cotton
Drusilla, 12/9/63, Henry Underhill, Mary Underhill, Amy Tom-
  linson
Howell, none given
Lucy, 3/21/67, Howell Hight, Sarah and Eliz. Cotton
Edmund, 3/20/69, Thos. Whitefield, Wm. Hight, Selah and Anne
  Hight
Susanna, 2/10/72, Thos. Moss, Sarah Moss, Mary Jennings

Henry and Sarah Cotton
Betty, 1/3/62, none given
Thomas, 5/21/66, Thos. and Lewis Adkins, Mary Adkins

Wm. and Eliz. Cotton
Selah, 12/14/60, Isam Cotton, Mary Cotton, Joyce Adkins

COTTON (Continued)
Wm. and Eliz. Cotton (Continued)
Jerimiah, 5/31/61, Wm. Cotton, David Cotton, Sarah Cotton
Wells, 12/31/63, Drury and Nath'l. Cotton, Susanna Cotton
Lucretia, 11/14/62, Wm. Heeth Jr., Mary Hill, Sarah Cotton
Hardy, 2/1/66, Wm. Hunter, John Ogburn Jr., Salley Cotton

Drury and Phoebe Cotton
Herbert, 10/17/62, Wm. and David Cotton, Eliz. Tatum
Littleberry, 3/10/64, John Crossland, Wm. Tatum, Mary Tatum
Mason, 2/14/68, Josh. Tatum, ------? (torn)

Harris and Deidamia Cotton
Wm., 10/13/76, Wm. Gary, Hartwell Hunter, Beck Cotton

CRAGG
Wm. and Anne Cragg
Susanna, 8/26/40, Nich. Partridge, Eliz. Freeman, Eliz. Ivy

Wm. and Susanna Cragg
Mary, 10/13/43, Wm. Rachael, Mary King, Mary Shrewsberry
Sarah, 2/9/45, David Stokes, Lucretia Stokes, Lucy Stokes
Mary, 7/15/48, Robert Jones Jr., Judieth Woodall, Mary Stokes
Mary Cragg, a child, died 11/8/46, reported by Wm. Cragg
Wm. Cragg died 8/27/47

CREACH-CROUCH
John and Kesiah Creach
Walter, 9/1/62, none given
John, 12/18/65, Joseph Hix, James Bane, Eliz. Bane
Peggy, none given, 3/1/70
Thos. Bevan, 8/2/71, Patrick Lashley, Lawrence Smith, Mary
    Smith

John and Judy Crouch
Eliz., 3/19/66, none given
Tabitha, 4/16/68, none given

CREEDAL
Wm. and Mary Creedal
John, 11/6/74, Henry Creedal, John Smith, Nancy Creedal

CREW
John and Eliz. Crew
Lucretia, 8/27/42, Thos. Addison, Mary Addison, Eliz. Pepper

CROSS
Edward and Eliz. Cross
Edmund, 1/6/64, none given

CROSS (Continued)
Edward and Rebbecca Cross
John, 7/15/66, Steven Pepper, Wm. Wilson, Eliz. Nicholson
Eliz., ?/?/?, Wm. Nicholson, Eliz. Nicholson, Eliza Sharp

CROSSLAND
John and Mary Crossland
Christopher, 8/11/54, Nath'l. Felts, Wm. Knight, Hannah Felts
Joshuah, 11/26/52, Wm. Mann, Joseph Coles, Mary Cotton
Nath'l., 12/21/66, Nath'l. Cotton, John Ray, Sarah Hunter
Susanna, 6/1/68, Thos. Partridge, Mary Adkins, Eliz. Cotton
John, 3/25/70, Thos. Johnson, Thos. Moss, Anne Ray
Henry, 5/12/72, Wm. and Hern Cotton, Rebbecca Cotton
Jane, 1/11/75, Thos. Whitefield, Mary Whitefield, Sarah Ivy

CULLAM
Thomas and Eliz. Cullam
William, 11/11/39, Sarah Tatum, Wm. Johnson, Jr., ------ Smith
Eliz., 7/13/42, none given
Frederick, 3/7/44, Nath'l. Johnson, Samuel Tatum, Susanna Johnson
Anne, 3/11/47, Edwd. Prince, Mildred Underhill, Susanna Johnson
Thomas, 12/8/50, Thos. Ivy, Wm. Saunders, Eliz. Cullam
Nich., 6/18/52, Travis Griffith, Israel Cullam, Mary Cullam
Anslem, 2/26/58, John Bane, Wm. Willie, Mary Cullam
Frederick Cullam, an idiot, died 9/22/58, reported by Thos. Cullam.

Wm. and Amy Cullam
William, 8/29/65, Thos. Cooper, John Hight, Anne Cullam
Jerimiah, 1/27/68, Travis Griffith, Thos. Cullam, Anne Griffith
Susanna, 1/28/73, John Hight, Lucy Gilbert, Kesiah Wallace

CURRY
John and Ava Curry
James, 9/1/48, Morris Prichard, Eliz. Prichard
Ava, 7/30/53, Wm. Longbottom, Rebbecca Longbottom, Eliz. Hargrave
Cary, 12/21/59, none given
Clairbourne, 8/5/65, Lewis Dunn, Geo. Long, Mary Rachael

Jean Curry died 12/2/43, reported by Sylvanus Stokes Jr.

CURTIS
John and Elenor Curtis
Sucky, --/--/--, David Walker, Mary Walker, Lucy Belches

34

CURTIS (Continued)
John and Sucky Curtis
John, 9/6/66, Abra. Winfield, Joseph Richardson, Suck Winfield

John and Anna Curtis
Lucretia, 12/15/61, John Wilkerson, Hannah Hill, Rebbecca Seat
Salley, 11/11/62, Rubin Malone, Lucy Malone, Sarah Redding
Bolling, 5/8/63, John Wynne, Jas. Cain Jr., Lucretia Cain
Wm. Willie, 6/5/64, Peter Green, Lewis Brown, Martha Brown
Elemelich, 5/9/69, none given
Tarpley, 7/7/70, John Walker, Joseph Richarson, Jane Raines
Hezikah, 7/19/72, Absolum Brown, Nath'l. Rainey, Phoebe Rainey
Civilia, 9/27/73, Burwell Wellborn, Mary Richarson, Polly Rainey

DANSEY
Wm. and Mary Dansey
Anne, 9/5/38, James Mason, Anne Mason, Mary Mason
John, 3/9/39, Cap't. John Mason, Joseph Mason, Anne Stevens
Wm., 5/4/41, John Mason Jr., John Gilliam, Anthony Hancock
Eliz., 1/3/42, Thos. Wrenn Jr., Eliz. Mason, Hannah Wrenn
Mary, 6/15/46, Hartwell Marriable, Mary Marriable, Eliz. Dobie
Archibald, 9/23/51, David Mason, Joseph Pennington, Anne Bevin

DAVIDSON
Wm. and Prissilla Davidson
Eliz., 2/23/39, Wm. Brown, Ann Turner, Eliz. Turner
Tomy (son), 2/18/41, Wm. Carlisle, Wm. Brown, Mary Richard-
son
Arthur 6/12/44, Arthur Richardson, Arthur Smith, Marg. Bryan
Mary, 2/7/46, John Smith Jr., Eliz. Vassor, Martha Smith

DAVIS
Hugh and Anne Davis
Christopher, 1/14/40, John Davis, Chris. Jean, Eliz. Temple

Wm. and Frances Davis
Frances, 12/27/45, Nath'l. Hood, Martha and Susanna Moore

Absolum and Katherine Davis
Zilpah, 2/15/52, Thos. Vines, Eliz. Vines, Sarah Banks

John Davis Jr. and Mary
Lucy, 4/29/40, Samuel Crew, Amy Davis, Mary Woodward
Mathew, 3/14/41, John Davis, Chris. Jean, Eliz. Rachael
James, 4/25/48, John Carter, Thos. Wade, Susanna Wade
Johannah, 2/11/49, John Woodward, Isabel Buckner, Amos Moss

Absolum and Anne Davis
Lucy, 5/7/51, Lewis Dunn, Katherine Harwood, Mary Land
Gidion, 12/14/52, Ben'g. Harrison, Richard Felts, Prissilla Gil-
liam

DAVIS (Continued)
Absolum and Anne Davis (Cont.)
Chislen, 1/17/55, Ralp'h. McGee, Thos. Southward, Agnes Carter

Thomas and Jane Davis
Abigail, 12/2/40, Richard King, Mary Keeton, Mary Bonner
Lucy, 3/10/50, Wm. King, Anne King, Frances Atkinson
Charles, 2/23/52, Chs. Wood, Nath'l. Hood, Sarah Hood
Jenny, 3/1/55, Edwd. Davis, Susanna Davis, Sarah Hutchens
Wyatt, 1/8/58, Edwd. Whittington, Thos. Davis Sr., Penelope
   Whittington
Beckey, 9/12/63, James Hern, Susanna and Fanny Davis

John and Rachael Davis
Cretia, 4/9/62, Nath'l. Green, Mary and Winny Atkinson
Baxter, 4/8/64, Wm. Carter, Wm. Carter Jr., Anne Wilkerson
Thomas, 5/7/66, Matth. Parham, Israel Melton, Rebbecca Blanks
Vina, Wina?, 4/5/71, John Milton, Martha and Mary Atkinson

DEAN
Thos. and Eliz. Dean
Jean, 6/1/40, Jas. Mathews, Eliz. Mathews, Phoebe Dean

DELAHAY - DE LA HAY
Chas. and Eliz. Delahay
John, 9/9/39, Wm. Richardson, Edwd. Farrington, Martha Rich-
   ardson
Arthur, 7/31/41, Henry Freeman Jr., Frances Hutchens, Sarah Ellis
Chas., 8/25/45, Thos. Woodland, Drury Robertson, Mary Rainey
Sarah, 8/12/47, Isacc Robertson, Frances Robertson, Eliz. Far-
   rington
Susanna, 7/4/50, John Rolland, Mary Rolland, Mary Rainey

Arthur and Sarah Delahay
John, 6/6/65, Ben'g. Wellborn, Burwell Hill, Mildred Hill
Edmund, 10/12/67, Robert Slate, Thos. Wynne Jr., Sarah Delahay
Eliz. Jones, 10/7/69, John Hill, Sarah and Susanna Delahay

Chas. and Anne Delahay
Wm., 5/21/70, Ben'g. Wellborn, Wm. Rainey Jr., Susanna Delahay
Peggy, 2/11/72, Nath'l. Robertson, Eliz. Dunn, Eliz. Hewitt
Charles Delahay, dead 9/20/73, reported by Mrs. Berryman

DENNIS
Joseph and Mary Dennis
Wilkes, 8/21/69, Jas. Bell, Sylvanus Bell, Eliz. Spane
Rebbecca, 5/20/72, James Spane, Thany Spane, Mary Davis

DENTON
Josiah and Rebbecca Denton
John, 10/9/59, Tim. Ezell, Joshuah Hawthorn, Anne Ezell

DENTON (Continued)
Josiah and Rebbecca Denton (Continued)
Wm., 2/3/62, Danl. Eppes, Warwick Gilliam, Jr.,Anne Eppes
James, 9/17/68, Nath'l. Duncan, Isacc Hawthorn, Mary Adams

John and Mary Denton
Edward, 3/9/43, Wm. Hutchens, John Hood, Frances Denton
Thos, (twin) 3/9/43, John Tatum, Thos. Tadlock, Frances Tatum
Sarah, 4/30/45, Josh. Hawthorn, Sarah Bird, Eliz. Williams'

DICKENS
Thos. and Anne Dickens
James, 9/7/58, John Land, Wm. Andrews Jr., Sarah Andrews
Rosanna, (twin) 9/7/58, Wm. Adams Jr., Lydia and Sarah Andrews

Alex. and Lydia Dickens
Peter, 2/18/39, Wm. McDade, Thos. Adkins, Mary McDade
Wm., 7/10/42, James Losbourne, Henry Bailey, Anne Dickens
Lucy, 11/11/44, Math. Whitehead, Mary Jennings, Eliz. Atkins
Frederick, 7/1/47, Edwd. Shelton, Chas. Dickens, Eliz. Atkins

DINKINS (likely Dickens)
Theophiles and Sarah Dinkens
Mason, 9/23/67, John Hill, Winney Ivy, Patty Green

Peter and Martha Dinkens
Salley, 2/20/61, Wm. Cullum, Anthony Hancock, Eliz. Pennington

DOBIE
Wm. and Hannah Dobie
Joseph, 8/12/40, Joseph Mason, Chas. Gee, Mary Dansey
John, 1/9/42, Ben'g. Moss, Joseph Hawthorn, Martha Moss

Nath'l. and Elenor Dobie
Nath'l., 11/19/53, Thos. Shands, Josh. Hawthorn, Hannah Dobie

Peter and Mary Dobie
John, 7/17/50, John Moss, David Wiggens, Susanna Lilly,
------ Lee.
Wm., 11/17/61, David Wiggens, Mathew Wynne, Susanna Clifton
Mary, 7/25/63, Richard Wiggens, John Moss, Charity Clifton

John and Mary Dobe
Joshuah, 1/21/44, Peter Vincent, Robert Tatum, Jane Underwood

DOONE
Morris and Rebbecca Doone
James, 3/2/63, Wm. Sammons, Edward -------, Amy Moss

DOWDY - DOWDEN

Edward and Sarah Dowden

Eliz., 1/27/21, none given - Mary, 3/16/27, none given - John, 8/2/34, Jesse, 12/13/36, none given - Sarah 11/15/24, none given, Susanna, 12/17/29, none given - Hannah, 6/17/39, none given

Thomas and Eliz. Dowdy

Lucy, 1/7/53, Robt. Parsons, Elenor Parsons, Eliz. Adkins.

Thomas and Lucy Dowdy

Thomas, 10/2/59, Ben'g. and Wm. Seaborn, Aggy Woodward
John, 4/24/62, Nath'l. Northington, John Sands, Martha Seaborn
George, 12/17/64, David Mason, John Sammons, Winefred Hutchens
Bartley, 8/8/70, Nath'l. Newsom, Jas. Burns, Mason Bird

DRAKE

Lazarus and Sarah Drake

David, 7/12/52, David Hines, Wm. Johnson, Christian Hines
Drury, 1/15/67, John Peters, Wm. Wrenn, Anne Wrenn

DUFF

Wm. and Mary Duff

Anne, 3/7/59, Wm. Wynne, Eliz. Wilkerson, Lucy Blaton

DUNCAN

Nath'l. and Agnes Duncan

Mely, 2/10/44, Hugh Ivy, Mely Underwood, Agnes Wilkerson
Agnes, 5/21/47, Wm. Wilkerson, Eliz. Tatum, Lucy Jones
Boyce, 8/6/49, Sarah and Eliz. Wilkerson, Danial Duncan
Miles, 3/1/53, Richard Wilkerson, Nath'l. Cotton, Mary Wilkerson
Sarah, 11/4/60, Wm. Hunter, Sarah Moss, Sarah Adkins
Wm., 12/16/61, Thos. Dunn, John Knight, Betty Beddingfield
John, 4/12/63, John Adkins, John Ray, Katherine McInnish
Nath'l., 10/5/65, Ben'g. Barker, Joseph Denton, Joyce Capel
Danial, 4/30/68, John Underhill Jr., Adam Eckman, Boyce Duncan
David, 3/13/69, Giles Underhill, Wm. Tomlinson, Sarah Underhill
Nath'l. Duncan reported the death of David Duncan 4/9/45

DUNN

John and Lucy Dunn

Isabell, 12/28/40, John Pennington, Rivena Harley, Eliz. Weaver
Lucy, 10/27/43, Wm. Dunn, Amy Dunn, Eliz. Hancock
Wm., 12/16/62, Thos. Dunn, John Knight, Betty Winfield

David and Frances Dunn

Ishmael, 1/13/48, Peter Hawthorn, Wm. Bird, Rebbecca Hawthorn

DUNN (Continued)

Thomas Dunn Jr. and Lucy

Gray, 3/1/44, Wm. Johnson, Harry Prichard, Mary Judkins
Ruth, 4/10/47, Edwd. Shelton, Eliz. Shelton, Eliz. Judkins
Lavina, 3/1/48, Burwell Bell, Jane Judkins, Mary Dunn
Dorothy, 1/2/50, Amos Atkinson, Frances Judkins, Susanna
    Stokes
Allen, 9/28/58, Thos. Bushby, Thos. Holt, Lucy Dunn
Barnaby, 4/13/61, Thos. Moore Jr., Lewis Dunn, Agnes Battle
Henry, 5/14/68, Jas. Battle, Wm. Moss, Lavina Dunn

Wm. and Amy Dunn

Nath'l., 7/23/46, Nath'l. Bedingfield, Thos. King, Eliz. Edwards
Wm., 5/4/50, David Mason, Beng. Wyche, Mary Moss
Drury, 2/21/52, Thos. Mitchell, Thos. Shands, Mary Mason
Eliz., 9/11/54, none given
Thomas, 10/1/55, Wm. Aldridge, David Simms, Mary Nunn
Lewis, 1/14/57, Wm. Bird, Thos. Hobbs, Mary Dobie
Mary, 9/2/58, Banks Meacum, Mary Gee, Jane Tuel
Thomas, 3/6/63, Wm. Belamy, Nath'l. Jones, Anne Hamilton
David, 1/14/64, John Adkins, Robert Glover, Fanny Biggons
Drury Dunn died 2/8/72, reported by Geo. Rives.

Eliz. Dunn, the wife of Thomas, died 8/28/67, reported by Wm.
    Dunn.

Nathanial and Rebbecca Dunn

Henry, 2/8/70, Wm. and Nathanial Parham, Lucy Malone
Frances, 6/8/72, John Petway, Rebbecca and Selah Parham

Nathanial Dunn died ------, 1749
Mary Dunn died ------, 1749.

ECCLES

Edward and Mary Eccles

Lucy, 2/10/41, Chas. Jackson, Eliz. Titmash, Susanna Jackson

Edward and Eliz. Eccles

Henry, 10/31/47, Edmund Pate, Wm. Rolland, Eliz. Roberts

Thomas and Eliz. Eccles

Sarah, 10/30/53, Rob't. Eccles, Betty and Susanna Eccles

John and Mary Eccles

Martha, 2/3/59, Nath'l. Freeman, Martha Freeman, Hannah
    Winfield
Eliz., 2/3/59. (twin), Josh. Winfield, Jemimma Freeman, Mary
    Bough
Molly, 11/26/60, none given
E. Winfield (son), none given
Hannah, 10/4/73, Robert Winfield, Lucretia Parham, Kesiah
    Freeman

ECKMAN - EKMAN
Adam and Amy Ekman
John, 4/19/71, Nath'l. Barker, Henry Underhill, Rebbecca Cotton
Robert, 7/1/69, none given
Eliz., 3/16/73, Wm. Willie, Jacobina Willie, Tabitha Mitchell

EDMUNDS
Wm. and Judieth Edmunds
Gray, 3/26/42, John Harrison, John Edmunds, Phylis Edmunds
Rebbecca, 7/23/45, Nath'l. Briggs, Hannah Peters, Lucy Bailey

David and Anne Edmunds
Howell, 1/25/43, Howell Jones, John Edmunds, Gray Edmunds,
   Sarah Hines
Archur - Arthur, 4/28/47, David Jones, John Jones, Amy Chap-
   pell

John and Rebbecca Edmunds
Jane, 1/24/62, Richard Blunt, Mary Irby, Mary Nicholson
Charlotte, 2/2/60, David Hunter, ------ Simmons, Eliz.Bridges

John Gray Edmunds and Eliz.
Lucy, 5/7/64, Henry Jarrett, Mary Chappell, Lucretia Jones
Tempe, 11/12/65, Fred Hines, Francis Briggs, Prissilla Edmunds
Susanna, 6/28/67, John Nicholson, Sarah Kennybrough, Olive Hines

William Edmunds died 3/9/39, reported by Mary Edmunds
Mary Edmunds died 10/3/65, reported by John Harrison

EDWARDS
Chris. and Sarah Edwards
W., 1/21/38, Wm. Willie, Chris. Tatum, Sarah Robinson

EDLESDISTA
David and Sarah Edlesdista
Molly, 6/20/62, Howell Hutchens, Fanny Davis, Chany Williams
John, 12/13/64, Wm. and Jesse Rodgers, Martha Hutchens

Eliz. Edwards died 2/3/52, reported by Chris. Tatum

ELDRIDGE
Thomas and Martha Eldridge
John, 4/22/41, Wm. Epps, Wm. Willie, Anne Bolling, Anne
   Eldridge
Judieth (twin), 4/22/41, Wm. Willie, Judieth Eldridge, Isabel
   Bedingfield
Mary, 3/11/42, Henry Bedingfield, Eliz. Eldridge, Isabel Bed-
   ingfield
Rolph, 12/29/44, Aug. Clairbourne, Wm. Clack, Anne Murry,
   Martha Eldridge

ELDRIDGE (Continued)

Cap't. Wm. and Anne Eldridge

Eliz., 3/25/62, John Eldridge, Mary and Judieth Eldridge
Robert, 1/4/64, Robert Jones, Wm. Willie, Jacobina Willie, Anne
Clairbourne
Thomas, 1/19/66, none given
Mary Aughustine, 8/22/68, Cyrill Avery, Martha Binns, Judieth
Avery
Anne, 2/7/71, Geo. Rives, Martha Belches, Sarah Petway

Thomas and Judieth Eldridge

Sarah, 5/14/40, Thos. Eldridge Jr., Agnes Kennon, Martha Eldridge

Judieth Eldridge died 10/14/59, reported by Wm. Eldridge
Thomas Eldridge died 11/4/40
Thomas Eldridge died 12/4/51, reported by John Hay
Eliz. Eldridge died 9/15/45, reported by Thos. Eldridge

Thomas and Eliz. Eldridge

Howell, 3/11/53, John Jones, Wm. Willie, Eliz. Willie
Aristotle, 10/30/51, Chris. Mason, Wm. Willie, Margaret Hay

ELLIS

John and Mary Ellis

John, 1/29/42, Edward Lee, Robert Sandefour, Lydia Weathers
Richard, 9/25/48, Wm. Rolland, Josh Rolland, Sarah Harwood
Mary, 9/26/51, Josh. Ellis, Agnes Adams, Eliz. Wiggens

Joshua and Sarah Ellis

Joshuah, 3/23/40, Robert Bulloch, Thos. Weathers, Eliz. Delahay

Joseph and Faith Ellis

Joseph, 5/5/46, none given
John, 11/27/46, Joseph Jones, Drury Davis, Rebbecca Jones
The above should be Joseph, 1/6/53
Edwin, 5/16/59, none given

Edward and Eliz. Ellis

Wm., 1/24/40, Alex. Dickens, Nath'l. Hawthorn, Susanna Haw-
thorn
Jerimiah, 5/7/44, John Ellis, Richard Wiggens, Mary Dickens
Edward, 8/27/45, Timothy Ezell Jr., John Ezell, Anne Ezell

Jonathan and Hannah Ellis

Richard, 1/22/52, Wm. Ellis, Thos. Person
Jonathan, 1/22/52, Richard Presson, Ben'g. Ellis, Eliz. Presson

Eliz. Ellis died 11/20/50

Wm. and Eliz. Ellis

Ben'g., 4/8/53, Ben'g. Ellis, Simon Stacey, Lydia Proctor
Drury, 1/18/55, Jonathan Ellis, Edward Wright, Hannah Ellis

ELLIS (Continued)

Wm. and Eliz. Ellis (Continued)

Susanna, 5/15/57, John Andrews, Sarah Andrews, Lucy Proctor
John, 3/4/59, Emanuel James, Henry Underhill, Mary Underhill
Wm., 1/25/61, Arthur Richardson, Fred Andrews, Mary Stacey
John, 12/13/65, Wm. and Jesse Rodgers, Martha Hutchens
Katherine, none given
Mary, 8/18/67, none given
Salley, 11/6/69, Sarah Bond, Anne James
Wright, 9/15/72, Thos. Smith, Ben'g. Ellis, Patience Blow

Wm. and Anne Ellis
Mary, 3/3/74, none given

EMERY
Green and Sarah Emery
Mary, 12/29/39, Geo. Ezell, Mary Sansick, Anne Felts
Eliz., 3/13/42, John Bulloch, Amy Bulloch, Agnes Bulloch

EPPES
Edward and Mary Eppes
Amy, 9/9/39, Wm. Reid Jr., Mary Eccles, Lucy Johnson
Sarah, 6/17/41, Gilbert Weaver, Mary Moore, Eliz. Denton
Anne, 9/15/43, Josh. Tatum, Frances Moss, Eliz. Weaver
Mary, 7/4/46, Epps Moore, Eliz. Gilbert, Prissilla Mitchell
James, 3/11/48, Jas. Clairbourne, James Anderson, Mary Tatum
Winny, 10/16/51, Drury Tatum, Mary Moss, Judieth Rivers (Rives?)
Susanna, 9/12/53, Richard Blunt, Susanna Moore, Martha Gilbert
Eliz., 6/3/56, Timothy Ezell, Lucy Dunn, Mary Moore
Frances, 1/6/59, Nath'l. Tomlinson, Jacobina Willie, Anne Wiggens

Eliz. Epps died 10/14/68, reported by John Adkins
Mary Epps, aged 79, died 6/13/55, reported by Edward Epps

Danial and Anne Epps
Pleasant, 12/9/67, Edward and Robert Slate, Sarah Slate
Rebbecca, 8/28/71, Wm. Rose, Mary Rose, Tabitha Rolland

Francis and Phoebe Epps
Mary, bab. 3/13/60, none given
James, 5/16/62, Jas. Parish, Nath'l. Green, Jane Rains
Francis, 1/22/65, Wm. Mitchell, Fred Green, Sarah Jones
Thomas, 11/6/67, Jones Freeman, Robert Slate, Lucy Freeman

ESKRIDGE
Thomas and Eliz. Eskridge
Judy, 7/4/70, Lawrence Gibbons Jr., Mary Moore, Eliz. Edmunds
Willoughby, 11/19/71, Wm. Yarbrough, Nath'l. Dunn, Lucy Gibbons

EVANS
Wm. and Prissilla Evans
Wm., born 3/7/47, none given

Ben'g. and Lucy Evans
John, 2/14/54, Mich'l. Jarrett, Mich'l. Hill Jr., Susanna Oliver
Wm., twin, Drury Spane, Burwell Green, Mildred Spane
Susanna, 1/1/56, Wm. Oliver, Mary Malone, Eliz. Pepper
Archer, 6/5/58, John Atkinson, Wm. Rolland, Mary Hill

Thomas and Frances Evans
Thomas, 6/7/61, Mark Harewell, Jas. Green Way, Mary Farrington

EZELL
Timothy Ezell Jr. and Anne
Isacc, 4/7/43, none given
Mary, 3/17/44, John Ezell, Penelope Green, Eliz. Ezell
Richard, 8/5/47
Ann, 2/27/48, Wm. Rose, Mary Ezell, Lucy Peerman
Timothy, 9/16/50; John Jenkins, John Bennett, Lucretia Peerman
James, 2/16/52, Richard Wiggens Jr., Sam'l. Wiggens, Mary
Lee
Note, Anne Ezell, a child, died Oct. 1749

George and Sarah Ezell
John, 9/22/41, Jerimiah Bulloch, Richard Wiggens, Eliz. Roberts

James and Kesiah Ezell
Jesse, 3/14/49, Richard Bulloch, Chas. Bulloch, Lucy Ezell

Thomas and Anne Ezell
Thomas, 1/20/44, Edmund Ellis, Wm. Rose, Mary Rose
John, 2/10/42, John Eaton, Rob't. Berry, Eliz. Rose
Anne, 1/29/46, John Ellis, ---- Rose, Sarah Roberts
Wm., 2/21/49, Wm. Rolland, Wm. Barns, Sarah Rose
Frederick, 4/28/52, Thos. Adkinson, Jesse Rolland, Faith Rose
Baalam, 9/7/56, Wm. Woodland, Sam'l. Northington, Agnes
Woodland
Abel, 9/20/58, Wm. Hill, Thos. Felts, Henretta Rains

David and Agnes Ezell
Gray, 11/22/59, Sloman Wynne Jr., Thos. Sturdivant, Eliz.
Sowersberry

Lambert and Anna Ezell
Mary, 6/29/60, Henry Porch Jr., Hannah Wren, Wilmouth Porch
Betty, 9/4/58, Timothy Ezell, Anne Ezell, Tabitha Wiggens

Thomas and Phoebe Ezell
Sally, 8/28/69, Jas. Bell, Susanna Felts, Rebbecca Rolland

EZELL (Continued)

John Jr. and Jane Ezell
Phoebe, 9/15/63, Nath'l. Felts, Phoebe Seat, Anne Ezell
Hartwell, 12/28/64, Thos. Ezell Jr., Jas. Hill, Rebbecca Seat
Lucy, 4/20/67, Andrew Felts, Mary Felts, Lucy Simmons

Wm. and Phoebe Ezell
Nancy, 4/25/75, Eph. Hutchens, Betty Southward, Lucy Maclamore

Timothy Ezell died 3/11/68, reported by Ellis Gilbert.

Wm. and Susanna Ezell
Delilah, 8/18/69, Andrew Felts, Anne Ezell, Anne Seat

Drury and Winny Ezell
Lucy, 5/17/65, Robert Whitehead, Amey Ezell, Anne Barr

Wm. and Martha Ezell
Anne, 3/10/43, Thos. Weathers Jr., Anne Nubins, Clara Wynne
Mary, 1/6/45, Henry Prichard, Lucy Prichard, Sarah Stokes
Susanna, 2/9/49, Richard King, Tabitha Ezell, Molly Stokes

George and Amy Ezell
Jesse, 3/22/66, Joseph Denton, Wm. Rives Jr., Eliz. Meacum

John and Eliz. Ezell
Isacc, 7/14/47, John Ellis, Thos. Ezell, Sarah Roberts
Eliz., 10/5/51, Thos. Adams, Mary and Eliz. Ezell
Sucky, 1/5/54, John Rawlings, Eliz. Harwood, Mary Adams
John, 9/13/56, John Hargrave, Wm. Ezell, Faith Pennington
Molly, 4/7/60, Sampson Moseley, Amy Freeman, Agnes Ezell
Molly, 12/13/61, Geo. Ezell, Anne Ezell, Tabitha Wiggens
Isam, 3/8/62, Lewis Johnson, Sarah Stokes, Wm. Rolland
Patty, 2/20/64, John Owen, Rebbecca Seat, Eliz. Woodland
Jesse, 4/6/66, Thos. Moore, Wm. Hern, Eliz. Sowersberry
Eliz., 2/21/68, Lewis Johnson, Sarah Stokes, Tabitha Rolland
Timothy, 4/17/71, Isam Gilliam, Lewis Hutchens, Susanna Ezell

Isam and Eliz. Ezell
Lucy, 11/15/54, Edward Carter, Eliz. and Fortune Stokes.
John, 10/13/56, John Hargrave, Wm. Ezell, Faith Pennington
Wm., 5/16/58, Jas. Williams Jr., Ben'g. Owen, Eliz. Williams
Molly, 5/7/60, Sampson Moseley, Amy Freeman, Agnes Ezell
Isam, 3/9/62, Young Stokes, Wm. Rolland
Robert, 3/30/64, Jas. Bell, Robert Owen, Sarah Stokes
Eliz., 2/21/68, Lewis Johnson, Sarah Stokes, Tabitha Rolland'
Timothy, 3/17/71, Isam Gilliam, Lewis Hutchens, Susanna Ezell

Peter and Amy Ezell
Betty, 5/21/60, Math. Sturdivant, Eliz. and Martha Roe
Becky, 5/26/67, Drury Parham, Patty Gilliam, Anne Barr

Isam Ezell died 4/18/75, reported by Thos. Moore

EXUM
Micajah and Anne Exum
Micajah, 7/19/71, Ben'g. Exum, Wm. Birdsong

FAISON
Henry and Lucy Faison
Wm., 1/2/60, Simon Stacey, Lawrence Smith, Mary Field
Edward, 4/13/63, Edward Wright, Franklin Clark, Anne Lane
Henry, 4/7/65, Wm. Ellis, Jas. Turner, Martha Hulin
John, 4/10/67, John Brown, Fred Smith, Eliz. Andrews
Lawrence, 12/25/69, Arthur Smith, John Freeman, Eliz. Turner
Richard Bland, 1/30/72, John Smith, Miles Birdsong, Mary Smith
Mary, 6/1/74, Mich'l. Smith, Mildred Smith, Mary Clark

FANNING
Bryan and Rachael Fanning
John, 5/24/6., Wm. Rolland, Littleberry Spain, Mary Rottenberry

FARINGTON
John and Eliz. Farington
Robert, 9/21/46, Edward Farrington, Wm. Rolland, Amy Freeman
Jane, 9/21/48, Jesse Rolland, Mary Rolland, Anne Felts

Robert and Mary Farington
Amy, 2/24/52, Nath'l. Green, Judy Love, Phoebe Green

Robert Farrington died 11/30/57, reported by Mary Farrington
Edward Farrington died 12/10/49, reported by Robert Farrington

FAWN
James and Anne Fawn
Sarah, 12/10/57, none given
Robert, 1/19/62, Fred Hobbs, John Chamberless, Eliz. Weeks
Wm., 3/13/68, Josh. and Eph. Moss, Elenor Hobbs
John, 9/16/65, Ben'g. Barker, Fred Hobbs, Sarah Wynne

FELTS
Nathaniel Felts and Hannah
Elenor, 8/9/40, Francis Felts, Sarah Roberts, Sarah Felts
Hannah, 1/21/42, Edward Shelton, Sarah Emery, Jean Felts
Lewis, 12/10/44, Lewis Adkins, Thos. Felts, Mary Seat
Sarah, 3/14/46, Robert Seat, Sarah and Eliz. Roberts
Jesse, 12/16/51, Nath'l. Felts Jr., Samuel Bulloch, Eliz. Felts
Winny, 7/11/54, Samuel Stokes, Mary Crossland, Jane Seat

Wm. and Sarah Felts
Lucy, 10/8/39, Nicholis Jones, Wm. Hicks, Eliz. Jones, Eliz. Hicks

Nathaniel and Eliz. Felts
Lucy, 4/23/49, Nath'l. Felts Jr., Agnes Bulloch, Hannah Seat

Wm. and Sarah Felts
Sally, 11/2/60, none given
Gary, 11/3/62, Petway Johnson, Wm. Ellis, Lydia Andrews
Jesse, 11/13/65, Jesse Land, Henry Creedall, Jane Jones

Helen Felts and -----??, John Hale, Sarah Warwick, Anne Ivy

Nathanial Felts Jr. and Anne
Frederick, 3/26/63, Nath'l. Felts, Thos. Adkins, Eliz. Rolland
Isam, 4/5/50, Thos. and John Felts, John Seat
Nathanial, 10/10/65, John Ezell Jr., Rebbecca and Susanna Seat
Archibald, 2/25/58, Thos. and Nathanial Felts, Agnes Felts
Aughustine, 1/28/62, Richard and Chas. Bulloch, Phoebe ------.
Nancy, 11/22/67, Ben'g. Phipps, Anne Seat, Suck Felts
Betsy, 9/11/69, Young Stokes, Eliz. and Sarah Woodland
Thomas, 3/26/74, Isam and Fred Felts, Mary Felts

John and Mary Felts
Andrew, 7/19/46, Nath'l. Felts, John Bulloch, Anne Seat
Sucky, 2/11/47, Nath'l. Felts, Anne Seat, Hannah Seat
John, 8/7/49, Thos. Felts, Thos. Felts Jr., Anne Rolland
Jordan, 7/16/51, Jas. Cooper, Wm. Hix, Jane Seat
Molly, 4/1/53, Lewis Adkins, Eliz. and Mary Felts
Nath'l., 1/25/55, Wm. Hill, Wm. Harris, Lucy Seat
Allen, 7/19/46, none given

Thomas Felts Jr. and Agnes
Sarah, 2/15/50, Thos. Felts, Hannah and Eliz. Felts
Susanna, 4/6/52, Jerimy Bulloch, Amy and Kesiah Bulloch
Burwell, 3/8/54, John Bulloch, Wm. Hill, Mary Bulloch
Eliz., 11/30/56, Nath'l. Felts, Rebbecca Seat, Mary Bulloch
Anne, 11/29/58, Thos. Ezell, Anne Felts, Agnes Bulloch
Bolling, 6/23/63, Robert Seat, Tubal Hix, Elenor Felts
Salley, 11/29/58, Thos. Ezell, Anne Felts, Agnes Bulloch

Richard and Mary Felts
Sucky, 11/15/54, David Clanton, Tabitha Felts, Eliz. Roe
Winny, 10/28/56, Sarah Arnold, Patty Roe
Patty, 9/24/60, Lewis Dunn, Amy Felts, Agnes Gilliam
Sarah, 10/10/58, Nath'l. Felts, Sarah Gilliam, Lucy Dunn
Frederick, 7/20/62, Wm. Gilbert, Peter Knight, Eliz. Cooper
Gray, 3/23/66, Lewis Hutchens, Jesse Rodgers, Anne McGee
Wm., 10/5/68, Edmund Gilliam, Wm. Roe, Anne Southard
Henry, 5/13/70, Wm. Gilbert, Peter Knight, Eliz. Cooper

Nathan and Mary Felts
Eliz., 2/1/53, Wm. Rolland, Eliz. Rolland, Eliz. Rowland
Randolph, 3/10/54, Robert Seat, Nathanial Felts, Eliz. Rolland
Rolland, 10/10/55, Nath'l. Felts, Jr., Ben'g. Adams, Jr., Lucy
    Rolland

FELTS (Continued)
Nathan and Mary Felts (Continued)
Sucky, 1/16/59, Thos. Adams, Jane Ezell, Lucy Harris
Wm., 12/7/60, Francis Felts, Isacc Rawlings, Rebbecca Harwood

FIELD,
Richard and Anne Field
Mary, 2/14/40, none given
Green, 4/21/49, Robert Nicholson, Barthowlemew Field, Lydia
    Smith
Pamelia, 7/10/50, Arthur Smith, Martha Gilbert, Mary Barrow

FIGG
Ben'g. and Mary Figg
James, 1/28/68, Jas. Barker, Jas. Cook, Anne Barker

FIGURES
Barthalemew and Mary Figures
Thomas, 12/18/17, none given
John, 3/30/23, none given
Richard, 9/18/25, none given
Rebbecca, 7/31/28, none given
Mary, 1/19/30, none given
Joseph, 1/13/33, none given
Wm., 3/24/36, none given
Eliz., 9/14/39, none given

FINCH
Wm. and Anne Finch
Isam, 7/5/61, John Robertson, Henry Porch, Eliz. Woodward

FIRE - FIER - FEAR all seem to be the same family
Wm. and Lucy Fire
Lucretia, 3/6/68, Thos. Weathers, Mary and Selah Atkinson
Drury, 12/5/70, Abel Mabrey, Lewis Mabrey, Patty Atkins
Thos. Lawrence, 6/12/74, John Davis, Amos Adkins, Rachael
    Davis

FITCHET
Wm. Fitchet and Dedimus Christian (his wife)
Eliz., 12/12/51, Wm. Smith, Mary Burgess, Eliz. Massengale

FITZPATRICK
Moses and Frances Fitzpatrick
Sarah, 11/28/38, Dan'l. Massengale, Ester Winkle

FITZPATRICK (Continued)
Moses and Hannah Fitzpatrick
Hannah, no date, but before 1743

FLOOD,
John and Selah Flood
Hannah, 12/13/61, Samuel Blizzard, Sarah Blizzard, Anne Kennedy

FORT
John and Rebbecca Fort
Arthur, 12/21/42, Wm. Land, Rob't. Land, Mary Land

Frederick and Mary Fort
Betsy, 9/25/62, John Knight, Jr., Eliz. Knight, Amy Harwood
Wm. Knight, 6/27/64, Jones Glover, Thos. Adams, Anne Adams
Mary Anne, 3/17/66, Wm. Newsom, Mary Crossland, Sarah
    Pennington
Frederick, 10/21/71, Jas. Barns, Nath'l. Newsom, Eliz. Barns
Doncha, 7/18/68, Nathan Northington, Susanna Felts

John and Lucy Fort
Flake, 12/14/65, Joseph Prince, Samuel Pullam, Sarah Long

Holyday and Lucy Fort
Phylis, ----------, Lewis Underwood, Tabitha Rolland, Anne
    Adams
Franky, 1/1/62, Jane Bell, Amy Moss, Martha Graves

FREEMAN
Wm. and Eliz. Freeman
Anna, 2/28/41, Wm. Moss, Susanna Freeman, Anne Sandefour
Mary, 12/9/43, Thos. Freeman, Mary Porch, Susanna Freeman
Henry, 7/28/45, Robert Sandefour, Thos. Brewer, Lucy Dunn

Henry Freeman Jr. and Amy
Sarah, 12/16/41, Burwell Gilliam, Mildred Gilliam, Eliz. Rolland
Arthur, 11/14/43, Richard Avery, Arthur Freeman, Eliz. Bell
Patty, 3/20/47, Hinchey Gilliam, Mary Rachael, Amy Gilliam
Prudence, 2/1/50, Isam Gilliam, Tabitha Gilliam, Molly Freeman
Henry, 10/20/53, Levi Gilliam, Jones Freeman, Prissilla Lofting
Frankie, 8/26/56, Josiah Freeman, Eliz. Carter, Martha Lofting
Mary. 3/20/59, none given
Lucy, 2/12/62, Wm. Griffin, Eliz. Gilliam, Selah Rachael

Wm. and Lucretia Freeman
Robert, 10/11/50, Lemuel Ezell, John Ivy, Elenor Freeman
Wm., 10/11/58, John Ezell, Robert Hancock, Betty Stokes

John and Ester Freeman
Mary, 7/20/40, Thos. Wilkerson, Martha Winfield, Eliz. Freeman

48

FREEMAN (Continued)

John and Ester Freeman (Continued)

Mary, 7/14/52, Thos. Eccles, Eliz. Eccles, Rachael Rottenberry
Kesiah, 11/18/55, John Wilkerson, Winefred Cain, Eliz. Tyus
John, 6/18/59, none given

Thomas and Susanna Freeman

Jesse, 5/24/49, Robert Sandefour, Thos. Bridges, Eliz. Freeman

Henry and Lucy Freeman

James, 3/10/74, Arthur Smith, Wm. Freeman, Rebbecca Hancock

Arthur and Agnes Freeman

Huson Stokes, 9/11/40, Robert Farrington, Henry Freeman Jr.,
Agnes Stokes
Jemimma, 2/13/41, John Rolland, Lucy Stokes, Mary Gilliam
Kesiah, 1/25/43, Wm. Green Jr., Lucy Stokes, Amy Freeman
Charlotte, 1/29/45, Wellington Dixon, Mary Randall, Eliz. Green
Henry, 12/10/45, John Weelborn, Joel Freeman, Anne Dixon

Jemimma Freeman died 8/5/48, reported by Robert Farrington

Frances Freeman by --------

Mary Brown, 4/25/63, Nath'l. Rainey, Mary and Eliz. Richardson

Frederick and Anne Freeman (dgh. of Henry
and Margaret Sturdivant)

James, 1/3/69, Joel Tucker, Wm. Sturdivant, Anne Sturdivant
Margarett, 12/12/69, Thos. Sturdivant, Anne and Lucy Parham

John and Naomi Freeman

Eliz., 10/16/62, Arthur Smith, Anne and Mary Field
Chas., 9/8/72, Wm. and Miles Birdsong, Mary Hancock

John and Amy Freeman

Sally, 9/17/67, Henry Freeman, Mary Birdsong, Lucy Hancock

Josiah and Phoebe Freeman

Cecillia, 7/13/56, Burwell Green, Lucy and Sarah Stokes
Prudence, 3/3/54, Fred Green, Susanna Green, Eliz. Stokes
Henry, 6/10/50, none given
Molly, 1/2/62, Arthur Delahay, Charlotte Freeman, Lydia Stokes
Baalam, 3/21/67, Peter Winfield Jr., Sylvanius Bell, Sarah Hern
Eliz., 1/23/70, Ro. Wynne Raines, Jane Raines, Lucy Green

James and Olive Freeman

Calib, 8/29/70, Arthur Smith, Jas. Cooper, Eliz. Rodgers

Thomas and Mary Freeman

Peter, 5/4/40, John Gilliam, Nath'l. Malone, Rebbecca Gilliam

Jones and Rebbecca Freeman

Amy, 8/31/46, Allen Addison, Eliz. Green, Eliz. Green
Lucy, 8/2/52, Nath'l. Green, Phoebe Parham, Hannah Seat

Hamlin Stokes Freeman and Aggy
Arthur, 1/17/62, Amos Love, Joseph Richardson, Lucy Stokes

Frederick and Martha Freeman
Hartwell, 3/6/74, Edward Powell, Burwell Rolland, Molly Wynnes

Jones Freeman died 5/19/71, reported by Henry Freeman.
Rebbecca Freeman died 10/11/70, reported by ------?, she was
the wife of Jones Freeman - she died of dropsy.

GARLAND
John and Patty Garland
Mary, 2/5/65, Simon Stacey, Mary Stacey, Eliz. Montgomery

GARY
Richard and Hannah Gary
Mary, 1/25/39, Edward Epps, Mary Epps, Amy Tomlinson

GEE
James and Boyce Gee
Eliz., 7/24/41, Chas. Gee, Amy Epps, Eliz. Gee
Boyce Gee died 6/6/50, reported by Cap't. Gee

Cap't. Chas. and Bridget Gee
John, 1/20/42, David Jones, Joseph Mason, Winefred Goodwynne
Jesse, 1/9/45, Jesse Goodwynne, Wm. Gee, Mary Chappell
Cap't. Chas. Gee died 10/28/59, reported by Henry Gee

Henry and Frances Gee
Jane, 1/6/60, none given
James, 1/28/62, none given
Eph. Parham, 3/18/70, Wm. Mason, John Gee, Winny Reaves
Frances Raines, 8/28/72, Thos. Vaughn, Rebbecca Dunn, Re-
becca Threwitt

Charles and Eliz. Gee
Joseph, 3/12/63, Thos. Adkins, Wm. Heeth Jr., Lucy Adkins
John, 11/30/66, Steth Parham, Jas. Mason, Eliz. Meacum
Patty, 8/27/68, Thos. Moore, Jane Mason, Eliz. Bedingfield
Salley, 4/25/71, Giles Underhill, Jemimma Handcock, Amy Gee

GIBBONS
Lawrence and Anne Gibbons
Eliz., 3/24/45, none given
James, 5/9/47, none given
Anne, 9/15/49, none given
Edmund, 6/11/52, none given
Sarah, 9/18/54, none given
Thomas, 6/21/58, Lawrence Gibbons Jr., Isaac Collier, Eliz. Gibbs

GIBBONS (Continued)
Thos. and Anne Gibbons
Mary. 12/7/62, Wm. Gilbert, Anne Ezell, Mary Epps
John, 3/26/67, Lawrence Gibbons Jr., James Mangum, Eliz.
    Gibbons
Thomas, 10/20/69, none given
Anne. 4/1/72, none given

Lawrence Gibbons Jr., and Lucy
Wm., 2/8/69, James Jones, John Bosseau, Eliz. Gibbons
John, 8/3/71, Lawrence Gibbons, Wm. Parham, Anne Gibbons

John Gibbons died 5/1/70, reported by John Nicholson

GIBBS
Mathew and Parnal Gibbs
Eliz., 3/24/39, John Leigh, Mary Leigh, Anne Williams
Howell, 2/4/44, Arthur Redding, Geo. Passmore, Eliz. Passmore
Wm., 6/22/41, Wm. Thompson, Thos. Barlow, Eliz. Thompson

John and Lucretia Gibbs
Molly, 3/18/63, Epps Moore, Molly Cotton, Betty Weeks

GILBERT
James and Lucy Gilbert
John, 3/22/61, John Barker, Thos. Cooper, Hannah Moss
Mary, 11/14/65, Lawrence Smith, Mary Briggs, Lucy Dunn
Sarah, 10/11/69, Jas. Barker, Mary Partridge, Mary Stacey
James, 1/29/72, Henry Barker, James Cooper, Eliz. Barker
Eliz., 9/18/58, none given

John and Eliz. Gilbert
James, 9/16/50, John Ellis, Wm. Rose Jr., Lucy Hams

Wm. Gilbert died 2/20/39

GILKS (probably Gilkerson)
Richard and Mary Gilks
Kinchen, 6/29/65, none given

GILLIAM
Wm. and Mary Gilliam
Charles, 6/27/59, Richard Hill, Richard Jones Jr., Sarah Hill
Eliz., 12/3/61, Joel Tucker, Judieth and Mary Tucker

Mary, the widow of Wm. Gilliam, died 10/20/71, reported by
    Richard Hill

John and Mary Gilliam
Moses Johnson, 11/22/69, John Clanton, Wm. Roe, Patty Clanton
Temperance, 2/21/71, Wm. Andrews, Anne and Eliz. Andrews

Warwick Jr. and Frances Gilliam
Mary, 8/14/71, Joseph Denton, Rebbecca Denton, Mary Jennings

GILLIAM (Continued)

Sarah Gilliam died 9/6/70, reported by Isam Gilliam

Hinchey Gilliam died Feb. 23rd, 1769, reported by Cap't. Jas. Jones

Marcus and Fanny Gilliam
William, 10/1/71, Wm. Stewart Jr., Wm. Lamb, Sarah Sommerville
Drury, 2/8/69, Wm. Rives Jr., Wm. Hern, Lucy Hern
Nath'l., 1/11/67, Wm. Stewart, Thos. Hall, Mary Horn

GLOVER
Robert and Mary Glover
Mary, bab. 12/16/39, Thos. Mitchell, Mary Mason, Eliz. Biggons
Sylvia, 12/8/51, David Mason, Eliz. Beddingfield, Anne Mason
Nenney, 12/13/61, Timothy Ezell, Lucy Adkins, Mary Jenkins

Jones and Anne Glover
Robert, 3/2/58, Wm. Richardson, Nath'l. Felts, Mary Harwood
Jones, 2/11/62, none given
Joseph, 12/30/63, John Battle, Ben'g. Owen, Eliz. Barns
Eliz., 5/19/71, Ben'g. Adams, Eliz. Newsom, Grace Morris

James Glover Jr. and Mary
Judieth, 4/5/75, Hartwell Marriable, Betty Marriable, Rebbecca Glover

James and Frances Glover
James, 11/20/52, Nath'l. Tomlinson, Thos. Young, Susanna Moore
Wm., 4/11/54, David Mason, Thos. Shands, Anne Whitefield
Anne, 1/31/57, none given
Rebbecca, 2/15/60, John Moss, Frances Moss, Eliz. Dunn

James and Anne Glover
Joseph, 12/30/63, John Battle, Ben'g. Owen, Eliz. Barns

Joseph and Mary Glover
Betty, 6/4/71, James Gray, no other
Thomas, 2/26/73, Joseph Smith, Beng. Gray, Rebbecca Smith

John and Mary Glover
Ben'g. 2/20/75, Jas. Cooper, John Kee, Mary Glover, Eliz. Brown

Mary Glover and --------?
Patrick, 3/25/68, Joseph Glover, Simon Stacey, Mary Glover

GOLIGHTLY
John and Grances Golightly
Reubin, 12/25/40, John Golightly, Wm. Martin, Eliz. Martin

GOLIGHTLY (Continued)

Wm. and Anne Golightly

Chris., 1/1/70, Aughustine Shands, Timothy Rives Jr., Eliz. Shands

GOOD

John and Sarah Good

Ruth, 9/25/44, Maurice Floyd, Eliz. Weaver, Mary Adkins

GOODWYNNE

John and Winefred Goodwynne

Robert, 3/15/39, none given
James, 8/16/41, Thos. Goodwynne, Josh. Tatum, Hannah Cook
Wm., 1/24/45, Wm. Clark, Wm. Goodwynne, Hannah Goodwynne
Francis, 11/7/49, Thos. Eldridge, John Rives, Martha Eldridge
Peter Potheriss, 1/15/52, Peter Potheress, Eliz. Potheress, Amy Mitchell

GORDAN

John and Jean Gordan

Eph., 3/11/40, none given

GRANTHAM

Edward and Catherine Grantham

Joshuah, 9/21/40, Robert Seat, Edwd. Shelton, Mary Seat

Thomas and Eliz. Grantham

Wm., 12/23/44, Wm. Johnson, David Stokes, Phoebe Stokes

GRAVES (sometimes spelled Groves - but all the same)

Faith Ray and John Groves

John Groves, 9/7/40, Thos. Eldridge Jr., Wm. Willie, Mary Eldridge

John Grove died 3/1/39

Soloman and Sarah Graves

Wm., 11/13/55, John Tyus, John Winfield, Eliz. Tyus
Thomas, 1/29/48, Wm. Gilliam Jr., John Curtis, Betty Winfield
David, 11/11/50, Richard Hill, Lewis Tyus, Margory Hill
Anne, 12/12/52, Peter Winfield, Eliz. Eccles, Rachael Rothenberry
Wm., 11/13/55, John Tyus, John Winfield, Eliz. Tyus
John, 5/22/62, Richard Jones Jr., Thos. Moore Jr., Eliz. Lofting
Rebbecca, 7/30/64, Henry Harrison, Eliz. Wyche, Eliz. Tyus
Patty, 6/21/68, Henry Gee, Judieth Avery, Martha Moore

Ben'g. and Ester Graves

Salley, 3/26/70, Cornelius Mabrey, Mary Hix, Sylvia Cornel

David and Martha Groves

Molly, 11/22/72, Wm. Graves, Rebbecca Graves, Lucy Gilliam

GRAY
Families who named children Gray

Wm. and Judieth Edmunds
Gray, 3/26/42, John Harrison, John Edmunds, Phylis Edmunds

Thos. Dunn Jr., and Lucy
Gray, 3/1/44, Wm. Brown, Wm. Hix, Martha Long

Chas. and Sarah Judkins
Gray, 8/28/48, Jane Carter, John Myrick, Eliz. Carter

David and Agnes Ezell
Gray, 11/22/59, Soloman Wynne, Jr., Thos. Sturdivant

Edward and Eliz. Jones
Gray, 6/12/64, Wm. Mitchell, Wm. Atkinson, Phoebe Rolland

Richard and Mary Felts
Gray, 3/23/66, Lewis Hutchens, Jesse Rodgers, Anne McGee

Steth and Sarah Wynne
Gray, 6/23/67, Robert Wynne, Chas. Sturdivant

George and Mary Anderson
Gray, 9/16/69, Thos. Parham, Edward Petway Jr., Anne Parham

John and Mary Judkins
Gray, 3/11/70, John Broadrib, Anderson Ramsey, Mary Tomlinson

By Agnes Gilliam
Gray Hutchens, 4/23/65, Chas. Long, Howell Cooper, Mary
    Gilliam

GREEN
People who named children Green

Richard and Anne Field
Green, 5/21/49, Robert Nicholson, Bathia Field, Lydia Smith

Richard and Marjory Hill
Green, 11/21/52, John Rolland, Soloman Grain, Frances Winfield

John and Agnes Wynne
Green, 9/4/65, John Sturdivant, Steth Wynne, Eliz. Wynne

Peter and Mary Green
Frederick, 11/11/32, none given
Peter, 5/22/34, none given
Wm., 5/10/37, none given
Jean, 3/29/39, none given
Mary, 4/24/41, John Farrington, Mary Randall, Mary Brook
Olive, 3/24/42, Wm. Green Jr., Eliz. Green, Eliz. Green
Millicent, 12/10/44, Wm. Yarbrough, Nath'l. Green, Rebecca
    Epps

GREEN (Continued)

Mary Green reported the death of Eliz. Parker, 11/14/48

Nathanial and Phoebe Green
Mildred, 12/19/50, Edward Powell, Frederick Green, Mildred
    Robertson
Sterling, 2/15/61, Mathew Parham Jr., Peter Green, Rebbecca
    Richardson
James, 3/15/64, Joseph Ingram, Geo. Randall, B. Ruth. Randall

Burwell and Lucy Green
J-----?, 2/27/55, Josiah Freeman, Lewis Tyus, Phoebe Freeman
Mary, 3/16/64, Phoebe Freeman, Peter Green, Mary Powell
Salley, 10/3/66, Samuel Mangum, Mildred Hill, Frances Ingram
Eliz., 5/26/69, Jas. Mangum Jr., Betty Mangum, Anne Avery

William and Lucy Green
Frances Burwell, 10/15/52, Lewis Tyus, Anne and Eliz. Tyus
Salley, 1/5/60, John Tyus, Susanna Green, Eliz. Tyus
Bureel, 4/12/65, Peter Green, Joel Knight

Frederick and Leticia Green
Thomas, 7/13/62, Robert Tucker, Henry Jackson, Mary Farington
Jane, 7/4/57, Peter Green, Judy Green, Mary Green
Clement, 6/15/60, Wm. Mitchell, Ro. Wynne Raines, Mary
    Prichard
Mark, 8/7/67, Wm. Parham, Thos. Hunt, Mary Hancock

Burwell and Susanna Green
James, 2/4/60, Jas. Richardson, Thos. Wynne Jr., Agnes Free-
    man
Ben'g., 8/21/54, Marcus and Sylvanus Stokes, Betty Stokes
J----?, 7/25/55, Josiah Freeman, Lewis Tyus, Phoebe Freeman
Drury, 3/26/58, Micajah Stokes, Robert Owen, Penelope Whit-
    tington

Bengiman Green died 1/9/49, reported by Mrs. Farington

Nathanial Green died 12/1/49

Wm. Green died 12/10/49, reported by James Jones

Peter and Judieth Green
Sarah Anne, 4/27/53, Amos Love, Mary Farrington, Francina
    Ingram
John Williams, 4/9/56, George Randall, Wm. Hunt, Marge
    Prichard
Eliz., 5/24/58, Joseph Ingram, Laticia Green, Anne Harper
Peter, 12/14/60; Thos. Wade, Ro. Wynne Raines, Anne Adams
Judieth, twin, 12/14/60, Frederick Green, Mary Tucker, Lucy
    Mangum
Miles, 6/6/67, Thos. Love, Peter Randall, Susanna Kelly

GREEN (Continued)

Sarah Anne Green died 9/2/58, reported by Mrs. Farington
Eliz. Green died 2/4/59, reported by Peter Green

GRIFFITH -
NOTE: This name is spelled Griffin and Griffith, both the same.

Richard and Grace Griffin
Richard, 3/15/39, Robert Jones Jr., Richard Hind, Ester Winkle
John, 1/6/44, John Bane, Thos. Wallace, Marv Briggs

Edward and Catherine Griffith
Thomas, 9/5/49, none given
Edward, 12/26/53, none given
John, 2/24/55, none given
William, 3/8/58, none given
Ede., 3/26/61, Nath'l. Johnson, Rebbecca Prince, Mary Pate

Thomas and Olive Griffith
John, 4/13/64, Arthur Richardson, John Carrell, Eliz. Hulin
Nath'l., 3/12/66, Thos. Newsom, Frederick Smith, Anne Carrell

Travis and Anne Griffith
Rebbecca, 4/29/51, Charles Sledge, Sarah and Eliz. Sledge
Allen, 11/15/58, John Crossland, John Tatum, Rebbecca Sledge
Joshuah, 3/9/62, Henry Underhill, Frederick Jarrett, Amy Sledge
Thomas, 4/28/70, Lawrence Smith, Edward Weaver Jr., Eliz.
   Rodgers

William and Rebbecca Griffith
Nancy, 6/11/62, John Land Jr., Lydia Gilliam, Moly Ezell

GROSSWIT
Thos. and Eliz. Grosswit
Wm., 3/3/46, Wm. Harper, Robert Farrington, Sarah Winfield
George and Amy Grosswit, Anne, 1/21/46, Thos. Grosswit,
Anne Grosswit, Mary Winkle

GUTHRIE

Sarah Guthrie died 3/9/42, reported by Danial Guthrie

HADDEN
Ben'g. and Martha Hadden
Martha, 8/3/39, Mathew Parham, Bridget Tatum, Jean Radcliff

Francis and Frances Hadden
Francis, 2/23/40, John Woodlief, Wm. Epps, Eliz. Jones

HALL
Ben'g. and Eliz. Hall
Herbert, 3/2/68, none given

HAMILTON
William and Jane Hamilton
Mary, 8/19/43, James Price, Elenor Dobie, Eliz. Williams
Thomas, 3/15/45, Chris. Tatum, Wm. Clifton, Mary Dobie

HAMLIN
Steven and -------- Hamlin
Molly, 4/10/54, none given

HANCOCK
Clement and Anthony Hancock
Hannah, 2/14/40, Edmund Pennington, Hannah Pennington, Sarah
Bird
Mary, 10/9/41, Edward Petway, Eliz. Brewer, Lucy Sill
Wm., 3/16/42, Wm. Clark, Wm. Dansey, Mary Dansey

Clement Hancock died 11/16/66, reported by Clement Hancock

John and Mary Hancock
Jean, 8/15/41, none given
Lucy, 12/25/43, Joseph Petway, Lucy Hancock, Jean Petway
Thomas, 5/1/49, Bengiman White, Richard Andrews, Mary Andrews
Randolph, 12/25/45, Aughustine Hargrave, Thos. Wrenn, Mary
Atkinson
John, 8/6/51, Wm. Lamb, James White, Sarah Baylis (Baley-
Bailey)

John and Susanna Hancock
John, 6/12/43, John Freeman, Thos. Freeman, Marjory Morris

Clement and Mary Hancock
Susanna, 11/14/58, John Harrisson, Susanna and Betty Harrisson

Ben'g. and Jane Hancock
Sarah, 4/6/47, none given
Lewis, 8/22/45, Nath'l. Felts, Nath'l. Felts Jr., Sarah Woodland
Steven, 1/27/49, none given
Mary, 2/6/50, none given
Wm., 2/8/53, none given
Rebbecca, 2/15/55, none given
John, 8/5/57, Richard and Harris Nicholson, Lucy Hancock
Samuel, 3/5/59, Wm. Collins, Mary Collins
Selah, 4/2/61, Wm. Collins, Mary Collins, Pamelia Hood
James, 9/1/63, Steven Pepper, Harris Nicholson, Lucy Hancock

Robert and Eliz. Hancock
Jemimma, 12/9/52, Clement Hancock, Antheny Hancock, Anne
Dansey
Robert, 3/6/55, Fred Green, David Mason, Antheny Hancock
Henry, 3/3/57, Thos. Peters Jr., Drury Sill, Sarah Underwood

William and Rebbecca Hancock
Eliz. Green, 10/27/66, David Jones Jr., Mary and Sarah Jones

HANCOCK (Continued)
William and Rebbecca Hancock (Continued)
Clement, 8/22/70, Jesse Williamson, John Gilliam Jr., Martha
Peters

HARDY
Richard and Frances Hardy
Patty, 3/24/65, Wm. Sturdivant, Sarah Sturdivant, Sarah Justis

HAREWELL
Mark and Sarah Harewell
Eliz., 7/8/62, Thos. Wade, Dorothy Vaughn, Lucy Butler
John, 7/15/64, Henry Broadnax, Thos. Collier, Anne Broadnax
Preston, 6/8/67, Wm. Yarbrough, Mason Harewell, Lucy Hare-
well

Peter and Phoebe Harewell
Joshuah, 3/28/54, Richard Woodruff, Eph. Price, Mary Spain

Richard and Phoebe Harewell
Littleton, 5/1/75, Mark Harewell, Thos. Parham, Sarah Harewell

HARGRAVE
Aughustine and Mary Hargrave
Katherine, 3/23/43, Richard Murphey, Faith Judkins, Mary Mur-
phey
Kesiah, 3/23/43, Richard Murphey, Faith Judkins, Mary Murphey

John and Katherine Hargrave
John, 9/6/42, Ralph McGee, John Gilliam, Anne Northington
Wm., 6/2/45, Morris Prichard, Samuel Seaward

John and Judieth Hargrave
Moses, 9/21/53, none given

Thomas and Letty Hargrave
Wm., 11/21/71, Jesse Lane, John Phipps, Sarah Lane

HARPER
Wm. and Frances Harper
Martha, 7/24/39, Drury Malone, Martha Malone, Mely Harper

Wyatt and Anne Harper
Wilkens, 11/24/61, Thos. Huson, Lewis Brown, Athalia Tucker
Wm., 4/22/63, Robert Winfield, Peter Green, Anne Winfield
Wyatt, 5/11/59, Thos. Huson, Peter Green, Mary Parham

Edward and Anne Harper
Wilkins, 10/24/61, Thos. Huson, Lewis Brown, Athalia Tucker
Wm., 4/22/63, Robert Winfield, Lewis Brown, Mary Keelly

HARRARD
Philip and Rebbecca Harrard
Mary, 9/1/39, Danial Roberts, Sarah Roberts

HARRIS
Joseph and Rebbecca Harris
Wm., 2/21/66, John Ezell,Jr., Lewis Harris, Phoebe Seat
Salley, 5/5/69, Thos. Ezell Jr., Mary Felts, Anne Seat

Joseph and Eliz. Harris
Simmons, 5/7/53, John Harrisson, Edwd. Crossland, Sarah
   Moss

John and Patience Harris
Mary, 4/15/49, Mich'l. Blow, Mary Porter
John and Lewis, twins, Richard Field, Beuford Pleasant, Anne
   Field, Joseph Petway, Nathan Lewis, Hannah Petway

Wm. and Lucy Harris
Lucy, 3/16/41, John Bulloch, Sarah Ezell, Jean Felts
Joseph, 1/6/44, Nathan and John Felts, Sarah Roberts
Lewis, 4/28/47, Nathanial Felts Jr., and Sr., Amy Bulloch
Rubin, 2/14/52, John Rawlings, Jerimiah Bulloch, Mary Rawlings
Nath'l., 3/5/56, Samuel Bulloch, Robert Seat, Mary Fetls
Hamlin, 10/9/59, David Owen, Wm. Hill, Eliz. Bulloch

Joseph and Rebbecca Harris
Wm., 2/21/66, John Ezell Jr., Lewis Harris, Rebbecca Seat
Salley, 5/5/69, Thos. Ezell Jr., Mary Felts, Anne Seat

HARRISON
Joseph and Eliz. Harrisson
Nanny, 4/4/41, Wm. Hight, Anne Hight, Susanna Simmons
William, 10/29/42, Chris. Tatum, Francis Moore, Bathia Tatum
Mary, 4/6/51, Wm. Partan, Mary Crossland, Mary Ricks
Patty, 9/25/57, Wm. Parsons, Anne Harrisson, Anna Gibbs

John and Anne Harrisson
Eliz., 9/12/43, Wm. Johnson, Eliz. Edmunds, Martha Moss

John and Mildred Harrisson
Elisha, 1/16/64, Peter Green, Henry Burrow, Mary Harrisson

John and Susanna Harrisson
Lucy, 9/4/41, Wm. Willie, Mary Edmunds, Mary Harrisson
Eliz., 9/12/43, Wm. Johnson, Eliz. Edmunds, Martha Moss
John, 4/2/45, Steven Hamlin, Thos. Peters Jr., Eliz. Jones
Wm., 8/1/47, Howell Jones, John Bane, Eliz. Chappell

Wm. and Anne Harrisson
Sarah, 2/18/71, Fred Andrews, Lydia Andrews, Sally Jarrett

Ben'g. and Anne Harrisson
Judy, 12/15/54, Richard King, Anne King, Mary Lofting

HARRISON (Continued)
Ben'g. and Anne Harrisson (continued)
Patty, 10/18/55, John Clanton, Amy Clanton, Jane Andrews

Henry and Eliz. Harrisson
Eliz., 7/5/59, Nic'h. Massengale, Lucy Massengale, Sarah
Avery
Peyton, 9/18/60, Moses Johnson, John Clanton, Mary Johnson
Henry, 3/14/62, John Cargil, Fred. Parker, Martha Avery

Charles and Mary Harrisson
Twins, Bengiman Henry and Betsy, born 1775, no sponsors given

John Harrisson died 12/14/76, reported by Wm. Andrews
Mary, the wife of Charles Harrisson, died 7/25/75, reported
by Col. C lairbourne

HARWOOD
Joseph and Sarah Harwood
Joyce, 2/5/25, none given
Eliz., 11/16/27, Sampson Mosley, Mary Pate, Rebbecca Seat
Sarah, 6/12/30, none given
Rebbecca, 5/27/33, none given
Joseph, 8/8/37, none given
Lydia, 12/15/35, none given
Anne, 1/12/41, none given
Absolum, 7/2/43, Wm. Knight, Chas. Ray Carter, Eliz. Wiggens
Mary, 12/14/46, John Wiggens, Eliz. Wiggens, Eliz. Harwood

George and Martha Harwood
Hannah, 9/11/59, none given
George, 11/17/65, Howell Cooper, John Mannery, Hannah Man-
nery

Danial and Nanny Harwood
Mary, 1/6/73, John Pate, Mary Barham, Anne Southern
Rebbecca, 3/30/75, Wm. Prince, Amy and Rebbecca Longbottom

Philip Harwood died 8/27/73, he had married Selah Rachael 3/20/73

Philip and Selah Harwood
Anne Bell, 10/19/72, Peter Randall, Rebbecca Robertson, Mar-
tha Randall
Philip, 10/19/73, Danial and John Harwood, Rebbecca Longbottom

Samuel and Agnes Harwood
Nath'l., 11/14/52, Sylvanus Stokes, Jr., Joseph Roberts, Eliz.
Harwood

HATTON
Goodrich and Anne Hatton
Wm., 4/23/63, Abra. and John Parham, Anne Parham

HAWTHORN

Rebbecca Davis, the mother of John, Peter, Nathanial and Joshuah
Hawthorn, died 4/20/63, she was aged 86 years.

Peter and Rebbecca Hawthorn
Ruth, 2/6/41, John Smith, Robert Hix, Eliz. Danton
John, 2/6/41, Josh. Hawthorn, Ruth Tatum, Eliz. Weaver

Nathanial and Susanna Hawthorn
Robert, 11/5/35, Richard Davis, John Painter, Elenor Weaver
Susanna, 7/4/37, John Hix, Eliz. Weaver, Agnes Oliver
Anne, 4/7/39, Peter Hawthorn, Francis Hawthorn, Eliz. Weaver
John, 9/29/40, Edward Ellis, John Bird, Sarah Allison

Peter and Sarah Hawthorn
Peter, 9/10/49, none given
John, 12/5/44, John Rives, Wm. Bird, Frances Denton

Peter and Sarah Hawthorn
John, 9/3/44, John Rives, Wm. Bird, Frances Denton
Fanny, 5/5/41, Joshuah Hawthorn, Elenor Weaver, Eliz. Denton

Joshuah and Eliz. Hawthorn
Isam, 9/16/44, Joshuah Tatum, Wm. Bird, Frances Denton
Joshuah, 12/14/46, Peter Hawthorn, John Vincent, Sarah Haw-
thorn
John, 3/12/48, John Bennett, Robert Sandefour, Sarah Bird
Frances, 2/16/52, James Ray, Anne Ray, Rebbecca Hawthorn
Joshuah, 10/26/54, Peter Hawthorn, Joseph Denton, Fanny Big-
gons
Eliz., 12/25/55, John Tatum, Fanny Hawthorn, Anne Hamilton
Mary, 7/28/60, James Cureton, Eliz. Weeks, Mary Biggons
Sarah, 4/25/62, Thos. Young Jr., Eliz. Dobie, Ruth Gilliam

Isam and Prissilla Hawthorn
Mary, 8/3/69, Wm. Chambless, Eliz. Chambless, Eliz. Gilbert
Eliz., 1/26/72, Wm. Rives, Amy Golightly
Martha, 4/23/74, John Hawthorn, Mary McInnish, Sarah Leasen-
bery

Peter and Rachael Hawthorn
John, 11/4/51, John Jenkins, Edward Epps, Anne Whitefield

Peter and Susanna Hawthorn
Rebbecca, 10/1/74, John Hight, Selah Wallace, Patty Williams

John Hawthorn, a child, died 11/19/48, reported by Peter Haw-
thorn
John Hawthorn, a child, died 10/14/49, reported by Peter Haw-
thorn
Sarah Hawthorn died 10/21/49
Peter Hawthorn died 7/19/53, on his birthday

HAY
Charles and Sarah Hay
Amy, 10/9/37, none given
Wm., 3/30/35, none given
Henry, 6/26/40, David Duncan, Eliz. Duncan

Richard and Frances Hay
Richard, 5/2/40, Lewis Soloman Jr., Mathew Hubbard, Mary
 Barlow
Seth, 3/6/54, none given
Baalam, 2/24/46, none given

Joshuah and Mary Hay
Mary, 2/9/40, Joseph Lane, John Phipps, Sarah Lane

John and Judieth Hay
Margarett, 11/5/51, none given

John and Susanna Hay
John, 2/5/63, Wm. Scoggin, Henry Porch Jr., Jane Scoggin

Richard Hay Jr. and Ede.
Molly, 7/2/71, David Mason, Ruth Hay, Mary Whitehead

Howell and Mary Hay
Lucy, 5/4/69, David Mason, Eliz. Prince, Mary Pate

HEETH - HEATH
Adams and Rebbecca Heeth
Eliz., 12/9/43, James Heeth, Sarah Gee, Rebbecca Heeth
Rebbecca, 2/14/45, Robert Rives, Mary Heeth, Eliz. Peebles
Joshua, 3/8/50, Chris. Tatum, Abraham Heeth, Eliz. Heeth
Adam, 9/25/51, Wm. Eldridge, Joseph Heeth, Susanna Heeth
Sarah, 5/20/5?, Joseph Heeth, Prissilla Shands, Rebbecca Heeth
Thomas, 12/9/43, Abraham and Richard Heeth, Mary Cureton

James and Rebbecca Heeth
John, 9/21/41, John Smith, James Tomlinson, Sarah Tomlinson
Sucky, 2/4/47, Samuel Griffith, Sarah Rives, Judieth Banks
Selah, 7/5/51, Charles Gee, Mary Griffith, Eliz. Hawthorn
Mary, 3/22/53, Ben'g. Tomlinson, Eliz. Moss, Eliz. Ro-----?
Rebbecca, 1/3/55, Henry Weaver, Mary Tomlinson, Mary Tom-
 linson
James, 2/6/61, Epps Moore, Robert Petway, Lucy Moore
LaVina, 4/29/62, none given

John and Eliz. Heeth
Mary, 6/24/43, Wm. Heeth, Rebbecca Heeth, Sarah Tatum
John, 4/8/48, James Heeth, James Tomlinson, Amy Ivy

William and Eliz. Heeth
Jesse, 6/29/43, John Smith, Anne Smith
John, 11/24/45, John and Chris. Tatum, Rebbecca Heeth

HEETH (Continued)

William and Eliz. Heeth (continued)
Nath'l., 7/27/50, Peter Tatum, John Bradley, Mary Heeth
Drussilla, 12/3/52, Abraham Heeth, Rebbecca and Anne Heeth

John and Mely Heeth
Woody, 10/14/53, John Bradley, Timothy Rives, Mary Cotton

Joseph and Sarah Heeth
Richard, 5/3/61, Epps Tatum, Robert Chappell, Phoebe Shands

Thomas and Sarah Heeth
Sarah, 12/7/41, James Heeth, Eliz. Adkins, Eliz. Titmash
Thomas, 1/25/43, John Smith, Peter Tatum, Frances Smith
Wm., 6/24/48, Wm. Heeth Jr., John Cotton, Mary Heeth
John, 6/16/52, Thomas Moody, Nath'l. Lee, Martha Tatum

Wm. Heeth Jr. and Margarett
Seth, 6/19/55, Abraham and Josiah Heeth, Rebbecca Heeth
Henry, 10/25/56, Ben'g. Tomlinson, Wm. Heeth, Rebbecca
    Heeth
Howell, 3/31/58, Henry Bonner, Joseph Heeth, Phoebe Smith
Margarett, 7/26/60, Thomas Heeth, Sarah Gee, Lucy Adkins
Aughustine, 5/30/62, Wm. Eldridge, no others
Jane, 12/15/63, John Heeth, Boyce Gee, Susanna Clairbourne
Jesse, 11/5/65, none given
Wm., 3/12/69, none given
Abner, 10/17/70, Charles Green, Thos. Tatum, Jemima Heeth

HERN, HORN, HORNE
Note: This is the same name spelled different ways.
James and Jean Hern
Eph., 12/2/39, Nath'l. Hood, Martha Whitehead, Sarah Hood
Eliz., 2/9/51, James Hern, Eliz. Hern, Thany Whitehead
Wm., 10/23/43, Richard Adkins Jr., Mary Adkins
Thomas, 11/15/44, James Yarbrough, James Spain, Eliz. White-
    head
Robert, 2/25/46, Wm. Hutchens, Robert Whitehead, Sarah King
Susanna, 5/9/47, John Owen, Susanna Hern, Eliz. Grantham
Anne, 2/27/48, Thomas Davis, Mary Carlisle, Mary Rose
Lucy, 2/27/48, none given

James and Mary Hern
Edmund, 9/3/39, Wm. Hix, John Turner, Anne Ellis, Faith Hix
James Jones, 5/19/42, Nich. Jones, Nath'l. Jones, Eliz. Jones
John, 3/12/45, Mariah Prichard, Richard Murphey, Jane Sawry
Mary, 4/5/47, Wm. Davidson, Eliz. Briggs, Rebbecca Jones
Nath'l., 12/3/49, John Stokes, Frances Sayers, Sarah Stokes
Eliz., 4/29/52, Charles Wood, Hannah and Jane Seat
Frederick, 9/3/54, Edward Shelton, John Knight, Mary Rose
Jane, 12/9/59, James Bell, Mary Knight, Sarah Freeman

HERN - HORN - HORNE (Continued)
Wm. and Sarah Hern
Freeman, 10/29/62, Wm. Richardson, John Hern, Lucy Moss
Beckey, 1/24/64, Nath'l. Jones, Betty Freeman, Sarah Rachael
Richard, 5/8/68, Wm. Rolland, Anne Felts, Mary Owen
Richard, 6/11/69, Wm. Rives Jr., Thos. Hern, Lucy Hern
Edmund, 2/24/70, Wm. Moss, Jones Stokes, Prudence Freeman
Herman, 10/21/71, Eph. and Jesse Hern, Ruth Hood
Robert, 1/13/74, Lewis Adkins, Wm. Hardy, Lydia Hern

James and Frances Horne
Joel, 9/14/67, Joel Knight, Wm. Horne, Elenor Rives

James and Jean Hern (Horn)
Wm., 10/23/43, John King Jr., Wm. King, Anne Evans
Jesse, 5/15/52, Danial Knight, Thos. Weathers, Eliz. Whitehead
Jane, 11/15/57, Wm. Malone, Marjory Hill, Rachael Fonnel

James and Mary Horn
Patty, 6/22/65, Charles Knight, Mary Hern, Patty Freeman
Elenor, 12/27/62, Wm. Longbottom, Robert Land, Amy Freeman

Thomas and Lydia Horn
Shadrack, 8/1/71, Robert Owen, James Cook, Eliz. Owen
Frederick, twin, John and Fred Owen, Sarah Threwitts
James, 11/15/73, Wm. and Jesse Hern, Sarah Owen

HEWETT
William and Eliz. Hewett
James, 11/25/52, George Robertson, Frederick Green, Mildred
Robertson
Thomas, 7/10/57, Thos. Collier, Seymour Robertson, Mary
Wynne
Martha, 2/20/60, Wm. Rainey, Mary Powell, Anne Adams

HIGHT
Wm. and Anne Hight
Susanna, 12/21/37, Nathanial Duncan, John Duncan, Mary Mabrey
Nath'l., 3/2/39, David Duncan, John Duncan, Mary Simmons
Howell, 3/16/44, John Atkins, Wm. Malone, Mary Atkins
John, 8/9/47, John Wilkerson, Warwick Gilliam, Susanna Sykes
Selah, 11/20/55, Giles Underwood, Eliz. Cotton, Susanna Hight
Hulda, 12/17/61, John Crossland, Amy Ivey, Anne Griffith

Thomas and Rebbecca Hight
Mar., 12/28/51, Ben'g. Moss, Frances Moss, Eliz. Cotton

Wm. Hight Jr. and Anne Cullom
Eliz., 3/20/68, Wm. Cullum, Eliz. Cullum, Sarah Wiggens

John and Eliz. Hight
Nanny, 10/2/65, Thos. Hight, Sarah Hight, Anne Cullum

HIGHT (Continued)

John and Eliz. Hight (Continued)
Herbert, 2/24/67, Howell Hight, Thos. Cullum, Jr., Eliz. Cullum

John, 10/19/71, Thos. Cooper, Joseph Johnson, Selah Hight

Simmons, 4/1/74, Julius Hight, Peter Jennings, ------ Underhill

Wm. and Eliz. Hight
Charnel, 8/24/73, Richard Painter, Henry Underhill, Selah Hight

James, 3/29/75, Gabrial Barr, John Moss, Betty Wilkerson

Thomas and Sarah Hight
Mary, 11/8/63, Arthur Smith, Sarah Smith, Selah Wallace

Robert, 2/8/69, Joseph Smith, Howell Hight, Selah Hight

Thomas, 8/29/71, Simon Stacey Jr., John Hight, Mary Jennings

William, 7/25/74, Peter Jennings, Thos. Soliman, Selah Jennings

Howell and Johana Hight
Henry, 2/16/74, James Johnson, James Cooper, Mary Cooper

HILL

Mary Hill, a child, died 11/2/61, reported by Richard Hill

Cap't Richard Hill died 7/9/75

The above Richard Hill, the husband of Anna, was dead when
Eliz. Mary was born, so says the register

Michael Hill died 12/30/69, reported by Robert Newsom

Ben'g. Hill died 7/3/72, reported by Lawrence Smith

Cap't. Richard Hill died 7/9/75, reported by Mrs. Broadnax

William and Hannah Hill
Betty, 8/1/55, John Hill Jr., Eliz. Felts, Rebbecca Seat

Robert, 12/13/56, Nath'l. Felts, Lewis Underwood, Rebbecca
Longbottom

Salley, 5/31/59, Thos. Felts, Judieth Soloman, Sarah Seat

John, 5/16/61, Eph. Hill, Chas. Bulloch, Mary Felts

Michael and Anne Hill
Isaac, 8/31/63, Wm. Wellborn, John Brown, Sarah Wellborn

Ben'g. and Eliz. Hill
Katy, entered 4/17/66, none given

Sally, 10/18/69, none given

Anne, 6/3/72, Lawrence Smith, Rebbecca Edmunds, Mary Wilcox

Green and Mary Hill
Wm., 3/12/75. Joel Wellborn, Wm. Chappell, Mary Chappell

Charles and Sarah Hill
Charles, 2/25/45, Thos. Bell, Ben'g. Clark, Rebbecca Bell

HILL (Continued)

John and Mary Hill
Mary, 7/12/41, none given (private baptism)
Mary, 8/12/46, Richard Hay, Mary Hix, Mary Mayne
James, 6/1/43, Edmund Pate, Richard Barlow, Jr., Mary Pate

John and Mely Hill
Mary, 1/14/43, Moses Johnson Jr., Mary Gilliam, Anne Johnston
Sarah, 3/12/44, none given
John, 3/9/50, John Wellborn, John Clanton, Sarah Wellborn
Eliz., 11/7/54, Wm. Richardson, Mary Hill, Eliz. Richardson
Susanna, 10/17/57, James Cain Jr., Amy Hill, Anne Wilkerson
Tabitha, 11/17/66, Mary Rowland, Eliz. Curtis

Nicholis and Eliz. Hill
Sarah, 12/12/47, James Wilson, Sarah Williams, Martha Gilbert
Mary, 4/25/49, Jas. Wilson Jr., Sarah Williams, Martha Hill

Richard and Margory Hill
Sarah. 9/24/43, Nath'l. Raines, Mary Raines, Lucy Hill
Wm. Gilliam, 3/3/45, Wm. Harper, Robert Farington, Sarah Winfield
Hannah, 12/15/48, Lewis Tyus, Lucy Tyus
Green, 11/25/52, John Rolland, Solamon Grain, Frances Winfield
Richard, 5/18/54, Wm. Gilliam, Wm. Gilliam Jr., Mary Eliz. Tyus
Thomas, 6/19/57, Nath'l. Parham, Thos. Tyus, Frances Parham
Henry, 12/?/62, Wm. Gilliam Jr., ------? ,Evans, Patty Dixon
William, 3/28/65, none given

John and Mildred Hill
Anne, 10/3/48, Arthur Smith, Sarah Carlisle, Eliz. Bane
Lucy, 8/24/61, Lewis Brown, Lucretia Hill, ------ Mangum

Thomas and Eliz. Hill
Amy, 1/18/47, Wm. Wiggens, Kesiah Tatum, Eliz. Tatum
Moses, 11/25/50, John Moss, Michael Weathers, Susanna Weathers

Michael and Mary Hill
Eliz., 10/15/56, Wm. Malone, Lucy Hill, Mary Malone
Michael, 5/3/59, George Robertson, Richard Hill, Frances Threwitts
Michael Hill died 12/30/69
Eliz. Hill, a child, died 2/19/50, reported by Rob't. Newsom
Eliz. Hill, a child, died 9/26/58, reported by Michael Hill

Richard and Anna Hill
Eliz. Mary, 3/28/65, Peter Winfield, Frances Threewits, Betty Wynne.

HILTON
Isacc and Susanna Hilton
Frederick, 2/28/64, John Wilkerson, John Moss, Sarah Slate

HINES
Wm. Hines Jr. and Rebbecca
-------- (sn.), 5/13/43, none given
Wm., 6/9/57, Henry Sawry, James Campbell, Jane Petway
Salley, 5/11/52, Samuel Peters, Mary Pate, Salley Hines
Susanna, 3/17/54, Thos. Moore Jr., Eliz. Hines, Eliz. Pete
Howell, 3/5/58, John Chappell, Wm. Hines Jr., Eliz. Pete
Micajah, 1/13/63, Wm. Hines Jr., John Mitchell, Susana Hines

David and Christian Hines
Susanna, 10/15/45, John Gray Edmunds, Phylis Edmunds, Jane
    Bane
Howell, 9/5/47, Danial Guthrie, David Edmunds, Eliz. Hines
Winny, 5/3/52, Wm. Hines Jr., Rebbecca Hines, Sarah Drake
Fanny, 10/30/55, John Jones, Mary Hines, Lucy Harrisson

Peter and Eliz. Hines
Eliz., 10/30/51, Henry Jarrett, Sarah Moss, Sarah Tomlinson

Hartwell and Eliz. Hines
Alex. Woosman, 9/30/71, Nic'h. Jarrett, Henry Chappell, Salley
    Chappell
Fred. Bryan, 9/30/71, Fred and Wm. Hines, Jr., Margarett
    Bryan

Richard and Mary Hines
Anne, 8/9/51, Ralph McGee, Anne McGee, Tabitha Gilliam
Drury, 11/6/52, David Hines, James Wrenn, Hannah Peters
Patty, 5/24/55, Thos. Hines, Eliz. Hines, Sarah Clanton
Sarah, 4/17/57, Wm. Howell, Christian Hines, Anne Wrenn
Hannah, 9/11/59, none given
Bob, 6/13/62, Wm. Wrenn, Howell Chappell, Susanna Hines
Betty, 10/22/63, Lewis Johnson, Eliz. Wrenn, Lucy Dowdy
Jesse, 5/22/65, John Gray Edmunds, Jehu Barker, Ann McGee

HINTON
Thomas and Sarah Hinton
Mary, 10/9/62, Thomas Lewis, Sarah Hams, Tabitha Jones

HIX
Wm. and Mary Hix
James ?/?/1735, none given
Eliz., 2/24/40, Joseph Hix, Eliz. Jones, Eliz. Hern
Tubal, 11/22/43, Geo. Long, Robert Bulloch, Eliz. Lloyd
Hannah, 10/15/45, Danial Roberts, Cecelia Stokes, Hannah Rob-
    erts
Jemimma, 12/6/47, John Ezell, Eliz. Ezell, Mary Lannery
Wm., 7/13/48, Nath'l. Jones, James Hix, Eliz. Dowdy
Mary, 12/14/49, Wm. Thompson Jr., Hannah Felts, Mary Man-
    nery

HIX (Continued)
Wm. and Mary Hix (Continued)
Micajah, 11/17/53, Edward Shelton, John Bulloch, Anne King
Wm., 7/5/60, Wm. Willie, Geo. Hogwood, Mary Hix

John and Mary Hix
Mary, 1/19/36, none given
Robert, 1/3/43, Thos. Grussett, John McGarity, Prissilla Hix
John, 8/15/48, Francis Hutchens, John Painter, Eliz. Cooper
Sarah, 12/22/37, none given

Joseph and Anne Hix
John, 7/19/42, John Roberts, Danial Massengale, Mary Roberts
Wm., 12/22/44, John McGarrity, James Massengale, Jr., Prissilla Davidson
Joseph, 8/29/55, Simon Stacey, Eph. Justice, Mary Wallace
Wm., 2/29/65, Arthur Turner, Fred Smith, Sarah Burgess

Robert and Mary Hix
Amy, 3/7/42, none given
Nath'l., 11/6/43, Edward Lee, John Ellis, Eliz. Lee

John and Eliz. Hix
Robert, 3/29/41, Robert Hix, Wm. Weathers, Mary Hix

Tubal and Hannah Hix
Fanny, 11/10/64, John Hales, Susanna Sledge, Hannah Mannery
Lorana, 1/2/71, Wm. Smith, Eliz. Graves, Elenor Felts

James and Eliz. Hix
Fanny, 6/24/68, Jesse Lane, Lucy Lane, Mary Johnson
Rheso, 12/28/70, Nath'l. Felts, Lucy Gilbert, Jenny Hix

HOBBS
Thomas and Sarah Hobbs
--------, 12/24/42, Wm. Tomlinson, Joseph Hobbs, Sarah Hobbs
Richard, 3/28/44, James and Joseph Mason, Mary Mason
Elenor, 10/10/45, Nathanial Mitchell, Elenor Tomlinson, Mary Dansey
Sarah, 6/11/49, Nath'l. Tomlinson, Frances and Susanna Moore
Isam, 3/12/50, David Mason, Alex. Tomlinson, Eliz. Bedingfield
Frances, 4/18/55, Wm. Tomlinson, Mary Tomlinson, Eliz. Hobbs
Mary, 7/19/58, none given

Frederick and Catherine Hobbs
Wm., 2/24/64, Ben'g. Barker, Joseph Denton, Mary Barker
Lucy, 1/22/66, Wm. Tomlinson, Rebbecca Ivy, Hannah Hancock
Bolling, 7/8/67, Nathanial Cotton, Danial Ivy, Agnes Dunn
Edmund, 8/25/71, Danial McInnish, David Lessenberry, Frances Barker

Catherine Hobbs death was reported by John Adkins 1/30/72

HOBBS (Continued)
John and Betty Hobbs
Howell, 11/22/60, none given
Frederick, 11/25/62, Henry Jackson, Ben'g. Lanier, Eliz. Powell
John, 5/1/64, John Powell, Seymour Robertson, Jemima Harrison
Eliz., 9/19/67, Jas. Mangum Jr., Sarah Batte, Susanna Harrison
Martha, 9/29/69, Braxton Mabrey, Martha Battle, Thos. Parham

HOGWOOD
Geo. and Mary Hogwood
Wm., 8/29/53, Samson Mason, Wm. Hix, Mary Rawlings
George, 11/17/65, Howell Cooper, John Mannery, Hannah Mannery
Sucky, 4/29/68, Lewis Underwood, Eliz. Prince, Ede. Newsom

HOLLOWAY
David and Frances Holloway
Mary, 10/3/44, Joseph Petway, Eliz. Davis, Jane Petway
James, twin, Ben'g. Clark, Wm. Owen, Mary Clarke
John, 8/7/49, Simon Stacey, Arthur Smith, Catherine Stacey
Rebbecca, 6/10/47, Wm. Willie, Mary Proctor, Hannah Owen

HOLT
Nath'l. and Abby Holt
Drury, 12/29/59, none given
Molly, 8/26/62, Drury Clanton, Nanny Jones, Patty Clanton
Betsy, 11/21/67, Charles Holt, Prissilla Gilliam, Mary Clanton
Amy Wyche, 8/21/70, Wm. Roe, Amy Clanton, Mary Rodgers

HOOD
Nathanial and Sarah Hood
Sarah, 3/29/33, Wm. Hutchens, Anne Hutchens, Sarah Bird
Eliz., 3/16/38, James Horn, Eliz. Horn, Eliz. King
John, 11/5/40, Chris. Tatum, John Bird, Bridget Tatum
Nathanial, 3/3/42, Thos. Weathers Jr., John Rolland, Sarah Felts
Lucy, 11/29/45, Frances Hutchens, Joyce Kellerman, Eliz. Adkins
Henry, 4/3/49, Jesse Gilliam, John King, Jane Gilliam
Frances, 5/9/47, Wm. Rives, Frances Rives, Penelope Whittington
Mely, 8/14/50, John Owen, Eliz. Owen, Sarah King
Ruth, 2/24/52, Thos. Davis, Jane Davis, Mary Rodgers
Sarah, 3/31/55, Lewis Adkins, Sarah Adkins, Hannah Felts
Peter, 9/22/56, Wm. Stuart, John Wellborn Jr., Sarah Northington

John and Eliz. Hood
Anne, 5/14/46, Chris. Tatum, Anne King, Eliz. Horn
John, 7/19/61, Wm. Cox, Levi Gilliam, Hannah Cox

HOOD (Continued)
John and Eliz. Hood (Continued)
Faithy, 7/27/63, Jordan Knight, Prissilla Jones, Lucretia Hood
Eliz., 6/16/66, James Williams Jr., Francis Woodruff, Martha
   Hutchens

Thomas and Mary Hood
John, 6/9/54, Warwick Gilliam, Joseph Denton, ------ Gilliam
Eph., 6/28/57, Josh. Hawthorn, Joseph Denton, Eliz. Dobie

HORTON
Amos and Sarah Horton
Jesse, 2/9/43, Sledge, John Thompson Jr., Mary Adkins
Rebbecca, 1/1/60, none given

Danial and Mary Horton
Lucy, 10/14/61, Timothy Ezell, Anne Ezell, Eliz. Horton
Martha, 9/25/63, Amos Horton, Sarah Horton, Eliz. Wilkerson

HOUSMAN
John and Bathia Housman
Steven, 2/27/37, none given
Amelia, 12/2/39, James Brown, Amelia Tatum, Elenor Doby
Mary, 7/15/40, none given

HOWELL
Nathanial and Susanna Howell
Eliz., 3/14/56, Jesse Mann, Anna Gibbs, Eliz. Redding

William and Hannah Howell
Mary, born 2/14/59, none given
Wm., born 10/27/60, none given

HUBBARD
Mathew and Mary Hubbard
James, 12/22/42, Thos. Pennington, John Rawlings, Rebbecca
   Martin
Eliz., 3/7/45, John Avent, Rebbecca Marriable, Eliz. Roberts
Sarah, 6/27/47, Richard Barlow, Eliz. Barlow, Lucy Prichard
Lucy, 11/13/52, Wm. Soloman, Rebbecca Sammons, Anne Pen-
   nington
John, 4/23/63, Howell Pennington, Thos. Walden, Jane Avery

HUFF
Howard and Olive Huff
Martha, 3/1/45, Wm. Stewart, Eliz. Wynne, Mary Stewart

HULIN
Wm. and Selah Hulin
Olive, 12/29/49, John Mangum, Betty Bradley, Eliz. Wright
Sealah, 5/10/52, Robert Prior, Olive Mangum, Frances Prior
John, 4/6/54, Wm. Waller, Wm. Carell, Olive Mangum

HUNT
Wm. and Eliz. Hunt
Eliz., 5/20/55, Peter Green, Amy Hill, Lucy Mahaney

Wm. and Lucy Hunt
John, 12/2/66, John Hunt, Wm. Jones, Sarah Hunt

John and Sarah Hunt
Patty, 5/28/68, James Bell, Patty Peters, Mary Hunt
Miles, 8/24/70, John Hargrave Jr., Samuel Clifton, Sarah Gilliam

Judkins and Martha Hunt
Wm., 1/9/72, Wm. and Thomas Batte, Eliz. Hunt
Judkins, 2/16/74, Sterling Harewell, Teasley Read, Nancy Hunt

John and Mary Hunt
Mary, 6/22/44, Mathew Wynne, Bridget Tatum, Eliz. Tatum

Thomas and Frances Anne Hunt
Goodwyne, 3/16/58, Henry Broadnax, Edward Harper, Anne
Harper

Thomas and Athalia Hunt
Sucy, 3/25/53, none given

Ben'g. and Eliz. Hunt
Susanna, 3/25/53, Lewis Tyus, Lucy and Jane Green

Howell and Rebbecca Hunt
James, 7/4/69, Burwell Lofting, Bird Land, Lydia Battle

Thomas and Dorothy Hunt
Sarah, 4/4/66, Frederick Green, Leticia Green, Olive Randall

Betty Hunt died 12/30/64, reported by Richard Wilkerson
Burwell Hunt died 1/10/74, reported by James Bonner
Wm. Hunt died 1/21/74, reported by James Bonner
Beng. Hunt died 7/21/68, reported by James Fawn
Thomas Hunt died 7/23/59, reported by (name not given)

HUNTER
William and Mary Hunter
Sarah, 4/26/50, Thos.Stafford, Eliz. Bladen, Mary Ricks
Hartwell, 11/8/53, Thos. Adkins Jr., Josh. Cotton, Eliz. Wilkerson
Patty, 9/4/56, David Mason, Anne Dansey

HURST
Howard and Olive Hurst
Anne, 11/1/44, Thos. Wynne, Mary Rives, Lucretia Wynne

HUSKY
John and Faith Husky
Suck, 8/30/60, John Mangum, Lucy Cain, Wimney Robertson

HUSON

Thomas and Tapenus Huson
Lucy, 6/12/34, none given
Thomas, 11/28/37, none given
Nath'l., 9/23/?, Wm. Wright, Edward Shelton, Lucy Stokes
Eliz., 1/1/42, Charles Mabrey, Eliz. Holt, Eliz. Holland
Charles, 2/12/44, John Clanton, Henry Prichard, Mary Gilliam
John, 1/14/46, John Thompson, Wm. King, Anne Holt

Amos and Agnes Huson
Hardy, 12/19/41, Jones Stokes, Edward Shelton, Anne Stokes
Lucy, 12/19/43, Thomas Bettle, Catherine Richardson, Lucy
    Stokes
Jones, 1/14/49, Samuel Longbottom, Thomas Northcross, Eliz.
    Stokes

Thomas and Sarah Huson
Rebbecca, 2/11/59, none given
John, 3/9/49, John Wilkerson, Wm. Banks, Susanna Richardson
Susanna, 12/25/52, Wyatt Harper, Mary Stevens, Mary Hams
Edward, 1/22/55, Churchill Curtis, Ben'g. Bell, Anne Harper
Anna, 1/17/57, Wm. Parham Jr., Martha and Eliz. Dickens

John and Nancy Huson
Eliz., 3/27/74, John Powell, Eliz. Parham, Mary Hewett

HUTCHENS

Lewis and Mary Hutchens
Robert, 4/29/69, John Hutchens, Curtis Land, Mely Land

Lewis and Winefred Hutchens
Prissillan, 6/2/63, Chas. Barham, Lucy Pennington, Selah Spain
Betty, 2/24/65, John Cox, Lucy Dowdy, Martha Seat

Howell and Lydia Hutchens
Mary Gilliam, 9/14/69, John Sledge, Aggy Gilliam, Betty Southard

Agnes Gilliam and -------
Gray Hutchens, 4/23/65, Chas. Long, Howell Cooper, Mely
    Gilliam

Francis and Jane Hutchens
Frederick, 10/11/41, John Pennington, John Stokes, Sarah Stokes
Mary, 10/22/45, Wm. Hutchens, Mary Moore, Anne Hutchens
Arthur, 10/8/48, Geo. Long, David Stokes, Mary Rodgers

Wm. and Anne Hutchens
Wm., 10/29/43, John Painter, Wm. King, Mary King
Martha, 2/27/46, Francis Hutchens, Susanna Hern, Sarah Long
Hutchens twin Francis Hutchens, Susanna Hern, Sarah Long
Lucy, 12/21/53, John King, Sarah King, Rebbecca Warwick

HYDE
Ben'g. and Mary Hyde
Rebbecca, 10/1/43, Wm. Carlisle, Rebbecca Figures, Sarah
    Bell
Mary, 3/5/45, Joseph Ellis, Mary Figures, Lucy Warren
Amy, 1/15/48, John Ivy, Sarah Bell, Hannah Carlisle
Cherry, 11/2/50, Richard Bell, Eliz. Belamy, Patty Bag----?
Hannah, 3/1/53, Joseph Bell, Judieth Pepper, Lucy Jordan

Ben'g. and Mary Hyde and some of their children were killed by
their crazy negro man. The Rev. Wm. Willie says that he talked
to the negro who seemed to think that he had done nothing wrong.

INGRAM
Joseph and Francina Ingram
Mary, 12/8/52, Peter Green, Jane Green, Mary Whittington
Charles, 1/29/55, Nath'l. Rainey, James Cain Jr., Mary Dela-
    hay
Winefred, 1/31/57, Edward Whittington, Mary Prichard, Mary
    Green
Grace, 9/17/59, Peter Green, Jane Green, Mary Whittington
Wm., 1/13/62, Frederick Green, Wm. Mitchell, Mildred Wil-
    kerson
Francina, 4/28/64, Burwell Green, Judieth Cooper, Anne Rainey
Johanna, 6/11/66, George Patterson, Eliz. Bonner, Martha
    Rives
Gaskins, 4/19/70, George Randall, Thomas Love, Mary Ingram

IRBY
John and Rebbecca Irby
Mary, 4/11/74, Samuel Cocke, Anne Cocke, Susanna Edmunds

IVEY
John Ivy Jr. and Eliz.
Wm., 10/22/34, none given
James, 12/13/36, none given
Sarah, 2/21/39, none given
Joel, 3/14/40, John Underhill, Wm. Jones, Eliz. Ivey
John, 8/6/43, John Jones, Thos. Ivey, Sarah Roe
David, 3/20/50, John Ogburn, Edward Prince, Amelia Anderson.

John Ivey died 2/21/53, reported by Hugh Ivey

Thomas Ivey
Betty, 9/23/58, (foundling), Thos. Ivey, Amey Ivey, Anne Ivey

Thomas and Anne Ivey
Curtis, 9/6/59, John Mason Jr., Wm. Gilbert, Eliz. Crossland

John and Mary Ivey
Wm., 5/11/46, Wm. Fitzgerald, Ben'g. Briggs, Eliz. Fitzgerald
John, 9/19/49, Howell Jones, J. Gray Edmunds, Eliz. Blunt
Wm., 10/28/52, none given

IVEY (Continued)
John and Mary Ivey (Continued)
Edmund, 1/29/55, Richard Blunt, Henry Nicholson, Rebbecca
Edmunds
Beng., 5/24/60, Joseph Prince, Ben'g. Adams, Eliz. Adams
Eliz., 9/16/61, James Jones, Mary Jones, Mary Nicholson

Wm. and Mary Ivey
Nath'l., 1/22/62, John Rawlings, John Pate, Anna Ivey

Henry and Lucretia Ivey
Rebbecca, 7/9/49, Joseph Prince, Mary Hubbard, Amey Jones

Joseph and Nancy Ivey
Lucy, 5/24/61, Thos. Felts Jr., Hannah Felts, Betty Scoggin

James and Mary Ivey
Littleton, 11/21/67, John Ivey Jr., Littleberry Mason, Anna
Ivey

Adam and Mary Ivey
Eph., 12/24/51, John Ivey Jr., John Wiggens, Eliz. Wiggens
Mely, 11/3/47, Eliz. Wiggens, Amy Jones
Jesse, 1/25/48, Robert Bulloch, David Wiggens, Sarah Brown
(Bonner?)
Peebles, 2/7/53, Jerimiah Bulloch, Henry Ivey, Lucy Ivey
Amy, 2/15/59, Edmund Pate, Sarah Cornet, Ede Ivey
Timothy, 9/15/57, Edward Shelton, Joseph Prince, Eliz. Stanford
Sampson, 1/18/61, Theophilas Dickens, Jocob Warwick Jr.,
Amy Ivey

Hugh and Eliz. Ivey
Mathew, 2/1/35, none given
Eliz., twin
Henry, 10/7/40, John Thompson, Wm. Craig, Martha Horton
Sarah, 7/20/46, John Wilkinson, Jane Cotton, Eliz. Ivey
Rebbecca, 3/17/48, John Ivey, Sarah Sledge, Martha Ivey
Jesse, 2/11/52, Giles Underhill, Wm. Cotton, Eliz. Ivey

David and Media Ivey
Lovell, 11/29/73, Edward Pate, Richard Mason, Prissilla Ivey
Peyton, 4/30/75, Ambrose Grizzard, John Pate, Rebbecca Ivey

Daniel and Salley Ivey
Littleberry, 12/4/70, Harris Cotton, John Underhill Jr., Rebbecca Cotton

JACKSON
Turner and Jane Jackson
Katherine, 4/13/55, Jesse.Jones, Susanna Hall, Frances Wyche

JAMES

Emanuel and Sarah James

Emanuel, 11/1/45, Joseph Rodgers, Nath'l. James, Martha
Davis
Anna, 7/27/59, Ben'g. Hogan, Eliz. Vassor, Eliz. Wright
Wm., 10/27/51, Wm. Judkins, John Birdson, Eliz. Ellis
Sarah, 10/22/58, Rubin Rodgers, Constant Sharp, Lucy Proctor
Edwin, 1/29/54, Simon Stacey, Wm. Ellis, Lydia Proctor
Martha, 2/22/61, John Jones, Rebbecca Gibbons, ------ Stacey

Abner and Sarah James

Eliz., 10/16/62., Wm. Brown, Mary Stacey, Mary Birdsong

Abner and Mary James

Eliz., 9/16/62, Wm. Brown, Mary Stacey, Mary Birdsong
Lucy, 7/14/64, Thos. Booth, Patience Porch, Sarah Johnson
Enos., 9/9/71, Henry Blow, Mic'h. Moore, Mary Birdsong

JANE

John and Anne Jane

Sucky, 4/14/75, Thos. Whitehead, Betty Andrews, Mary Lessenberry

JARRETT

Henry and Eliz. Jarrett

Mary, 6/20/47, Samuel Magget, Mary Jarrett, Mary Judkins
Nic'h., 2/24/48, Nic'h. Jarrett, Wm. Maggett, Eliz. Jarrett
Eliz., 4/6/51, Samuel Maggett, Mary Maggett, Rebbecca Hines
Wm., 7/28/65, David Jones, Jarrett Wallace, Mary Jarrett,
Mary Jones
Sarah, 5/19/53, John Lamb, Judieth Pepper, Eliz. Ivey
John, 4/1/55, Micajah Maggett, Fred Jarrett, Anne Maggett
Henry, 12/2/59, John Irby, Richard Blunt, Susanna Gray

Nicholis and Jane Jarrett

Mary, 12/18/50, Henry Jarrett, Mary Weaver, Lucy Warren
Lucy, 6/21/53, Richard Cotton, Mary Jarrett, Sarah Barker
Henry, 9/12/55, Henry Weaver, Fred Jarrett, Mary Adkins
Nancy, 10/16/72, Henry Jarrett, Lucy Jarrett, Lydia Battle

Frederick and Martha Jarrett

Sarah, 10/14/54, Jesse Jones, Mary Weaver, Eliz. Adkins
Howell, 2/11/56, Henry Jarrett, John Parker, Salley Tomlinson

Richard and Jane Jarrett

Salley, 10/3/69, Wm. Richardson, Amy Richardson, Molly Jarrett

John Jarrett died 6/9/63, reported by Thos. Wallace

JEFFREYS

John Jeffreys Jr. and Eliz.

Rebbecca, 3/13/28, none given

75

JEFFREYS (Continued)
John Jeffreys Jr. and Eliz. (Continued)
Richard, 8/26/32, none given
Mary, 7/26/34, none given
Anne, 5/6/38, none given

JENKINS
John and Mary Jenkins
Thos., 8/16/53, Thos. Eldridge, Aug. Clairbourne, Sarah Hobbs
Eliz., 11/5/56, Timothy Ezell Jr., Anna Ezell, Frances Glover

JEAN also JANE
Wm. and Hulin Jean
Beckey, 11/14/53, Jas. Tomlinson, Martha Gilbert, Mary Jean

JENNINGS
Eliz. Jennings and --------- ?
Mary, 5/7/45, none given

Peter and Selah Jennings
Rebbecca, 1/27/71, James Bane Jr., Selah Knight, Mildred
    Field
Laban, 10/26/73, Thos. Moss, Josh. Cotton, Mary Crossland
Wm. and Peter (twins), 12/2/75, Henry Jarrett, Jas. Cooper,
    Sarah Hight, James White, Hartwell Hunter, Milly Field

JOHNSON
William and Mary Johnson
James, 8/22/41, Thos. Cooper, John Roberts, Hannah Gilbert
Mely, 1/15/43, John Gilbert, Martha Gilbert, Eliz. Cullam
Mary, 2/28/52, Thos. and Amy Ivey, Anne Gilbert
Eliz., 9/7/60, Wm. Gilbert, Mary Huskins

Moses Johnson died Jan.--, 1763
Mary Johnson, wife of above, died Oct. 18, 1772

Lewis and Eliz. Johnson
Ben'g., 8/19/50, John Judkins, Wm. Hines Jr., Sarah Johnson
Mary, 2/11/53, Thos. Moore Jr., Mary Gilliam, Anne Harrisson
Jemimma, 8/4/55, Richard Johnson, Mary Judkins, Anna Moore
Eliz., 5/31/66, Joseph Wrenn, Martha Freeman, Mary Rachael Jr.
Peggy, 11/55/57, Levi Gilliam, Lucy Johnson, Eliz. Gilliam

Lewis and Mary Johnson
Edmund, 12/7/69, Joseph Wrenn, Sylvanus Bell, Sarah Horn
Robert, 12/6/70, Wm. Lofting Jr., John Hern, Eliz. Hern

Eliz. Johnson died 2/14/67, reported by Thos. Moore
Mary Johnson died April --, 1771, reported by Lewis Johnson

Nath'l. and Hannah Johnson
Eliz., 6/23/53, none given
Drury, 5/5/51, Thos. Cooper, John Threadgale, Anne Gilbert

JOHNSON (Continued)
Lewis and Lucy Johnson
Eliz., 10/20/68, Joseph Denton, Eliz. Wilkerson, Eliz. Tatum
John, 4/21/73, Drury Stokes, Lewis Newsom, Anne Southard

James and Jane Johnson
Lucy, 11/23/68, Kath'l. Felts, Sarah Jones, Anne Johnson

William and Eliz. Johnson
Charlotte, 3/11/48, James Jones, Lucy Prichard, Mary Moore
Rebbecca, 9/7/47, none given
Eliz., 8/30/50, none given
James, 11/18/53, John Harrisson, Robert Hancock, Mary Parker
Nath'l., 8/25/62, Peter Smith, Henry Jones, Elenor Smith

William Johnson Jr. and Mary
Joshuah, 7/29/47, none given
Mely, 1/15/43, John Gilbert, Martha Gilbert, Eliz. Cullam
Wm. Gilbert, 1/18/58, Petway Johnson, James Gilbert, Susanna
 Thompson
NOTE: Wm. Johnson Jr. and Wm Johnson are evidently the same

Thos. and Eliz. Johnson
Aggy, 1/26/54, Thos. Ivey, Eliz. Ivey, Anne Gilbert
Eliz., 10/20/68, Joseph Denton, Eliz. Wilkerson, Eliz. Tatum
Thomas, 12/18/73, Richard Cook, Ben'g. Cooper, Aggy Johnson

Waddell and Aggy Johnson
Mary Pennington, 5/16/69, none given
John, 6/15/72, Isam Gilliam, David Graves, Mary Williams

Petway and Mary Johnson
Rebbecca, 11/2/60, none given
Mary, 2/19/68, James Gilbert, Lucy Gilbert, Mary Smith
Thany, 12/19/69, Nath'l. Felts, Eliz. Montgomery, ---- Ellis

Richard and Lucy Johnson
Wm., 12/4/62, John Gilliam, Thos. Gilliam Jr., Sarah Johnson

Thomas Johnson died 4/17/72, reported by Joshuah Cotton

JONES
David and Susanna Jones
Jas. Bosseau, 4/23/31, none given
Rebbecca, 2/4/32, none given
John, 12/10/36, none given
Holmes, 1/24/39, none given
Susanna, 1/13/40, James Jones, Bridget Tatum, Bridget Gee
Sarah, 8/8/43, Thos. Goodwynne, Hannah Cock, Eliz. Cock
Eliz., 5/18/45, Holmes Bosseau, Eliz. Barns, Sarah Bosseau
Mary, 2/4/47, none given
Robert, 11/17/52, John Hay, Wm. Eldridge, Rebbecca Jones

JONES (Continued)

James Bosseau Jones and Anne (Gilliam)

Samuel, 7/2/55, David Jones, David Jones Jr., Rebbecca Jones
Eliz., 7/21/57, David Jones Jr., Susanna Gray, Susanna Jones
Robert, 11/6/59, none given
Jean, 9/30/61, none given
James, 12/30/63, none given
Mary, 6/4/69, Willett Roberts, Lucretia Jones, Sarah Andrews
Ben'g., 2/19/72, Wm. Lackey, Ben'g. Roberts, Mary Jones

David Jones Jr. and Sarah

David, 9/27/52, none given
Robert, 3/6/55, none given
Abraham, 6/1/56, none given
Holmes, 6/15/58, none given
Littleberry, 5/5/65, Henry Jarrett, Howell Chappell, Hannah
  Jones
Charlotte, 9/11/67, John Sledge, Mary Jones, Sarah Jones

John and Judieth Jones

Eliz., 3/5/53, Robert Jones Jr., Rebbecca and Susanna Jones
Peter, 3/3/55, John Tatum, Geo. Rives, Frances Rives
Petty, 4/2/56, David Jones, Mary and Sarah Parker
Burwell, 10/12/58, none given
Sarah, 12/26/61, Peter Jones, Eliz. Fitzhugh, Martha Bryan

Robert Rives Jones and Anne

Eph., 1/2/40, Philip Bailey, Thos. Thrower, Phoebe Thrower

Robert Jones Jr. and Sarah

Allen, 12/26/39, none given
Martha, 8/22/43, Wm. Cocke, Anne Cocke, Eliz. Jones
Charlotta, 2/17/45, Thos. Eldridge, Jas. Gee, Eliz. Willie,
  Eliz. Jones
Robert, 2/2/49, none given

Robert Jones, Att'y. Gen. N.C., died 10/2/66. He was son of
  Robert Jones Sr.

Jesse and Mary Jones

Eliz., 3/22/64, Thos. Fitzhugh, Judieth and Rebbecca Jones
Jesse, 2/18/66, John Weathers, Wm. Nicholson, Eliz. Nicholson
Mary, 7/10/65, David Jones (torn)-------

Jesse Jones died 3/28/71, reported by Mrs. Hannah Jones

John and Agnes Jones

Frederick, 9/14/45, Wm. Wilkerson, Henry Gerrard, Mary Ger-
  rard
Salley, 10/24/47, John Underhill, Amelia Underhill, Lucy Oliver
Jesse, 1/25/49, Dan'l. Duncan, Wm. Fluellen, Eliz. Ivey
Betty, 6/19/64, Thos. Moss, Mary Adkins, Sarah Jones

JONES (Continued)

James and Rebbecca Jones

Patty, 9/15/66, Robert Jones, Molly Jones, Lucy Jones
Frederick (twin), Richard and Robert Jones, Molly Jones
Edmund, 8/5/68, Geo. and Gilliam Booth, ------ Tucker

Thomas and Anne Jones

Betty, ---- 1740, Wm. Richardson, Eliz. Richardson, Amy
   Rainey

Thomas and Eliz. Jones

David, -- -- 1744, Thos. Peters Jr., Richard Jones, Mary Barham

Frederick and Susanna Jones

Fred-Aughustine, ---- ----, Cadwaller Jones, Aug. Clairbourne,
   Anne Jones, Herbert Clairbourne

Thomas Jones, a blacksmith, fell from his horse and was killed
   11/8/68

Richard Jones died 2/18/74 - he was 72 years old
Anne, wife of above, died 2/21/74 - she was 66 years old, re-
   ported by Hamilton Jones
Richard Jones died 12/29/71 (he was called Jr.,) reported by
   Robert Jones
Howell Jones died 10/13/72, reported by David Mason

Richard Jones Jr. and Sarah

Howell, 7/25/60, Lawrence Gibbons, Eliz. Myrick, James Jones
Anne, 3/16/62, Soloman Graves, Eliz. Barns, Sarah Avery
Richard, 2/17/65, Wm. Parham, Robert Jones, Phoebe Epps
Martha Myrick, 1/11/68, Lawrence Gibbons, Eliz. and Lucy
   Gibbons
Samuel, 3/18/71, Wm. Myrick, David Graves, Rebbecca Lucas

John and Mary Jones

Sarah, 5/3/44, Thos. Dunn, Jr., Sarah Judkins, Lucy Judkins
Richard, 12/1/45, Ethelerid Jones, Nath'l. Green, Sarah Judkins
Jemimma, 12/25/50, Chas. Mitchell, Phoebe Parham, Molly
   Robertson
Laurana, 1/13/53, Ben'g. Bell, Martha Bell, Mary Moody
John, 3/10/55, Mathew Parham, Thos. Tyus, Rebbecca Maclin
Susanna, 3/21/57, Dorothy Vines, Martha Woodward, John
   Malone

Robert Jones Jr. and Molly

Willie, 5/25/41, Howell Briggs, Wm. Willie, Lucy Briggs, Eliz.
   Willie
Geo., 9/10/59, Lawrence Gibbons, Henchey Petway, Agnes Free-
   man
Eliz., 7/27/66, Hinchey Petway, Lucy Jones, Eliz. Gibbons
Patty, 10/30/67, Lawrence Gibbons Jr., Mary Petway, Rebbecca
   Jones

JONES (Continued)

Robert Jones Jr. and Molly (Continued)
Mary, 1/3/72, Hamilton Jones, Rebbecca Lucas, Anne Gibbons

James and Hannah Jones
Sarah, 3/5/50, none given
Ben'g., 5/7/53, John Irby, John Jones, Sarah Jones
Prissilla, 4/10/62, Henry Jarrett, Mary Jones, ----- Lanier

Thomas Jones, son of the above James and Hannah, reported
the death of his mother 1/25/74
James Jones, of High Hills, died 3/18/72

Wallace and Mary Jones
Wallis, 12/3/39, John Clark, Jones Stokes, Eliz. Shelton

William and Salley Jones
Thomas, born 12/11/64, none given

Robert and Eliz. Jones
Abraham, 10/19/39, Robert Jones Jr., James Jones, Sarah
Jones, Sarah Parker
Rebbecca, 10/19/39, none given

William and Mary Jones
Lucretia, 1/6/51, Thomas Thrower, Phoebe Thrower, Sarah
Bird

James Jones and Mary Judkins
Rivana, 1/27/52, Lewis Johnson, Lucy Dunn, Sarah Judkins

Robert Jones died 2/14/75, he was born Nov. 1694, reported by
Edward Epps
Richard Jones died 8/22/42, reported by James Jones

James and Sarah Jones
Edmunds, 12/13/42, James Jones, Wm. Willie, Eliz. Jones,
Sarah Chappell

Thomas and Mary Jones (Mulatto)
James, 11/23/71, Timothy Santee, Joseph Clark, Eliz. Blizzard
Becky, 7/12/73, none given

James and Rebbecca Jones
Edmund, 9/5/68, Geo. and Gilliam Booth, ------ Tucker
Wm., 3/28/70, Nathanial and Hamilton Jones, Rebbecca Lucas
Patty and Frederick, twins, Robert Jones, Molly Jones, Lucy
Jones, Richard and Robert Jones, Molly Jones

Allen and Mary Jones
Martha Cobb, 9/12/64, Willie Jones, Wm. Willie, Jacobina Willie, Eliz. Willie

JONES (Continued)

Henry and Amy Jones
Sally, 10/30/61, John Pare, Anne Pare, Elenor Smith
Molly, 12/14/67, Wm. Rowland, Eliz. Green, Agnes Smith
Wm., 5/1/70, Joseph Prince, Joshuah Smith, Mildred Santee

Nathanial and Frances Jones
Robert, 8/24/62, John Cargil, John Mason Jr., Eliz. Mason
George, 1/28/65, George and Timothy Rives, Sarah Rives
Willie, 12/27/75, Geo. Rives, Wm. Dunn, Martha Rives

Nathanial and Sarah Jones
Wm., 5/17/61, Wm. Hern, Jesse Wallace, Lucy Wallace
Eliz., 9/26/63, Wm. Evans, Sarah Davis, Selah Wallace
Patty, 12/8/65, Thos. Lane, Lucy Lane, Rebbecca Wright
Peggy, 12/26/69, Nath'l. Felts, Mary Chappell, Anne Hix
Nath'l., 6/11/71, Henry Jarrett, Franklin Clark, Ansula Wilkerson
Nich., 12/22/73, James Gilbert, Jesse Lane, Anne Batts

John and Sarah Jones
Beckey, 6/20/69, Thos. Pate, Mely Ivey, Mary Adkins
Molly, 5/7/71, John Pate, Christian Ivey, Mary Adkins
Salley, 3/21/74, Nath'l. Newsom, Mary Bulloch, Eliz. Pate

John and Anne Jones
Wm., 12/22/73, Thos. Avent, Wm. Smith, Alice Newsom

Hamilton and Jocobina (Willie) Jones
Willie, 12/15/75, Wm. Willie, Nathanial Jones, Eliz. Willie, John Cargil

Joseph Jones died 11/29/49, reported by Wm. Mumford

Edward and Eliz. Jones
Chamberlaine, Nove --, 1754, none given
Irwin, July 13, 1756, Thomas Vaughn, Ben'g. Bell, Elizabeth Jones
Susanna, Jan. 10, 1759, Mark Harewell, Eliz. Harewell, Martha Pepper
Patty, July 13, 1760, George Randall, Temperence Wellborn, Jemimma Winfield
Lucy, 7/23/62, John Robertson, Sarah Jones, Eliz. Mangum
Gray, July 12th, 1764, Wm. Mitchell, Wm. Atkinson, Phoebe Rowland
Betty Jordan, Oct. 16, 1768, Robert Petway, Phoebe Petway, Mary Butler
Sarah, 3/30/71, Danial Mabrey, Sarah Smith, Selah Mabrey
Thomas, Oct. 5, 1773, Edward Powell, Chamberlaine Jones, Olive Randall

Ben'g. and Mary Jordan
Thos., 3/12/48, Wm. Wallace, Danial Rodgers, Sarah Carlisle

Jesse and Prissilla Jordan
John, 4/9/73, Wm. and Rubin Rodgers, Mary Rodgers
Ben'g., 3/22/75, none given

JUDKINS

Wm. and Catherine Judkins
Wm., 3/22/39, Robert Seat, Thos. Pennington, Eliz. Grantham
James, 3/5/41, Joshuah Rolland, Wm. Rolland, Eliz. Rolland

Charles and Sarah Judkins
John, 1/19/37, Richard Avery, John Gilliam Sr., Sarah Avery
Susanna, 2/14/40, John Avent, Eliz. Rolland, Hannah Hatley
Frances, ------ 1741, none given
Charles, 2/16/41, John Jones, Gregory Rawlings, Eliz. Jones
Gray, 8/28/48, James Carter, John Myrick, Eliz. Carter

Charles Judkins died 2/24/74, reported by Robert Jones Jr.

William and Sarah Judkins
John, 10/3/46, Nich. Judkins, Nich. Magget, Sarah Tomlinson
Wm., 10/22/48, Henry Jarrett, Nich. Maggett, Mary Judkins
Mary, 11/29/50, Wm. Maggett, Lucy Nicholson, Jane Willer
   (Wallace?)

Robert and Sarah Judkins
Eliz., 1/5/59, none given
Susanna, 5/2/61, John Gibbons, Rebbecca Gibbons, Sarah Judkins

John and Mary Judkins
Charity, 1/14/64, Simon Stacey, Betty Ellis, Mary Stacey
Martha, 12/4/65, Simon Stacey Jr., Patty Stacey, Olive Hulin
   (Huson?)
Gray, 4/11/70, John Broadrib, Anderson Ramsey, Mary Tom-
   linson
Howell, 12/28/72, Lawrence Stacey, Ben'g. Ellis, Mary Stacey

Charles Judkins Jr. and Martha
Lucy, 10/2/69, John Judkins, Agnes Freeman, Sarah Webb
Thomas, 1/28/74, Cyril Avery, John Rivers, Jemimma Atkinson

JUSTICE

John and Eliz. Justice
Judieth, 11/20/54, Frame Justice, Sarah Johnson, Eliz. Griffith.

JUSTICIAN

John and Eliz. Justician
Eliz., 10/17/51, Levi Gilliam, Anne McGee, Sarah Roe
John, 3/11/55, Micajah Jarrett, Fred Jarrett, Anne Maggett

KELLERMAN
Nicholis and Joyce Kellerman
Henry Weaver, 4/21/40, John Weaver, John Painter, Eliz.
Weaver

KELLY
John and Eliz. Kelly
Patty, 3/30/46, none given
Mary, 12/18/48, none given
Susanna, 2/16/49, Thos. Huson, Mary Winfield, Eliz. Curtis
Eliz., 5/16/52, Thos. Hunt, Susanna Richardson, Eliz. Cain
Sylvia, 4/5/54, none given
Salley, 5/6/56, none given
John, 12/12/65, David Tucker, Lawrence Gibbons Jr., Mary
Kelly

KENNEDY
Uriah and Anne Kennedy
Jo---?, 4/9/68, Timothy Santee, Samuel Blizzard, Sarah Bliz-
zard

KENNERBROUGH
John and Sarah Kennebrough
John, 6/19/56, none given
Peggy, 9/25/58, none given
James, 2/12/61, Thomas Bryan, Steven Pepper, Lucretia Jones
Nancy, 2/22/63, Simon Stacey, Rebbecca Jones, Mary Jarrett
Sarah, 1/14/66, Thos. Presson, Martha White, Anne Parton
Mary, 1/7/69, Fred Andrews, Judieth Smith, Sarah Jarrett
Mary, 2/29/75, none given

KERSEY
Steven and Sarah Kersey
---------, 1/2/52, Joseph Roberts, Chas. Blizzard, Hannah
Felts

KINCHEN - Families who gave children first name of Kinchen
Richard and Mary Gilks
Kinchen, 6/11/55, none given

John and Sarah Hines
Kinchen, 9/9/59, none given

Joseph and Faithey Stacey
Kinchen, 1/18/63

James and Eliz. Chappell
Kinchen, 2/9/69

KING
John and Mary King
Moses, 1/21/42, Wm. King, Richard King Jr., Anne King
Amy, 2/14/46, Nath'l. Hood, Thos. Battle, Anne King

KING (Continued)
John and Mary King (Continued)
James, 2/14/46, Wm. King, Mary Rodgers, Anne Evans
Joel, 11/17/50, Francis Redding, David Woodruff, Frances Williams

John and Sarah King
Joshuah, 4/8/40, Wm. Knight, Richard Knight, Eliz. Hern

Richard King Jr. and Anne
Sarah, 1/14/42, Richard Woodruff, Mary King, Hannah Fisher
Arthur, 2/22/48, Wm. Ezell, James Carter, Agnes Ezell
Sarah Anne, 3/2/60, John Owen, Mary Moore, Rebbecca Rawlings

Thomas and Mary King
Sarah, 9/13/49, Joshuah Moss, Martha Stafford, Eliz. Crossland

Thomas and Sarah King
Rebbecca, 5/13/45, Henry Moss, Eliz. and Ruth Moss

Andrew and Faith King
James and John, twins, Nath'l. Green, Wm. Willie, Alice Watts, Mary Allen

Richard and Eliz. King
Mason, 4/22/49, Jesse Gilliam, David Stokes, Eliz. Hill

William and Eliz. King
Jas. Hugh Clark, 3/7/49, John Eaton, Wm. King, Rosana Eaton
Olive, 3/21/52, John Painter, Anne King, Mary Doby

James and Sarah King
Molly, 9/17/69, Wm. Cocke, Selah Spane, Lucy Hood

KIRKLAND
Joseph and Joyce Kirkland
Patty, 3/10/52, Nath'l. Peebles, Mary Jones, Martha Griffin

KNIGHT
John and Eliz. Knight
Peter, 1/8/39, Peter Hawthorn, Chauncy Tatum, Mary Epps
Sarah, 8/25/42, Peter Knight, Wm. Gilbert, Lydia Stokes
Mary, 9/2/49, Wm. Hutchens, Sarah Evans, Anne King
Lydia, 4/27/57, Josiah Freeman, Phoebe Freeman, Lucy Stokes
Walker, 5/24/62, Peter Knight, Wm. Gilbert, Lydia Stokes
Lucretia, 4/21/60, none given
Lewis, 12/25/63, Levi Gilliam, Wm. Newsom, ----- Freeman
Frank Epps, 2/11/66, Micajah Stokes, Jesse Rodgers, Eliz.
    Rodgers
Wm. and Mary Knight
Charles, 10/7/42, Thos. Andrews, Wm. Land, Eliz. Shelton

KNIGHT (Continued)

Wm. and Mary Knight (Continued)

John, 9/17/45, Edward Shelton, Samuel Wright, Eliz. Alsobrook
Sarah, 1/19/48, Samuel Harwood, Sarah King, Eliz. Harwood
Joel, 11/17/50, Francis Redding, David Woodruff, Frances
    Williams
Archibald, 1/10/50, John Avent, John Moss, Eliz. Carter
Wm., 3/18/53, James Carter, Wm. Ezell, Mary Bass

Richard and Martha Knight

Martha, 10/28/46, John Bell, Rebbecca Hubbard, Agnes Ezell

Richard and Eliz. Knight

Rebbecca, 4/10/50, Boyce Tatum, Mary Andrews

Joel and Hannah Knight

Mary, 8/11/65, James Spane, Margory Hill, Hannah Parham,
    Temperance Wellborn
Lucretia, 10/22/67, Henry Burrows, Lucretia Burrows
Sylvia, 9/13/69, Isam Hawthorn, Sylvia Porch

Moses and Judieth Knight

Patty, ?/25/60, James Cocke, Eliz. Shelton, Amy Whitehead
Betsy, 10/29/65, Wm. and Anna Sturdivant, Polly Wynne
Moses, 1/24/67, Wm. Sturdivant, Nath'l. Newsom, Frances
    Sturdivant
Eph., 8/2/72, Thos. Stokes, Abel Mabrey, Anne Hood
Wm., 9/20/74, Rubin Rodgers, Thos. Weathers, Mary Whitehead
James, 5/31/70, John Cocke, Wm. Stewart Jr., Amy Cocke

John and Anne Knight

Wm., 12/30/69, Fred Fort, Charles Mabrey, Fanny Huson
Ben'g., 1/30/72, Lanier Newsom, Wm. Knight, Martha Newsom

Jordan and Eliz. Knight

John, 9/29/66, James Horn, Thos. Moore, Jane Horn
Lucy, 5/15/68, John Knight, Eliz. Rodgers, Lucy Hern
Mary, 2/3/70, Curtis Land, Mary Rachael, Lucretia Gilliam
Danial, 11/20/71, Joseph Wrenn, Rubin Rodgers, Lucy Horn

Charles and Mary Knight

Temperance, 10/27/73, Joel Bulloch, Mary Bulloch, Anne Capel

LAMB

John and Mary Lamb

Thomas, 1/10/49, Humphrey Baily, John Peirson
Danial, 2/22/56, Mildred Christian, Wm. Hunter, Danial Lamb
Mary, 1/21/60, Peter Jones, Wm. Lamb, Mildred Chesman
Robert, 1/30/58, Rob't. Nicholson, Nannie Cleary, Mary Briggs

Wm. and Mary Lamb

John Curtis, 2/6/69, John Lamb Jr., Jas. Chappell Jr., Salley
    Bird

LAMB (Continued)
Wm. and Mary Lamb (Continued)
Eliz., 11/27/70, Mark Nicholson, Nancy Cleary, Mary Stacey
Thomas, Patrick, 11/27/70, Wm. Ellis, Lawrence Smith, Mary
    Tomlinson

John and Salley Lamb
Acril, 4/9/73, Wm. Tomlinson, Robert Lamb, Eliz. Keer

LANCASTER
Samuel and Eliz. Lancaster
Levi, 1/20/38, Joseph Rodgers, Joseph Ellis, Sarah Ellis
Mary, 10/21/41, Wm. Rodgers, Francis Rodgers, Susanna Ellis

Lawrence and Mary Lancaster
Lawrence, 7/22/47, Joseph Holloman, Arthur Williams, Martha
    Holloman

Wm. Lancaster died 3/24/40, reported by John Andrews Sr.
Etheldred Lancaster died 2/2/40, reported by John Andrews Sr.

LAND
Curtis and Prissilla Land
Rebbecca, 2/2/39, John King, Martha Ezell, Eliz. Hern
Winefred, 2/28/41, Wm. Land, Sarah Robertson, Anne King
Mely, 8/10/47, Jonathan Williams, Mary and Amy Gilliam
Wm., 11/2/49, Wm. Longbottom, Levi Gilliam, Prissilla Lofting
Prissilla, 3/3/52, Burwell Gilliam, Agnes Battle, Phoebe Lofting
Ruth, 2/2/55, Geo. Long, Eliz. Mabrey, Eliz. Harwood

Robert and Mary Land
Suckey, 6/20/42, Richard King Jr., Mary King, Eliz. Grantham
John, 2/19/45, Jonathan Williams, Ralph McGee, Eliz. Grantham
Robert, 11/13/47, Richard Rawlings, Jones Longbottom, Anne
    Evans
Webb, 3/4/50, Thos. Capel, Wm. Longbottom, Amy Battle
Mary, 7/14/52, Wm. Hutchens, Sarah and Mary Rose
Betty, 10/26/55, Robert McGee, Sarah Rawlings, Lucy King
Ben'g., 6/21/58, Robert Armstrong, Eph. Clanton, --- -----?
Nath'l., 9/7/60, John Land, Wm Hern, Sarah King
Isam, 11/13/71, Frederick Fort, Howell Cooper, Milly Land
Lavina, 12/15/67, James Bell, Hannah Parham, Fanny Davis

John and Jane Land
Charlotte, 5/24/52, Wm. Longbottom, Lydia Di-------? s?

Bird and Rebbecca Land
Lucas, 6/21/61, Abner Sturdivant, John Rolland, Winefred Land
Lucretia, 12/23/70, John and Curtis Land, Sarah Flood
Lewis, 12/28/65, Jesse Rodgers, Eliz. Rodgers, Amy Cocke
Lewellen, 10/21/67, James Cocke, Abel Mabrey, Mary Land

LANE

Joseph and Lucy Lane
Jesse, 9/3/41, Joshuah Ray, Ben'g. Kinchen, Eliz. Richardson

Jesse and Anne Lane
Samuel, 6/29/66, Joseph and Thomas Lane, Mary Johnson
Peter, 6/21/68, John Blow Jr., Nath'l. Felts Jr., Eliz. Hix
Rebbecca, 12/13/72, Wm. Birdson, Mary Birdson, Anne Cleary

LANIER

Samuel and Hannah Lanier
Thomas, 7/6/33, none given
John, 10/28/38, none given
Lemuel, 4/12/41, Joseph Halsey, Nath'l. Briggs, Hannah Peters
Eliz., 1/10/35, none given

LEE

Henry Lee Jr. and Eliz.
Peter, 10/4/41, Peter Hawthorn, Thos. Musselwhite, Anne
    Meacum
Isacc, 9/21/42, Chris Tatum, Henry Lee, Anne Lee
Wm., 10/4/44, John Tatum, Wm. Dunn, Amy Dunn
Rebbecca, 6/5/50, Wm. Barrow, Amy Barrow, Eliz. Rolland

Edward and Eliz. Lee
Anne, 2/20/39, Robert Hix, Anne Lee, Eliz. Freeman
Rachael, 5/4/41, John Atkins, Agnes Wilkerson, Jean Cotton
Steven, 9/11/43, Wm. Moss, John Ezell, Mary Hix
Mary, 2/23/45, Timothy Ezell Jr., Mary Porch, Eliz. Hay
Levi, 8/21/48, Peter Hawthorn, Francis Niblet, Sarah Hawthorn
Henry, 5/23/50, Ben'g. Harrison, Henry Lee, Susanna Weathers
Betty, 9/7/55, John Ezell, Lydia Weathers, Mary Dobie

Edward and Lucy Lee
Mary, 2/12/44, Timothy Ezell Jr., Mary Porch, Eliz. Hay
Jemimma, 2/27/61, Geo. Ezell, Anne and Rebbecca Lee
Mary, 7/8/63, Travis Weaver, Salley Pennington, Eliz. Meacum
Betsy, 8/4/66, Fred Holt, Anne Holt, Molly Pennington

Danial and Sarah Lee
Amy, 11/24/72, none given

LEIGH

John and Mary Leigh
Mary, 3/6/39, Mathew Gibbs, Mary Griffin, Helen Moreland
Angelica, 8/5/51, Epps Moore, Francis Smith, Eliz. Leigh
John, 8/25/54, Goodrich Hutton, Edward Epps Jr., Eliz. Parham

LESSENBERRY

John and Isabel Lessenberry
Eliz., 11/4/69, Thos. Lessenberry, Eliz. Bedingfield, Mary
    Lessenberry

LESSENBERRY (Continued)

John Lessenberry and Sylvia Glover

John Lessenberry, 10/3/73, Wm. Rives, Thos. Young, Eliz. Bedingfield

LISTER

Andrew and Patty Lister

Andrews, 7/18/52, Wm. Carlisle, Ben'g. Hyde, Mary Mears---?

LOFTING

Cornelius and Eliz. Lofting

Mary, 4/15/39, Edward Shelton, Mary Johnson, Mary Mabrey
John, 11/29/40, Moses Johnson, Robert Land, Mary Johnson
Moses, 12/1/42, Wm. Johnson, John Rachael, Eliz. Mabrey
Sarah, 10/7/44, Moses Johnson Jr., Anne Johnson, Mary Gilliam
Moses, 9/7/46, Richard Johnson, Mary Lofting, Lydia Pennington
Patty, 3/22/64, Isam Gilliam, Eliz. Avery, Eliz. Johnson
David, 9/25/52, Richard Johnson, Burwell Gilliam
Wm., 10/22/48, Wm. Johnson, Wm. Knight, Martha Johnson.
Eliz., 11/15/56, Richard Johnson, Mary Lofting, Lydia Pennington

Wm. and Mary Lofting

Martha 9/17/39, Wm. Dunn, Amy Gilliam, Lucy Dunn
Frederick, 2/14/41, Thos. Gilliam, Thos. Wiggens, Mary Gilliam
James, 9/5/48, Wm. Rodgers, Philip Harwood, Anne King

Wm. and Eliz. Lofting

Mary, 2/28/62, Anslem Gilliam, Prissilla Gilliam, Mary Lofting
James, 7/17/64, Drury Gilliam, Fred Lofting, Agnes Battle
Betty, 10/7/67, Thomas Moore, Phoebe Moore, Patty Clanton

Wm. Lofting Jr. and Eliz.

Phoebe 4/20/63, Isam Gilliam, Anne Wrenn, Mely Clanton
Thos., 1/2/70, Burwell Lofting, John Fort, Anne Southard
Randall, 3/24/72, Burwell Lofting, Wm. Moss, Leah Pennington
Lucy, 8/6/74, Thos. Newsom Jr., Lucy Sanders, Eliz. Dunn

Burwell and Sarah Lofting

John, 7/5/70, Thos. Moore, John Rachael, Lydia Battle
Margarett, 2/7/72, Isam Gilliam, Jemmimma Rachael, Lucy Gilliam

Wm. and Lavina Lofting

Henry, 11/16/72, Lewis Johnson, Dan'l. Harwood, Mary Dunn

Frederick and Judieth Lofting

Fanny, 2/7/70, Burwell Lofting, Prissilla and Betty Gilliam
Henry, 2/5/73, Isam Gilliam, Wm. Lofting, Anne Moore

LONG

Robert and Hannah Long

Sarah, 6/7/40, John Brittle, Catherine Barker, Martha Long
George, 12/27/42, Wm. Brown, Wm. Hix, Martha Long
George, 5/30/45, John Phipps, Wm. King, Catherine Richardson

LONG (Continued)

George and Eliz. Long

Gessey, 3/26/41, David Williams, Anne Warren

George and Sarah Long

George, 4/30/45, John Phipps, Wm. King, Catherine Richardson

Charles and Winny Long

Fanny, 1/2/67, Ben'g. Adams, Rebbecca Long, Sarah Adams

Rebbecca, 9/14/71, Nath'l. Newsom, Sucy Newsom, Agnes Carter

Jesse, 1/11/74, Jones Cornet, Curtis Land, Eliz. Southard

George Long Jr. and Amy

Wm., 11/19/69, Samuel and Philip Harwood, Agnes Harwood

Edwin, 2/27/70, James Williams Jr., Danial Harwood, Anne
  Cassel

John and Eliz. Long

James, 3/23/50, Wm. Brown, Chas. Barker, Sarah Brown

Mary, 7/19/53, Wm. Smith, Sarah Smith, Eliz. Sawry

Edward and Sarah Long

Salley, 11/9/60, John Mannery, Eliz. Carter, Hannah Mannery

LONGBOTTOM

Wm. and Rebbecca Longbottom

Eliz., 9/21/52, Thos. Nothcross, Amy Freeman, Alice Knight

Rebbecca, 12/6/59, Gregory Rawlings, Amy Harwood, Aggy
  Harwood

Samuel, 2/27/62, Ben'g. Seaborn, Chas. Williams, Lydia Pennington

Bolling, 1/11/64, Robert Land, Chas. Barham, Eliz. Williams

Prissilla, 12/6/59, John Rosser, Mary Harwood, Frances Adams

Martha, 3/16/72, Charles Mabrey, Martha Freeman, Agnes
  Gilliam

Jones, 10/6/74, Drury McGee, Wm. Grizzard, Anne Williams

LOVE

Amos and Mary Love

Mary, 8/21/53, Peter Green, Judieth Green, Mary Rainey

Alecia, 12/?/57, Ro. Wynne Raines, Jane and Mary Green

Eliz., 7/11/60, Wm. Richardson, Eliz. Richardson, Frances
  Richardson

Thos. and Betty Love

Mary, 7/18/69, Burwell Green, Phoebe and Patty Bonner

Sally, 12/29/67, Charles Love, Mary Bonner, Lucy Gibbons

Margarett, 9/26/71, Peter Green, Mary Ingram, Patty Bonner

LUCAS

Charles and Rebbecca Lucas

Martha, 3/19/74, Henry Gee, Mary and Eliz. Mason

LYNN

Robert and Anne Lynn
John, 3/10/56, Henry Tudor, Richard Rawlings, Lucy Harris
Charles, 12/9/63, Nath'l. Northington, Andrew Felts, Fanny
  Bird
Claremond (dgh), 1/2/70, David Mason, Eliz. Lynn, Judieth Dig-
  bie

Curtis and Anne Lynn
Winny, 1/15/74, Davis Mason, Selah Sammons, Sarah Tudor

McDADE

Wm. and Sarah McDade
Willis, 2/7/39, Alex. Dickinson, John King, Lydia Dickens

MacGARRITY

John and Mary MacGarrity
Patrick, 1/5/45, Richard Murphey, Arthur Smith, Lucy Wyndham

McGEE

Ralph and Anne McGee
John, 12/29/44, John Wellborn, Etheldred Jones, Sarah McGee
Anne, 4/14/47, Burwell Gilliam, Anne Evans, Mary Dunn
Wm., 12/13/52, David Clanton, Edmund Gilliam, Aggy Clanton
Jemmy, 12/5/61, Lewis Dunn, Joseph Wrenn, Anne McGee

Robert and Prissilla McGee
Herman, 7/7/60, Richard Johnson, John Pennington, Phoebe
  Moore
Lucy, 5/5/63, Burwell Gilliam, Amy McLamore, Martha Seaborn
Judieth, 7/22/65, Anslem Gilliam, Anne McGee, Sarah Hern
Beckey, 1/7/69, John Hutchens, Mary Southern, Aggy Gilliam
Robert, 12/7/71, Drury and Wm. McGee. Anne Andrews
Clemens, 8/5/74, David Mason, Wm. White, Eliz. Southard

Ralph and Fortune McGee
Willie, 10/16/58, none given

Patty Gilliam, widow, and Wm. McGee
Martha McGee, 2/23/70, Richard Felts, Sucky Felts, Jane Lane

Drury and Fortune McGee
Molly, 3/14/64, John McGee, Agnes Gilliam, Anne McGee
Gilliam, 1/21/66, Edmund Gilliam, Burwell Lofting, Rebbecca
  Sowersberry
Drury, 11/9/71, Wm. McGee, Eph. Hutchens, Phoebe Gilliam
Nancy, 4/13/69, John Gilliam, Mary and Annie Southard
John, 10/23/64, John Gilliam, Wm. Longbottom, Eliz. Southard

McINNISH

Danial and Sarah McInnish
Wm., 7/27/46, Wm. Stewart, John Weaver, Sarah Hill

McINNISH (Continued)
Donald and Sarah McInnish
Wm., 5/6/66, Wm. Willie, Henry Underhill, Jacobina Willie
Rebbecca, 7/9/69, Joseph Epps, Eliz. Willie, Jacobina Willie
Jesse, 1/24/73, Isam Hawthorn, Steth Moss

Katherine McInnish and --------?
Littleberry,?/?/?, Timothy Ezell, Charles Wood, Mary Sullivan

McLAMORE
John and Faith McLamore
Joel, 1/7/39, Wm. Thompson, Ralph McGee, Mary Lane

Burwell and Amy McLamore
Salley, 6/2/54, Ralph McGee, Samuel Gilliam, Lydia McGee
Molly, 7/24/60, Wm. Hill, Mary Knight, Mary Harwood

MABREY - MAYBERRY
Charles and Rebbecca Mabrey
Amy, 12/8/40, Simon Gale, Amy Freeman, Mary Gilliam

Francis and Mary Mabrey
3/10/? before 1740, Francis, no sponsors given

Cornelius and ------ Mabrey
Eliz., 7/19/61, James Williams, Eliz. Prince, Mary Pate

Charles and Jane Mabrey
Charles, 1/20/52, Wm. Knight, Edward Carter, Mary Richardson

Charles and Martha Mabrey
Wilkinson, 4/20/71, Charles Holt, Nath'l. Newsom, Susanna
Mabrey

Abel and Susanna Mabrey
Peter, 10/23/59, Wm. Rose, Wm. Woodland, Mary Rose
Lucretia, 5/13/62, Danial Mabrey, Eliz. Randall, Susanna
Brown Bell
Jordan, 2/22/65, Charles and Cornelius Mabrey, Eliz. Tyus
Frederick, 11/7/67, Joseph Harne (Harns?), Danial Epps, Sarah
Hubbard
Olive, 12/18/69, Ben'g. Phipps, Sarah Hood, Sarah Woodland

MAGGETT
Micajah and Susanna Maggett
Wm., 5/7/62, Michael Blow, Henry Jarrett, Eliz. Jarrett

MALONE
Wm. and Mary Malone
Nathanial, 1/24/39, Wm. Green, John Smith, Anne Malone
Wm., 1/29/44, Wm. Wellborn, John Oliver, Anne Patterson
Danial, 2/13/50, Michael Hill Jr., Wm. Wellborn, Frances Hill

MALONE (Continued)

Thomas and Millicent Malone
Lucy, 10/23/45, Nath'l. Malone, Lucy Robertson, Phoebe Malone

David and Mary Malone
Mary, 5/6/45, John Moss, Sarah Malone, Sarah Malone
Nath'l., 5/18/43, John Mason, Jr., Wm. Willie, Eliz. Eldridge

Rubin and Lucy Malone
Jordan, 2/10/66, John Curtis, Anne Winfield, Anne Curtis
Nanny, 3/3/68, Wm. Winfield, Sarah and Sucky Winfield

John and Mary Malone
Nath'l., 6/6/64, Robert Jackson, Webb Rolland, Frances Oliver
Lucy, 12/?/60, Peter Green, Lucy Mahaney, Eliz. Delahay
Wm., 2/8/67, Wm. Winfield, Wm. Malone, Jr., Anne Hill
John, 9/8/68, James Harrisson, Geo. Parham, Lucy Mahaney
Eliz., 9/5/72, Danial Malone, Eliz. Chappell, Mary Delahay

Danial and Amy Malone
Wm., 6/11/74, Mich'l. Malone, Lawrence Gibbons Jr., Mary
  Chappell

Thomas Malone died 2/2/59, reported by John Malone
Christian Malone died 3/4/59, reported by John Malone

MANGUM

William and Martha Mangum
James, 2/2/34, none given

William and Mary Mangum
Wm., 5/16/36, none given
Sarah, 10/14/43, James Mangum, Prissilla Rodgers, Mary
  Mangum
Arthur, 5/2/44, none given
Henry, 1/24/73, Peter Randall, Seth Williams, Lucy Green

NOTE: It is quite possible that there were two Wm. and Mary
Mangums, as there is so much difference in the ages of children.

James and Mary Mangum
Lucy, 7/26/41, Wm. Stanhope, Eliz. King, Eliz. Stanhope
James, 1/22/43, Wm. and Samuel Mangum, Mary Mangum
Wm., 1/4/46, Wm. Rodgers, Richard Woodruff, Mary Rodgers

John and Mary Mangum
Wm., 11/12/56, James Milner, John Bailey, Anne Pare
Lucy, 11/30/58, none given
Sarah, 11/6/60, John Rolland, Sarah Andrews, Agnes Carter

Samuel and Eliz. Mangum
Sarah, 7/10/69, Wm. Wellborn, Sarah Battle, Sarah Delahay

John and Lydia Mangum

MANGUM (Continued)
John and Lydia Mangum
Rebbecca, 2/14/62, James Mangum Jr., Lucy Mangum, Mary
Richardson

Wm. Cook Jr. and Agnes Mangum
Christopher, 2/10/56, Wm. Stewart, James Cook, Eliz. Clifton

MANLOVE
Christopher and Eliz. Manlove
Jane, 11/25/72, Bolling Stark, Sarah Field, Eliz. Robertson

MARKS
Richard and Sarah Marks
Wm., 1/28/63, Moses Knight, Wm. Rives, Judieth Knight

Joseph and Sarah Marks
Joseph, 6/17/62, Drury Parton, Jane Pare, Mildred Partam

MASON
James and Mary Mason
Eliz., 9/21/39, Capt. John Mason, Eliz. Mason, Elenor Tom-
linson
James, 3/4/41, John Mason, Wm. Willie, Eliz. Willie
Mary, 11/1/43, Peter Rives, Mary Rives, Sarah Gee
John, 12/31/44, John Mason, Thos. Mitchell, Martha Moore
Sarah, 6/18/46, none given
Richard, 10/27/47, Hartwell Marriable, Mary Marriable, Su-
sanna Moore

Joseph and Phoebe Mason
Seth, 10/16/41, John Mason, John Mason Jr., Eliz. Mason
John, 8/10/43, Wm. Shands Jr., Christopher Mason, Eliz.
Shands
Wm., 1/1/46, Wm. Shands, Wm. Petway, Eliz. Bedingfield

Thomas and Taphenus Mason (May be Huson)
Eliz., 1/1/42, Charles Mabrey, Sarah Hill, Eliz. Rollings

David and Mary Mason
Littleberry, 3/7/53, John Mason, Nath'l. Tomlinson, Anne Eppes
Thomas, 1/7/55, John Jenkins, James Glover, Thomas Glover
Nath'l., 1/28/57, Nath'l. Beddingfield, Wm. Dunn, Eliz. Mason
Eliz., 3/2/60, John Mason, Eliz. and Rebbecca Mason
Frances, 3/13/62, none given
Mary, 7/27/64, John Cargil, Mary Mason, Eliz. Carter
David, 3/7/69, James Mason, Wm. Richardson, Eliz. Mason
Henry, 6/4/71, John Rives, Littleberry Mason, Mary Peebles
Littleton, 2/5/74, Chas. Stewart, John Mason Jr., Anne Stewart

James and Betty Mason
Edmunds, 4/10/70, Wm. Harrisson, Wm. Mason, Mary Peebles
Lucy Adkins

MASON (Continued)
Richard and Mary Mason
Patsy, 5/2/74, Robert Mabrey, Laurana Jones, Susanna Mangum
David, 3/25/77, Henry Jarrett, Thos. Newsom, Jemimma New-
  som

John and Eliz. Mason
John, 2/28/71, Nath'l. Newsom, Eph. Hutchens, Martha Gilliam

Wm. and Lucretia Mason
Joseph, 6/31/75, Aug. Clairbourne, John Mason, Eliz. Mason,
  Eliz. Rives

John Mason Jr. and Jane
Eliz., 5/20/72, Christopher Rives, Eliz. Rives, Sarah Rives
John Raines, 4/24/70, John and Wm. Mason, Eliz. Mason
Jane, 3/4/74, Wm. Willie, Jacobina Willie, Rebbecca Mason

John Mason Jr. and Eliz.
John, 4/17/41, James Chappell, Wm. Dansey, Eliz. Chappell
Eliz., 4/10/42, Charles Gee, Sarah and Mary Gee
James, 2/19/43, Joseph Mason, Thos. Bridges, Sarah Chappell
Henry, 4/12/45, John and James Mason, Eliz. Edwards
Rebbecca, 12/16/46, James Chappell Jr., Mary Dansey, Reb-
  becca Chappell
Wm., 11/15/48, David Jones, David Mason, Sarah Jones
David, 8/16/52, David Mason, John Harrisson, Mary Mason
Lucretia, 6/1/56, Aug. Clairbourne, Mary Clairbourne, Eliz.
  Binns

Christopher and Sarah Chappell Mason
Isacc, 12/16/48, Christopher Tatum, Robert Jones Jr., Martha
  Chambliss
Sterling, 8/2/47, John Mason Jr., Eliz. Mason, Rebbecca Chap-
  pell

Isaac and Anne Mason
John, 12/21/52, Solman Wynne, Thos. Parham, Mary Dansey
Eliz., 6/6/58, Edward Petway, Eliz. and Phoebe Petway

Cap't. John Mason died 9/3/55, reported by Cap't. John Mason
Eliz. Mason, the wife of John, died 8/21/63, reported by Maj.
  John Mason
James Mason died 2/2/52, reported by Isacc Mason
Isacc Mason died 10/29/57, reported by Dr. Hay
Joseph Mason died 12/7/49, reported by Christopher Tatum
Eliz. Mason died 3/22/50, reported by Christopher Tatum

MEACUM
Joseph and Anne Meacum
Henry, 9/12/37, none given
Joshuah, 4/9/40, Henry Meacum, John Thompson, Frances
  Meacum

MEACUM (Continued)

Joseph and Anne Meacum (Continued)

Eliz., ------, Henry Lee, Anne Lee, Frances Lee
Susanna, 1/29/44, Henry Meacum Jr., Susanna Moss, Anne
    Threadgale
Mary Anne Caroline, 11/18/68, Thomas Whitefield, Eliz. Ezell

Nathanial and Frances Meacum

Nath'l., 4/1/51, Banks Meacum, Nath'l. Dobie, Mary Dobie

Joshuah and Mary Meacum

Anne, 2/7/53, Wm. Shands, Prissilla Shands, Frances Moss
Mary, 3/17/57, John Moss, Sarah Underhill, Mary Handcock

Henry and Anne Meacum

Mary, 12/26/49, John Moss, Amelia Underhill, Rebecca Haw-
    thorn
Lewis, 6/10/52, Richard Rives Jr., Richard Bird, Martha Gilbert
Nanny, 1/26/55, Timothy Ezell Jr., Anne Ezell, Anne Gilbert

Banks and Martha Meacum

Lucy, 4/7/57, John Verrell, Eliz. Gee, Lucy Moore
Winney, 8/26/59, Edward Walker, Anne Simmons, Frances Big-
    gons
Martha, 10/22/61, Hollum Southall, Martha Binns, Eliz. Dunn
Jemimma, 4/9/63, John Adkins, Nath'l. Bedingfield, Eliz.
    Meacum
Jemimma, 11/8/64, David Mason, Sarah Wynne, Mary Epps
John Simmons, 4/5/67, Wm. Rives, Henry Moss, Jr., Amy
    Dunn, Jr.
Dianna, 4/7/71, Thos. Adkins, Sarah McInnish, Mary Adkins
Banks, 3/28/73, none given

MEANLEY

Wm. and Lucy Meanley

Beckey, 8/15/71, Green Hill, Jane Raines, Patty Bonner

MITCHELL

Peter and Mary Mitchell

Hannah Jones, 11/7/32, none given
Martha, 12/5/34, none given
Eliz., 3/3/36, none given
Steven, 1/26/42, none given
Peter, 4/11/44, Thos. Addisson, John Curtis, Sarah Judkins

Wm. and Mary Mitchell

Edward, 2/29/39, Geo. Randall, Lazraus Yarbrough, Eliz. Cain
Susanna, 1/13/42, Lawrence Buckner, Eliz. Tynes, Eliz. Mitchell

John and Eliz. Mitchell

Tabitha, 9/11/38, none given
Jacob, 6/3/41, none given
Hannah, 7/12/44, none given

MITCHELL (Continued)
Henry and Sarah Mitchell
Samuel, 6/17/45, none given

Thomas and Anne Mitchell
Dorothy, 9/1/55, John Jones, Tabitha Mitchell, Eliz. Jones

John and Anne Mitchell
James, 12/4/69, none given

Henry Mitchell Jr. and Prissilla
Mary, 12/20/42, Arthur Redding, Ruth Moss, Permillia Gibbs
Henry, 8/31/45, Thomas and Nathanial Mitchell, Eliz. Williams
Jones, 6/?/52, John Bradley, Henry Gee, Prissilla Parham
Rubin, 7/14/55, Henry Tatum, Wm. Petway Jr., Amy Mitchell
Reaps, 2/13/58, Epps Moore, John Petway, Fanny Biggons
Frankey, 12/14/60, Christopher Rives, Mary Petway, Anne Epps
Tabitha, 1/22/67, Wm. Dunn, Eliz. Weeks, Angelica Mabrey
See Temple

Nathanial and Eliz. Mitchell
John and Tabitha, twins, 1/31/56, John Shands, Henry Mitchell,
    Frances Shands, James Harewell, Lucy Shands, Mary Go-
    lightly
Lewis, 7/18/63, John Rains, Thos. Parham, Mary Temple

Branch and Eliz. Mitchell
Noel, 8/14/68, Henry Mitchell, Susanna Clanton, Margarett Hay

Henry Mitchell died 3/27/54
Tabitha Mitchell died 1/15/52, reported by Ben Welden
John Mitchell died Oct. 1770, reported by Thos. Vaughn
Nathanial Mitchell died 11/30/68, reported by Branch Mitchell

MONTGOMERY
John and Eliz. Montgomery
Sarah, 3/25/62, Peter Jones, Eliz. Briggs, Lucretia Jones
John, 1/19/66, Petway Johnson, Mildred Gray
Ben'g., 10/19/68, James Jones, John Lane, Rebbecca Jones
Agnes, 2/23/71, James Gilbert, Lucy Gilbert, Mary Johnson
Peter, 3/7/74, Steven Andrews, Josh. Johnson, Eliz. Bane

MOORE
Thomas and Mary Moore
Anna, 10/22/39, none given
Mary, 6/7/42, Lewis Delahay, Bridget Tatum, Phoebe Thrower
Wm., 2/27/44, John Gilliam, John Rachael, Anne Phillips
Susanna, 5/17/48, Thomas Moore Jr., Eliz. Johnson, Mary
    Judkins

Thomas and Sarah Moore
Wm., 2/27/44, Thomas Moore Jr., Rebbecca Stewart, Mary
    Rachael

96

MOORE (Continued)

Thomas and Sarah Moore (Continued)

Martha, 2/15/53, James Gilliam, John Rachael, Anne Philipps
Rebbecca, 9/11/55, Wm. Ezell, Sarah Rawlings, Faith Pennington
Sarah, 5/27/57, James Carter, Eliz. Carter, Eliz. Carter, Sr.

Thomas and Phoebe Moore

Charles, 5/24/58, Isam Gilliam, Gregory Rawlings, Anne Moore
James, 6/4/60, John Judkins, Young Stokes, Agnes Battle
Bob, 2/8/63, Lewis Johnson, Wm. Moore, Martha Seaborn
Thomas, 8/29/65, Arthur Williamson, Nath'l. Newsom, Selah
     Rachael
Wm., 9/27/67, Josias Wrenn, Burwell Lofting, Mary Grub
Mary, 9/28/70, Barham Moore, Salley Gilliam, Salley Lofting
Susanna, 5/14/75, Ben'g. Seaborn, Mary Stewart, Mary Gilliam

Drury and Martha Moore

Patty, 3/27/41, John Delahay, Martha Moore, Anne Parham

Wm. and Anne Moore

Betsy, 6/9/71, Lewis Johnson, Jemimma Johnson, Rebbecca
     Moore
Patsy, 4/12/73, none given
Wm, twin, 7/4/75, John Cargil, Richard Mason, Sarah Hern
Littleton, twin, 7/4/75, same sponsors as Wm.

John and Mary Moore

Wm., 2/7/67, Frederick Freeman, Lucy Wilkerson
Rebbecca, 2/7/72, Wm. Stewart Jr., Anne Moore, Jemimma
     Johnson

MORGAN

Edward and Eliz. Morgan

Edward, 11/27/50, Wm. Carlisle, Richard Bell, Sarah Carlisle

Robert and Betty Morgan

Mary, 5/17/59, Bryan Fanning, Mary Echolds, Martha Freeman

John Morgan and Mary Tudor

Johnie, 1/2/68, Penrose Grizzard, Richard Hay, Lucy Tudor

MORRIS

Thomas and Mary Morris

Robert, 8/30/45, John Steagle, Samuel Chappell, Agnes Jones
Mary, 3/16/46, John Threadgale, Martha Moss, Mary Chappell

MOSELEY

Sampson and Joyce Moseley

Carey, 2/3/60, none given
Wm., 4/9/63, Robert Armstrong, Isacc Rawlings, Susanna Land
Fanny, 12/18/67, Lewis Newsom, Patty Rose, Eliz. Ezell

George and Martha Moseley

Ferrebe, 2/12/70, Bengiman Phillips, Mary Mannery, Eliz. Knight

MOSS

Henry and Susanna Moss

Lewis, 5/6/42, James Moss, Henry Meacum, Jr., Frances
  Moss
Joshuah, 6/23/44, Wm. and Henry Moss, Susanna Cheese
Henry, 5/6/47, none given
Frances, 4/3/50, John Moss, Anne Meacum, Sarah Parham
Gabrial, 6/16/52, Wm. Moss, Peter Hawthorn, Sarah Moss
Sampson, 9/5/55, Henry Meacum, Thos. Stafford, Frances
  Mason
Edmund, 12/17/57, John Adkins, Edward Lee, Eliz. Adkins
Susanna, 4/12/61, Thos. Gibbons, Mary Hancock, Anne Epps
Martha, 3/7/64, Drury Cotton, Lucy and Amy Adkins
James, 8/28/53, none given

James and Anne Moss

John, 1/22/40, Ben'g. Moss, Edward Epps, Frances Denton
Henry, 2/13/43, Wm. Moss, Henry Moss, Mary Johnson
Sampson, 3/20/45, Thos. Wade, James Moss, Mary Moss
Steth, 11/19/48, Wm. Banks, James Woodward, Angelica Cain
Wm., 4/14/62, Wm. Yarbrough, Henry and Winny Robertson

William Jr. and Eliz. Moss

Wm., 1/3/41, Ben'g., and Henry Moss, Mary Barker
Lucy, 8/22/40, Peter Hawthorn, Anne Sandefour, Mary Moss
Thomas, 2/17/43, Wm. Moss, Wm. Shands, Mary Moss
Eliz., 8/22/40, John Marcum, Eliz. King, Sarah Hawthorn
Anne, 10/8/50, Samuel Northington, Eliz. Rose, Sarah Rose

John and Frances Moss

Sarah, 5/7/43, Henry Moss, Susanna Moss, Mary Moss
Eph., 11/12/46, Henry Moss, Richard Cotton, Martha Gilbert
Seth, 6/16/50, Bengiman Moss, James Glover, Mary Denton
John, 8/12/55, Epps Moore, Joseph Denton, Sarah Mitchell
Swanna, ?/?/?, Joshuah Meacum, Mary Meacum, Anne Ezell

Henry and Ruth Moss

Christopher, 5/5/43, Christopher Tatum, Wm. Moss Jr., Eliz.
  Tatum
Howell, 4/3/45, Peter Tatum, Wm. Moss, Mary Moss
Winney, 1/10/46, Bengiman Moss, Rebbecca Hawthorn, Mar-
  tha Tatum

Bengiman and Rebbecca Moss

John, 4/21/43, James Mason, Christopher Mason, Mary Moss
Wm., 5/3/45, Joseph Mason, Wm. Shands Jr., Eliz. Edwards
Patty, 10/16/49, David Mason, Bright Tatum, Eliz. Mitchell
Frederick, 9/13/41, Wm. Moss, Henry Moss, Mary Johnson

Bengiman Moss and Ann (Williams) Moss

Moss, 7/27/43, Wm. Hutchens, Richard Woodruff, Eliz. Edwards

Joshuah and Anne Moss

Alfred, 6/20/70, Eph., and Gabrial Moss, Mary Moss

MOSS (Continued)

Thomas and Salley Moss

Wm., 3/29/66, Thomas Adkins, Giles Underhill, Sarah Underhill
John, 2/4/71, John Underhill Jr., Richard Ogburn, Anne Gee
Betsy, 11/13/74, Richard Cock, Salley and Milly Underhill

Henry Moss Jr. and Mary

Epps, 5/17/70, Banks Meacum, James Epps, Martha Meacum
Gabrial, 1/24/73, Eph. Moss, none others

Henry and Milly Moss

Collier, 5/30/68, Peter Cain, Phillip Burrow, Patty Burrow
Mary, 2/3/70, James Cain, Angelica Cain, Mary Abernethy

MULLENS

Thomas and Anne Mullens

Thomas, 7/19/41, Thomas Cotton, John Cotton, Amy Malone
John, 8/11/43, James Brown, James Gilliam, Mary Brown

MURPHY

Simon and Eliz. Murphey

Lucy, 5/6/38, Michael Sanders, Sarah Hern, Mary Sanders

Ben'g. and Eliz. Murphey

Eliz., 2/19/41, James Hooper, Eliz. Bladen, Eliz. Clarke
Wm., 2/20/43, Francis Niblet, Henry Moss, Ruth Moss

Richard and Lucy Murphey

Simon, 4/9/45, John Hines, John Hargrave, Eliz. Hines

Arthur and Charity Murphey

Sarah, 3/9/53, none given

MUSSLEWHITE

Thomas and Mary Musslewhite

Amy, 9/4/40, John Steagle, Eliz. Tatum, Elenor Smith

NASH

John and Eliz. Nash

John, 8/20/60, Aug. Clairbourne, Nath'l. Clairbourne, Mary
  Clairbourne, Eliz. Briggs

NELSON

Thomas and Olive Nelson

Martha, 11/1/76, none given

NEWSOM

Robert and Catherine Newsom

Anne, 1/11/40, James Brown, Anne Threwitts, Amy Bobbett

NEWSOM (Continued)

Robert and Catherine Newsom (Continued)

Winney, 5/6/42, Frances Walker, Mary Bobbett, Amy Bobbett
Richard, 7/25/46, John and Peter Threewit, Mary Randall
John, 3/1/48, Wm. Brown, Nath'l. Sturdivant, Eliz. Brown
Sarah, 1/8/50, Thomas Weathers, Anne Ezell, Eliz. Wynne

Amos and Agnes Newsom

Randall, 2/1/61, Isam Ezell, Wm. Rowland, Eliz. Ezell

Ben'g. and Mary Newsom

Crawford, 2/3/60, Joseph Armstrong, Edmund Pate, Alice
Newsom
Carter, 4/26/61, James Horn, Charles Barham, Eliz. Carter Jr.
Ben'g., 11/15/62, Thomas Barham, Wm. Hern, Sarah Barham
John, 10/11/65, James Barns, John McLamore, Sarah Knight
Holloday, 6/6/66, Nath'l. Holt, Charles Barham, Ede Newsom

Wm. and Eliz. Newsom

Frank, 5/22/64, Sampson Moseley, Philip Harwood, Patty Free-
man
Baalam, 5/26/66, Chas. Knight, John Fort, Rebbecca Long
Eldridge, 8/7/69, Danial Harwood, John Knight, Fanny Newsom
Baalam, twin, 8/7/69, Danial Harwood, John Knight, Fanny
Newsom
Fanny, 9/15/72, Wm. Longbottom, Jemima Rachael, Eliz. Moss

Thomas and Alice Newsom

Thomas, 12/9/58, Andrew Troughton, James Carter
Charles Stagg, 5/26/65, Lewis Dunn, Mary Newsom
Charlotte, 8/30/67, Gregory Rawlings, Mary Barham, Hannah
Arrington

Nath'l. and Susanna Newsom

Thomas, 1/5/67, John Hargrave, John Knight, Eliz. Moore
Barham, 2/16/69, Wm. Burrows, Chas. Knight, Mary Johnson
Anthony, 4/7/71, John Rives, Thos. Avent, Martha Moore

Jesse and Eliz. Newsom

Lucy, 4/23/61, Ben'g. Arrington, Aggy Newsom, Sarah Rawlings

Sylvia Newsom and ------

Peggy, 8/30/67, Fred Fort, Mary Fort, Sarah Grizzard
Rebbecca (by John Prince), 9/7/68, Drury Parham, Susanna Lilly

NIBLET

Francis and Jean Niblet

John, 9/13/44, Edward Weaver, Joseph Harrisson, Mary Hix
Sterling, 10/23/53, Richard Scoggin, Nath'l. Cotton, Mary Parsons
John, 9/10/55, Thos. Adkins, Nath'l. Bedingfield, Mary Tomlinson

NIBLET (Continued)
Francis and Eliz. Niblet
John, 9/4/44, Edward Weaver, Joseph Harrisson, Mary Reeks
Sarah, 10/21/50, Thomas Stafford, Sarah and Mary Reeks
Lucy, 11/21/58, Thos. Adkins, Lucy Adkins, Fanny Hawthorn

Alexander and Jean Niblet
Strachan, 3/21/62, John Dunbarre, James Gowan, Jacobina
Willie

NICHOLSON
Robert and Mary Nicholson
Mary, 7/25/44, Arthur Smith, Eliz. Blow, Jean Brittle
Harris, 12/14/46, David Hunter, Wm. Briggs, Eliz. Blow
Mary, 2/15/48, Wm. Evans, Beuford Pleasant, Anne Blunt
Mark, twin, 2/15/48, John and Danial Lamb, Anne Field
Samuel, 11/8/54, Wm. Evans, Beuford Pleasant, Anne Blunt

Edward and Mary Nicholson
James, 3/28/46, Peter Housman, Peter Parham, Jane Pillar

James and Anne Nicholson
James, 5/7/49, Beng. Ellis, Wm. Bailey, Lucy Warren (Weaver?)
Archibald, 2/25/46, Arthur Smith, Eliz. Pepper

Richard and Jane Nicholson
Thomas, 11/24/68, Floyd and Robert Nicholson, Mary Gibbons

John and Eliz. Nicholson
Wm., 12/16/65, Wm. Nicholson, Steven Andrews, Eliz. Nicholson
Buckner, 1/26/67, Harris and Robert Nicholson, Mary Andrews
Ben'g., 10/3/68, Floyd and John Nicholson, Mary Gibbons
Jane, 11/16/70, Thomas Smith, Eliz. Tharp, Susanna Andrews
John, 3/23/72, John Irby, Howell Briggs Jr., Jane Blunt
Susanna, 10/3/73, Richard Andrews, Susanna Edmunds, Susanna
Ellis

Harris and Susanna Nicholson
Charles. 11/11/70, John and Mark Nicholson, Rebbecca Briggs

Wm. and Eliz. Nicholson
Thomas, 11/24/68, Flood and Robert Nicholson, Mary Gibbons
James, 2/23/70, John and Harris Nicholson, Jane Blunt

Henry and Mary Nicholson
John, 12/21/69, Howell Chappell, Wm. Lamb, Mary Andrews
Robert, 3/2/70, Flood Nicholson, Thomas House, Prissilla
Edmunds

NORTHCROSS
Richard and Jane Northcross
Thomas, 7/13/57, Edward Powell, Wm. Hewett, Henretta Rosser.

NORTHCROSS (Continued)
101
Richard and Jane Northcross (Continued)
Susanna, 9/10/53, James Northcross, Abigail and Hannah Northcross
Wm. Wrenn, 10/14/60, John Addison, Abel Mabry, Dorothy Wood.
James, 3/26/65, Thomas Ezell, Abel Mabrey, Phoebe Battle
Beckey, 9/11/71, George Randall, Salley Underwood, Rebbecca
  Rowland
Eph., 8/20/72, none given

NORTHINGTON
Samuel and Phylis Northington
Nanny, 8/26/47, J. Gray Edmunds, Lucy Dunn, Hannah Thompson
Sterling, 11/7/49, Robert McGee, (Ralph ?), Joshuah Rolland,
  Hannah Seat
Samuel, 11/14/51, Sylvanus Stokes, Jesse Rowlands, Mary
  Rachael
Eliz., 12/29/55, John Wellborn, Jr., Hannah Wyche, Lucy
  Stokes
Molly, 5/26/58, Danial Owen, Mary Battle, Eliz. Brown
Jesse, 7/10/61, John Battle, Wm. Hill, Eliz. Holt
John, 8/5/65, Wm. Rose, Abel Mabrey, Amy Clanton
Wm., 7/30/67, Thos. Peebles, Ben'g. Owen, Rebbecca Owen
Samuel, 7/7/69, Mathew Davis, Samuel Northington

Nathan and Rebbecca Northington
(Rebbecca Chappell)
Jabez, 7/10/52, Wm. Tomlinson, John Chappell, Eliz. Pepper
Judieth, 12/26/53, James Tomlinson, Sarah Tatum, Sarah Moss
Eliz., 8/27/55, Charles Gee, Eliz. Mason, Amy Tatum
Rebbecca, 4/17/57, Isam Ezell, Micajah Stokes, Mary Rose
Nathan, 1/15/59, John Mason, Ben'g. Wyche, Eliz. Harrisson
Sarah, 2/20/60, Geo. Ezell, Eliz. Chappell, Rebbecca Mason
John, 4/18/63, Thomas Dowdy, Young Stokes, Lucy Baird
James, 4/7/67, Samuel Northington, James Chappell Jr., Lu-
  cretia Chappell
Elijah, 10/26/70, Ambrose Grizzard, Jabez. Northington, Eliz.
  Northington

Richard and Jane Northington
Thomas, 1/8/67, John Owen, Andrew Felts, Frances Woodruff

NUN-NUNS
John and Phoebe Nun
Wm., 11/4/46, Wm. Willie, Edward Shelton, Eliz. Shelton

John and --------- Nun
Eph., 12/7/60, James and Robert Armstrong, Mary Armstrong

OGBURN
John and Phoebe Ogburn
Aughustine, 12/28/51, Thomas Shands, Richard Partridge,
  ------ Hay

OGBURN (Continued)
John and Phoebe Ogburn (Continued)
Seth Mason, 6/5/58, John Jones, James Cook, Sarah Cook
Chlorine, 4/19/61, John Ogburn Jr., Anna Mason, Anne Tomlinson

John Ogburn Jr. and Mary
Mary, 2/12/64, Wm. Broadrib, Mary Mason, Sarah Ogburn

John Ogburn Jr. and Selah
John, 11/16/66, Thomas Hargrave, John Broadrib, Sarah Ogburn

Nicholis and Anne Ogburn
Wm., 12/20/71, Wm. Golightly, John Shands, Mary Adkins
Sterling, 12/4/74, Thomas Ogburn, Thomas Moss, Tabitha Mitchell

OLIVER
William and Frances Oliver
Isacc, 3/25/47, John Wellborn, Michael Hill, Lucy Hill
Isacc, 12/25/51, none given
Lucy, 9/5/58, Wm. Wellborn, Amy Hill, Lucy Mahaney
Anna, 8/30/61, James Jones, Sarah Wellborn, Mary Hill
Jane, 7/13/65, John Hood, Amy Freeman, Anne Hill
Frances, 3/25/66, John Malone, Frances Freeman, Lucy Oliver
Rebbecca, 11/8/70, Michael Malone, Mary Mahaney, Eliz. Malone

John and Eliz. Oliver
John, 7/16/41, John Painter, John King, Mary Rodgers

Isacc and Eliz. Oliver
Martha, 7/30/51, Thomas Dillard, Amy Hill, Mildred Oliver

OWEN
Wm. and Hannah Owen
Rebbecca, 10/4/45, Barthowlemew Figures, Rebbecca Figures, Eliz. Maggett
John, 10/15/47, Wm. Carrell, Ambrose Grizzard, Hannah Carrell
Hulda, 1/27/49, Arthur Smith, Mary Carrell, Sarah Grizzard
Mary, 3/25/52, Arthur Richardson, Lucy Nichols, Fanny Greffis
Eliz., 10/30/55, Thomas Carrell, Sarah Carlisle, Lucy Smith
Wm., 2/15/60, Wm. Brooks, Emanuel James, Selah Huson
Hannah, 10/20/62, Richard Blunt, Selah Smith, Rebbecca Richardson

John and Eliz. Owen
Mary, born 3/27/59, none given
Sarah, 3/20/57, David Owen, Mary Tanner, Mildred Hill
Peter, 4/22/60, Peter Threewit, Jesse Sturdivant, Eliz. Owen
John, 9/31/62, Wm. Rawlings, Robert Owen, Anne King
Patty, 9/31/62, Wm. Rowland, Robert Owen, Anne King
Mely, 9/4/66, Thomas Wynne, Jr., Selah Spane, Sarah Threewits
Robert, 9/25/71, Lewis Harnes, Fred Owen, Eliz. Owen
Drury, 6/24/74, Thomas Hern, Robert Whitehead, Sarah Owen

OWEN (Continued)
David and Mary Owen
Baalam, 4/15/56, Wm. Rowland, James Cain, Eliz. Gilliam
Joshuah, 9/15/59, Ben'g. Owen, Wm. Richardson, Lucy Harris
David, 7/6/61, James Bell, John Owen, Mildred Bell
Nancy, 6/5/63, Samuel Harwood, Rebbecca and Phoebe Rowland
Wm., 2/6/65, Wm. Spane, Jesse Sturdivant, Salley Threewitt
Suckey, 12/20/67, Robert Owen, Sarah Roland, Lucy Stokes
Mary, 3/10/70, Sylvanus Bell, Tabitha Wiggens, Anne Epps
Nathan, 11/3/72, Abel Mabrey, Wm. Newsom, Eliz. Rolland

Ben'g. and Eliz. Owen
Edmund, 5/4/62, David and Robert Owen, Mary Green
Bengaman, 3/9/66, Ro. Wynne Raines, Wm. Rowland, Phoebe
    Rowland
James, 6/8/68, James Bell, Thomas Stokes, Sarah Threewitts
Salley, 3/6/71, Young Stokes, Agnes Rowland, Eliz. Spane

John and Eliz. Owen
Lydia, 12/7/49, Lewis Adkins, Mary Spane, Sarah Roberts
Frederick, 11/12/51, John Atkinson, Edward Whittington, Mary
    Emery
John, 10/31/61, Wm. Rolland, Robert Owen, Anne King

Beng. and Betty Owen
Robert, 1/25/64, Webb Rolland, Isam Ezell, Sarah
    Threewit
Ben'g., 6/1/66, Robert Wynne Raines, Wm. Rolland, Phoebe
    Rolland

Valintine and Agnes Owen
James, 10/26/60, John Carter, Thos. Huson, Amy Carter

Richard and Lucy Owen
Herbert, 1/30/65, James Bell, David Owen, Mildred Bell

Frederick and Sarah Owen
Lewis, 12/2/72, Anderson Sturdivant, Peter Threewits,
    Jemimma Sturdivant

Sarah Owen and --------
Anny, 5/14/71, Wm. Broadnax, Mary Broadnax, Martha Winfield

John Owen died 2/26/39

PAINTER
John and Mary Painter
Eliz., 12/19/49, John Wilkerson, Rebbecca Cotton, Parnel Gibbs
Samuel, twin of above, none given

Richard and Agnes Painter
Richard, 2/16/46, Richard King, Richard King Jr.

104

PAINTER (Continued)
Richard and Agnes Painter (Continued)
John, 3/27/72, Nath'l. Cotton, Miles Duncan, Anne Duncan
Wyatt, 4/13/74, Miles Duncan, Harris Cotton, Betty Wilkerson

PARE
Wm. Pare Jr. and Jane
James, 7/8/58, Nath'l. Hood, Charles Williams, Rebbecca Pare
Rebbecca, 5/27/60, none given
Lavina, ?/?/?, Abel Mabrey, Sarah Williams, Sarah Adkins
Eliz., 11/3/62, Joseph Dobie, Keisah Tatum, Anne Gilliam
Mary, 2/25/64, Moss Williams, Mary and Eliz. Rodgers
Nancy, 6/5/69, John Cock, Lucretia Cock, Sarah Hood
Wm., 12/19/71, Wm.Stewart Jr., Eph. King, Lucretia Hood

John and Susanna Pare
Winney, 4/14/58, Mathew Wynne, Anne Pare, Mary Dobie
Wm., 9/19/60, Jesse Parton, John Clifton, Mildred Parton
John, 10/27/62, Joseph Pennington, Richard Wilkerson, Lilly
------?
Bob, 2/9/65, John Ray, Charles Gee, Lucy Lanier
Marcus, 8/31/68, John Walker, John Pennington, Salley Pennington
Nancy, 8/27/69, Drury Partan, Mary Clifton, Mary Partan
Mary, 4/27/73, Fred Lilly, Sarah Bendall, Betty Wynne

Thomas and Mary Pare
Lotta, 12/20/52, Wm. Willie, Anne and Aggy Pare

PARHAM
James and Eliz. Parham
Pattie, 1/16/39, Thomas Wilkerson, Sarah Malone, Ann Malone
Frances, 2/6/46, Abraham Parham, Mary Lee, Sarah Heath

Wm. and Susanna Parham
Charles, 3/16/33, none given

Mathew and Susanna Parham
Eliz., 7/30/39, John Bell, Francis Rainey, Hannah Bell
Cap't. Mathew Parham died 3/18/75, aged 81 years

Mathew and Martha (Wynne) Parham
Robert, 1/17/47, Sloman Wynne, Wm. Willie, Eliz. Parham
Mathew, 2/27/50, Robert Wynne, Thos. Parham, Eliz. Parham

Mathew Parham Jr. and Rebbecca
Eph., 9/25/56, Eph. and Wm. Parham, Judieth Green
James, 9/23/60, Edward Powell, Thos. Vines Jr., Mary Lilly

William and Martha Parham
Nancy Lucas, 3/17/69, Nath'l. Parham, Mary Gilliam, Rebbecca Lucas

Cap't. William Parham died - no date.

PARHAM (Continued)

Eph. and Rebbecca Parham
Frances, 5/31/41, Wm. Parham, Frances Parham, Jean Allen
Wm., 3/14/44, Wm. Johnson, Abra. Brown, Phoebe Parham
Rebbecca, 5/10/52, Wm. Green, Mildred Gilliam, Jane Parham

Steth and Eliz. Parham
Jane, 2/17/52, Thomas Parham, Prissilla Parham, Eliz. Hams
Phoebe, 6/25/53, Guthridge Hadden, Martha and Anne Parham
Eliz., 12/17/55, Robert Wynne, Susanna Hall, Eliz. Wynne
Mathew Anderson, 1/25/61, Mathew and Wm. Wynne, Aggy Wynne
Anne, 1/16/63, Abraham Parham Jr., Lucy Massenburg, Lucy
    Wynne

William and Mary Parham
Thomas, 8/26/56, Mathew Parham Jr., Thomas Huson, Laticia
    Green
Eliz., 8/20/58, Eliz. Smith, Olive Green, Charles Collins
John, 10/15/64, Eph. Parham, Richard Jones, Sarah Rainey
Frances, 11/25/65, Burwell Banks, Anne Wilkerson, Eliz. Gib-
    bons
Sarah, 2/28/69, Robert Wynne Raines, Sarah Batt, Anne Collier
Lewis, 8/19/70, Joel Wilkerson, James Parham, Molly Jones
Wm., 3/6/72, Wm. Battle, Wm. Mason, Frances Parham
Wm., 10/4/73, Wm. Kelly, Thomas ------?, Patty Kelly
Stevens, 8/15/74, Ambrose Brown, Ben'g. Mathews, Rebbecca
    Dunn

Thomas and Anne Parham
Wm., 7/15/46, Steth Parham, John Oliver, Eliz. Parham
Steth, 5/5/49, Peter Northcross, Isacc Oliver, Prissilla Parham
John, 6/26/52, Guthridge Hollum, Mathew Gibbs, Anne Wynne
Thomas, 12/11/56, Wm. Wynne, Ben'g. Tomlinson, Mary Nun

John and Mary Parham
Mathew, 1/17/41, Mathew Parham, Mathew Gibbs, Sarah Malone

Geo. and Mary Parham
Mary, 3/30/54, Wyatt Harper, Athalia Porch, Eliz. Echols
Wm., 5/13/59, none given

Nathanial and Selah Parham
Robert, 9/18/59, John and Robert Petway, Phoebe Petway
Lewis, 5/31/60, Eph. Parham, Frances Epps, Rebbecca Parham
Mary, 2/27/66, John House, Agnes Freeman, Phoebe Epps
Eph., 3/7/68, Edward Petway, Sylvanus Bell, Mary Banks

Geo. and Mely Parham
Wm., 5/13/59, none given
Nancy, 8/3/64, James Warren, Selah Warren, Rebbecca Jones
Booth, 8/1/70, Peter Green, Ro. Wynne Raines, Betty Love

Eph. and Ruth Parham
Betsy, 3/11/68, Gray Dunn, Mary Parham, Vina Dunn

PARKER
William and Rebbecca Parker
John, 4/2/42, Geo. Rives, Wm. Weathers, Penelope Green

William and Sarah Parker
Eliz., 4/6/41, Richard Jones Jr., Mary Johnson, Eliz. Jones
Wm., 12/25/45, Amelius Dowdning, John Nicholson, Mary
Nicholson
Patty, 6/14/51, John Jones, Lucretia Throder??, Susanna Har-
risson
Susanna, 4/28/54, Jesse Jones, Eliz. Willie, Mary Parker
Judy, 3/29/57, John Chappell, Sarah Jones, Alice Stagg

William Parker died 3/7/68, reported by Mrs. Hannah Jones

Thomas and Sarah Parker
Eliz., 3/1/61, David Jones, Sarah and Rebbecca Jones
Elizabeth Parker died 11/14/48, reported by Mary Green.
William and Susanna Parker
James, 12/29/71, James Peters, Fred Hines, Lucy Peters

William and Mary Parker
Archibald, 11/3/72, Flood Nicholson, John Blunt, Eliz. Peters,
Frances Jones
America, 10/23/74, Thomas Peets, Sarah Hunt, Mary Collier

PARSONS
Robert and Elenor Parsons
Amy, 8/20/46, none given
Henry, 8/12/49, Wm. Duff, Wm. Wilkerson, Eliz. Parsons
Elenor, 11/23/52, Francis Niblet, Eliz. Niblet, Mary Parsons

William and Mary Parsons
Robert, 3/20/64, Robert Parsons, Geo. Ezell, Mary Adams

Henry and Eliz. Parsons
Robert, 11/27/74, Robert Parsons, Wm. Harrisson, Anne Harrisson

PARTAN
Charles and Anne Partan
Robert, 1/4/39, John King, Wm. Partan, Johanna Partan
Lucy, twin, Wm. Partan, Mary Shelton, Jean Woodruff
Peter, 3/17/41, none given
Eliz., 6/24/44, Richard King, Anne Ezell, Johannah Briggs

Wm. and Johannah Partan
Mildred, 7/18/39, Samuel Smith, Mary Smith, Mary Shelton
Wm., 12/28/36, none given
Johannah, 4/11/46, none given
Jane, 9/24/55, John Gilliam, John Pare, Anne Gilliam
James, 9/24/55, Isacc Mason, Martha Gilbert, Anne Mason

PARTAN (Continued)
William and Hannah Partan
Jesse, 9/3/42, Wm. Moss Jr., John Steagal, Amy Dunn

Drury and Mary Partan
Wm., 7/25/68, Wm. Partan, Steth Wynne, Winefred Lilly

PARTRIDGE
Nicholas and Eliz. Partridge

Wells, 10/23/39, Peter Bailey, Peter Rosser, Sarah Partridge
Henry, 1/31/46, Nicholas Partridge, Thomas Adkins, Eliz.
    Adkins
Thomas, 2/14/47, Thomas Adkins Jr., Richard Tomlinson Jr.,
    Mary Tomlinson
Jesse, 12/29/49, John Barker, John Adkins Jr., Sarah Barker
Mary, 11/26/51, Nich. Jarrett, Eliz. Adkins, Eliz. Adkins
Eliz., 12/21/55, Thomas Adkins Jr., Mary Rosser, Mary Tom-
    linson
Amy, 12/31/58, John Adkins, Sarah Rosser, Lucy Adkins
Burwell, 7/4/62, Burwell Tomlinson, Wm. Peebles, Sarah
    Peebles
NOTE: Called Nich. Jr. in 1747

Richard Partridge Jr. and Eliz.
Mary, 11/26/51, Richard Jarrett, Eliz. Adkins, Eliz. Adkins
Eliz., 12/21/56, Thomas Adkins Jr., Mary Rosser, Mary Tom-
    linson

Wells and Anne Partridge
Nicholis, 5/25/58, Nicholis Partridge, John Barker Jr., Eliz.
    Jarrett
Mary, 7/13/60, Henry Jarrett, Sarah Barker, Charity Maggett
Charity, 3/8/62, John Adkins, Eliz. Adkins, Mary Jarrett
Bramley, 2/20/64, Edward Weaver Jr., Mary and Amy Adkins

Thomas and Sarah Partridge
Henry, 1/20/70, Jesse Partridge, Thos. Tomlinson, Mary Part-
    ridge
Betsy, 10/2/71, Wm. Partridge, Mary Adkins, Eliz. Partridge
Thomas, 12/11/73, Nicholis Partridge, Wm. Hunter, Phoebe
    Shands

PATE
Thomas and Mary Pate
Thomas, 8/24/39, John Bell, Wm. Thompson, Anne Pate
Sarah, 1/2/46, Edmund Pate, Sarah Thompson, Eliz. Pate

Thomas and Sarah Pate
Edward, 7/17/42, Edward Pate, Thos. Barlow, Anne Pate

Thomas Pate Jr. and Mary
Lydia, 1/26/62, Ephriam Hill, Sarah Pate, Mary Felts

PATE (Continued)
Thomas Pate Jr. and Mary (Continued)
Winney, 11/23/63, Samuel Pate, Ruth and Mely Pate
Thomas, 3/12/67, John Jones, Ben'g. Graves, Hannah Hix
Jesse, 9/24/68, Nath'l. and Lucy Sammons
Sucky, 9/13/70, Drury Felts, Eliz. Prince, Mildred Santee

Edmund and Mary Pate
Mary, 3/5/42, Wm. Cooper, Agnes Buten, Mary Rodgers
Edmund, 11/13/44, Wm. Knight, John Bulloch, Eliz. Adams

Edmund and Sarah Pate
Sarah, 11/13/47, Wm. Hix, Sarah Harwood, Sarah Roberts

John and Eliz. Pate
Clairbourne, 8/16/72, Ben'g. Adams, Wm. Prince, Mary Adkins

Edward and Lucretia Pate
Herbert, 11/23/67, Ben'g. Phipps, John Irby, Mildred Pate

PATRICK
John and Wilmouth Patrick
Reubin, 2/3/61, George and Peter Randall, Mary Hill
Wm., 2/27/63, Wm. Yarbrough, Wm. Threewits, Olive Randall

PATTERSON
George and Rebbecca Patterson
Eliz., 4/18/66, Joseph Ingram, Samuel Harewell, Mildred Hill

PEEBLES
Thomas and Sarah Peebles
Nathanial, 5/15/31, John Smith, Isabel Burrows
Thomas, 10/21/32, Thomas and Peter Tatum, Mary Wise
Wm., 1/1/34, Wm. Peebles, Wm. Rives, Mary Epps
Sarah, 6/26/37, John Weaver, Mildred Vincent
Henry, 3/3/41, Chris. Tatum, Timothy Rives, Hannah Dobie

John and Eliz. Peebles
Mary, 1/28/40, (bab), David Peebles, Mary Hix, Whitson Cooper
Eph., 9/23/40, (bab), none given

David and Sarah Peebles
Rebbecca, 1/27/42, John Underhill, Eliz. Gerrard, Eliz. Partridge

David and Mary Peebles
Wm., 8/29/62, Wm. Cocke, Wm Horn, Francis Rives
Baalam, twin, Robert Whitehead, Thos. Hern, Winefred Newsom
Hamlin, 11/9/60, Nathanial Hood, James Hern, Thany Spane

Thomas and Mary Peebles
Mary, 12/4/65, Wm. Harrisson, Lucy Adkins, Eliz. Mason
John, 1/12/68, John Judkins, Samuel Northington, Sarah Judkins

PEEBLES (Continued)
Thomas and Mary Peebles (Continued)
Susanna, 10/2/69, David Mason, Mary Mason, Prissilla Gilliam
Nathanial, 5/14/72, Cole Harrisson, Thos. Tomlinson, Eliz.
  Shands
Thomas Edmunds, 5/8/74, David Heeth, David Mason Jr., Mary
  Hay, Lucretia Mason

Jesse and Martha Peebles
Betsy, 12/23/73, John Potts, Mary Lessenberry, Susanna Epps

PEETE - PITT
Samuel and Mary Peete
Martha, 8/25/48, James Wrenn, Sarah Parker, Anne Wrenn
Wm., 7/22/54, Wm. Hines, James Carter, Rebbecca Hines

Thomas and Judieth Peete
Thomas, 7/30/71, Wm. Blunt, Wm. Nicholson, Martha Blunt

PENNINGTON
Thomas and Rebbecca Pennington
Faithey, 3/19/34, none given
Mary, 4/3/36, none given
Howell, 2/2/42, Mathew Hubbard, Francis Hutchens, Mary Hub-
  bard
Joel, 8/8/44, Wm. Ezell, Wm. Rachael, Mary Ezell
Wm. Thomas, 7/11/53, Gregory Rawlings Jr., Isam Ezell, Faith
  Pennington

Thomas and Rebbecca Pennington died 2/18/----, Nathanial Holt

John and Mary Pennington
Joshuah, 11/7/41, Francis Houtchens, John Pennington, Martha
  Moore
Marcus, 9/25/44, James Sasensick, Jesse Gilliam, James An-
  drews
Sarah, 10/27/50, Wm. Longbottom, Francis and Sarah Williams

John Pennington Jr. and Anne
Jesse, 8/10/40, Thomas Wrenn, Robert Hancock, Hannah Pen-
  nington
Lucy, 1/16/41, John Pennington, Mary Pennington, Eliz.Natty??
Lewis, 1/4/43, Thomas Pennington, Thos. Brewer, Mary Bailey
Sarah, 8/29/46, David Stokes, Rebbecca Pennington, Mary Hub-
  bard
Mary, 3/6/48, Joseph Pennington, James Andrews, Sarah Raw-
  lings
Frederick, 3/25/51, Charles Atherton, John Land, Anne Davis
Lucretia,?/?/?,Moss Pennington,Eliz. Pennington,Anne Dansey

Edmund and Sarah Pennington
Wm., 9/7/41, Wm. Cook, Timothy Ezell, Jr., Eliz. Willie

PENNINGTON (Continued)
David and Susanna Pennington
Holmes, 3/19/37, none given

Joseph and Eliz. Pennington
David, 6/1/53, Moses Pennington, Robert Wynne, Anne Dansey
Frederick, 4/24/55, John Clanton, Ben'g. Wyche, Lydia Pennington
Rebbecca, 11/10/58, Henry Gee, Mary Dansey, Mary Troughton
John, 12/1/60, Andrew Troughton, Eliz. Stevens
Mary, 6/7/63, Henry Porch Jr., Hannah Porch, Sarah Wrenn
Eliz., 1/7/66, Francis Walker, Lucy Pennington, Mary Land
Edward, 3/8/68, Jesse Williamson, Nath'l. Holt, Salley Pennington

David and Lydia Pennington
Leah, 5/8/55, Charles Wood, Phoebe Lofting, Eliz. Pennington
Tabitha, 9/8/58, none given
Kinchen, 1/18/61, John Judkins, John Shands, Sarah Freeman
Ned, 8/22/63, Joshuah Pennington, John Gilliam, Eliz. Moore
Jane Green, 2/8/65, Anslem Gilliam, Martha Clanton, Selah Rachael
Sarah Gilliam, 7/5/60, none given
Nelson, 7/25/67, Wm. Wrenn, Richard Hamlin, Eliz. Gilliam
Tempe, 3/27/69, Isam Gilliam, Patty Clanton, Peggy Newsom

Marcus and Anne Pennington
Eliz., 9/6/70, David Graves, Mary Hay, Martha Moore
Wm., 4/16/72, Wm. Graves, David Mason, Sarah Moore

PEPPER
Richard and Eliz. Pepper
Martha, 12/23/36, none given
Rebbecca, 10/15/37, none given

Richard and Martha Pepper
Richard, 8/16/42, Thos. Addison, Thos. Wade, Mary Addison

Steven and Jean Pepper
Anna, 9/16/41, Richard Pepper, Simon Murphey, Sarah Allison, Susanna Ellis

Martha Pepper died 6/20/43, reported by Richard Pepper

See Richardson, Northington, Jones

PETERS
Thomas Peters Jr. and Hannah
John, 9/24/40, Lemuel Lanier, Joseph Halsey, Mary Philips
Anne, 11/9/42, Lemuel Lanier, Hannah Lanier, Sarah Parker
Thomas, 3/7/44, David and John Edmunds, Anne Turner
Mary, 11/16/47, Richard Hines, Mary Hines, Mary Moore
Mathew, 3/31/52, James Armstrong, Thos. Parker, Mary Peete
Temperence, 12/20/61, James Miller, Betty Hunt

PETERS (Continued)
Walter and Catherine Peters
Thos. Dunlop, 3/3/68, James Buchannon, Wm. Short, Eliz.
   Peters, ------ Cocks

John and Martha Peters
Henry, 8/7/69, Eldridge Clack, John Chappell, Sarah Hunt
Salley, 4/6/67, Wm. Wrenn, Mary Peters, Mary Parker
Eliz., 11/23/74, Wm. Parker, Eliz. Mason, Hannah Peters

James and Lucy Peters
Nancy, 11/6/69, Thos. Sisson, Eliz. Hunt, Eliz. Parker
Susanna, 8/5/71, Wm. Parker, Susanna Parker, Hannah Peters

PETTYPOOL
John and Anne Pettypool
John, 2/14/62, none given

PETWAY
Edward and Eliz. Petway
Mary, 12/24/39, none given
Robert, 7/22/45, Thos. Eldridge, Thomas Mitchell, Eliz. Shands
Eliz., 9/1/56, Wm. Willie, Eliz. Willie, Anne Sturdivant
Susanna, 1/12/54, Theophilas Field, Selah Petway, Anne Moore

Elizabeth Petway died 11/27/63, reported by Edward Petway

Robert and Phoebe Petway
James, 9/26/60, none given
Robert, 5/25/63, Wm. and John Petway, Sarah Petway
Wm., 8/23/67, Nathanial Parham, Edward Petway Jr., Frances
   and Susanna Petway
Eliz., 1/27/70, Lawrence Gibbons Jr.
Edward, 1/30/72, Edward Petway, Edmund Gibbons, Eliz. Petway

Wm. Petway Jr. and Sarah
Eliz., 9/20/59, none given
Molly, 4/23/62, none given
Salley, 1/14/71, Cyrill Avery, Martha Binns, Jacobina Willie

Joseph and Hannah Petway
Sterling, 10/3/49, Nathanial Lewis, John Bradley, Patience
   Harris
Lucy, 1/5/52, John Harris, Eliz. Bradley, Jane Adkinson

Micajah and Amy Petway
Peyton, 7/30/57, Charles Mabrey, John Bulloch, Martha Lofting
Selah, 5/11/59, Wm. Rose, Mary Battle, Jane Mabrey

Nicholis Petway Jr., and Eliz.
Wm., 10/2/53, John Ogburn, Wells Partridge, Phoebe Ogburn

PHIPPS
Bengaman and Martha Phipps
Suscey, 11/16/59, none given
Anna, 10/30/62, Samuel Harwood, Eliz. and Selah Richardson
Jordan, 7/2/69, Abel Mabrey, John Ezell Jr., Eliz. Richardson

Benjamin and Salley Phipps
John, 6/19/72, Wm. Rowland, Samson Newson, Milly Richardson

PLATT
John and Alice Platt
Wm., 10/14/45, James Richardson, Charles Humphrey, Sarah
Ellis

PLEASANT
Beuford and Mary Pleasant
John, 3/9/45, Ben'g. Clark, Simon Stacey, Prissilla Rodgers
George, 3/4/48, Thomas Bell, Joseph Rodgers, Mary Bell
Thomas, 10/21/50, Robert Nicholson, Katherine Stacey

William and Mary Pleasant
Burwell, 12/17/63, Beuford Pleasant, Henry Underhill, Molly
Davis
Wm., 10/25/66, Simon Stacey, Thos. Hargrave, Jane Bane

Peter and Abigail Pleasant
Ben'g., 3/27/63, Wm. Ellis, Fred Andrews, Lucy Proctor

PORCH
James and Eliz. Porch
James, 9/9/40, John Thompson, Wm. Bird, Anne Ivey
Martha, 3/14/41, John Moss, Francis Moss, Mary Porch
Joshuah, 7/16/43, Joshuah Meacum, Henry Mason, Mary Moss
Sylvia, 3/3/44, Henry Meacum Jr., Susanna Cheves, Eliz. Part-
ridge
Isam, 6/4/46, Nicholis Partridge, Henry Moss, Mary Prescot
Soloman, 12/29/47, Wm. Petway, Wm. Wilkerson, Martha Gil-
bert
Isareal, 8/26/50, Christopher Tatum, Aug. Clairbourne, Anne
Ezell

Henry and Mary Porch
Thomas, 11/16/43, Richard Scoggin, Warwick Davis, Susanna
Crossland
Peter, 5/6/46, Peter Hawthorn, Henry Lee Jr., Rachael Prescot

Peter and Anne Porch
Wm., 10/5/75, Thos. Whitefield, John Ray, Susanna Scoggin

James Porch Jr., and Eliz.
Jeany, 11/26/70, Lewis Johnson, John Bell, Jemima Johnson
Peter, 1/8/73, Moses Knight, Thomas Hornsby, Patty Spane
Lucy, 4/21/74, Burwell Wellborn, Frances Oliver, Eliz. Cocke

PORCH (Continued)
Henry Porch Jr. and Hannah
Mary, 1/1/63, Bridges Porch, Anna Ezell, Sarah Wrenn
Hartwell, 3/7/70, John Petway, John Adkins, Jemima Hancock
Nancy, 11/25/72, Nathan Wrenn, Hulda Wrenn, Mary Sturdivan

POTTS
John and Mary Potts
Wm., 7/31/74, Eph. Moss, Thos. Tomlinson, Amy Duncan

POWELL - Bristol Register
John and Mary Powell
John, b. 1725, Anne, b. 1728, Robert, b. 1733

Edward and Eliz. Powell
Thomas, b. 1727, Mar'g., 1733

Hezikiah and Bathia Powell
Ann b. 1726, Wm. b. 1730, Rebbecca b. 1734

PRESSON
Thomas and Sarah Presson
Nicholis, 2/14/59, none given
Jane, 1/18/60, none given
Eliz., 12/7/65, James Turner, Anne Holt, Lucy Richardson
Jeaney, 11/6/69, John Presson, Lucy Presson, Sarah Kenny-
brough
Betsy, 11/17/71, James White, Sarah Smith, Jean Bean
Thomas Lamb, 8/20/74, Wm. Lamb, Wm. Stacey, Patty White

John and Lucy Presson
Danial, 12/14/60, Richard Johnson, John Lamb, Sarah Johnson
Hannah, 11/7/62, Thos. Presson, Sarah Presson, Mary Banks

PRICHETT - PRICHARD (spelled both ways, evidently PRICHARD)

Morris and Eliz. Prichard
Mary, 9/31/39, John Ellis, Joyce Washington, Eliz. Prichard
Richard, 11/8/45, Richard Blunt, John Irby, Anne Phillipps
Carey, 1/5/47, Henry Prichard, John Curry, Lucy Prichard

Henry and Lucy Prichard
Henry, 3/13/42, Henry Troughton, Thomas Dunn Jr., Eliz.
Shelton
John, 12/29/44, John Clanton, Wm. Ezell, Eliz. Prichard
Charles, 11/24/46, Wm. Johnson, Ben'g. Wyche, Tabitha Ezell
Wm., 9/18/49, Charles Atherton, John Moss, Anne Atherton

Thomas and Eliz. Prichard
Eliz. Breeden, 2/27/64, Charles Williams, Eliz. Gilliam, Betty
Moore

Thomas and Mary Prichard
Thomas Moore, 7/25/68, John Cocks, Wm. Hern, Agnes Gilliam

PRINCE
Joseph and Mary Prince

John, 4/20/40, John Prince, Daniel Prince, Elizabeth Hay
William, 3/3/41, none given
Mary, 3/3/43, John Underhill, Mary Chappell, Elizabeth Peebles
Amy, 1/20/45, none given
Joseph, 1/12/47-48, none given

Joseph and Elizabeth Prince

Joseph, 3/17/49, Agnes Oliver
Joel, 12/23/50, none given
Elizabeth, 3/10/53, none given
Judith, 4/8/55, none given

Edward and Hannah Prince

John, 3/24/47, none given
Isham, 5/21/47-48, none given
Nicholas, 7/5/51, Nath. Johnson, John Tatum, Sophrana Johnson

William and Elizabeth Prince

Joseph, 5/17/64, Rebecca Prince
William, 5/28/66, Rebecca Prince
Francis, 4/15/71, none given

James and Cecelia Prince

John, 10/3/45, Gilbert Prince, Peter Brooks, Sarah Brooks.

Thwaite Prince, death certified by Edward Prince Nov. 29, 1739.

PULLAM
Samuel and Eliz. Pullam

Molly, 7/7/66, Ben'g. Adams, Eliz. Newsom, Sarah Long

PULLY
Robert and Hannah Pully

Salley, 3/17/48, Joseph Norton, Alice Norton, Sarah Hay

PURRIER
Robert and Frances Purrier

Eliz., 6/10/53, Wm. Purrier, Sarah Pepper, Olive Mangum

PYNES
William and Jane Pynes

Nathanial, 8/23/48, James Bane, John Smith, Rachael Groves

RACHAEL - ROCHELLE
Ralph and Eliz. Rachael

Miles, 1/19/44, Christopher Jane, John Southerland, Mary Davis

Wm. and Laura Rachael

John, 10/21/43, Wm. Craig, John King Jr., Sophia Stokes

RACHAEL - ROCHELLE (Continued)
Wm. and Laura Rachael (Continued)
Mary, 10/18/45, Thomas Pennington, Eliz. Rose, Eliz. Adams
Cecelia, 11/25/47, John Berryman, Eliz. Ellis, Mary Stokes
Winefred, 9/10/49, Thomas Weathers, Naomi Bulloch, Mary
  Bulloch
Sarah, 9/7/41, David Stokes, Eliz. Gilliam, Cecelia Stokes
George, 6/24/52, John Rachael, Robert Bulloch, Martha Ezell
Wm. Stokes, 6/3/54, Wm. Houchens, Wm. Willie, Kesiah Bul-
  loch

John and Mary Rachael
John, 9/26/46, John and Burwell Gilliam, Eliz. Lofting
Selah, 2/6/47, Wm. Ezell, Temperence Hill, Winefred Woodruff
Mary, 9/30/49, Thomas Gilliam, Amy Freeman, Anne Gilliam
Henchie, 6/11/51, Hinchae Gilliam, Wm. Rodgers, Mary Rod-
  gers
Jemima, 11/9/53, Robert Bulloch, Mely Hill, Sarah Moore
Levi, 1/19/56, Levi Gilliam, James Bell, Eliz. Rodgers
Nathanial, 6/18/58, Nathanial Clanton, Andrew Troughton, Mary
  Gilliam

RAINES
William and Angelica Raines
Robert Wynne, 6/25/39, none given
Richard, 3/2/40, none given
Jean, 8/26/36, none given
Jefferson, 11/20/44, Wm. Gilliam, John Freeman, Anne Oliver,
  Eliz. Holloway
Nathanial, 3/21/48, Charles Williams, Thos. Bonner, Amy
  Raines
Anna, 7/22/46, Nathanial Raines, Anne Raines, Eliz. Parham
Theodosia, 12/10/49, Danial Wagon, Martha Tucker, Lucy
  Mathews

John and Amy Rains
Thomas, 6/27/63, Geo. Reives, Wm. Belomy, Anne Fawn
Amy, 2/10/73, none given

R. Wynne Raines and Jane
Peter Green, 8/28/60, Peter Green, Martha Freeman, Fred
  Green
Wm., 2/10/62, Francis Epps, Wm. Mitchell, Mary Gilliam
Littleton, 1/26/66, Robert Tucker, Ben'g. Owen, Mary Tucker

RAINEY
Nathanial and Phoebe Rainey
Phoebe, 4/12/58, Peter Green, Olive Green, Susanna Richardson
Wynne, 2/12/60, Thomas Wynne Jr., Fred Green, Francina In-
  gram
Eliz., 3/2/61, Wm. Richardson, Eliz. Wynne, Angelica Cain
Mary, 10/8/62, Wm. Rainey, Anne Rainey, Patty Freeman
Nath'l., 7/6/64, Lewis Brown, James Cain, Anne Rainey

RAINEY (Continued)

Nathanial and Phoebe Rainey (Continued)

Anne, 10/19/57, John Wynne, Mary Farrington, Mary Rainey
Wm., 3/15/66, Wm. Winfield, John Powell, Betty Ruthford Randall
Thomas, 12/5/68, Robert Tucker, Joseph Ingram, Mary Powell
Hannah, 3/25/72, Jarrell Burrow, Martha Rainey, Martha Wynne

Wm. Rainey Jr. and Mary

Mary, 10/11/58, Wm. Hewett, Penelope Whittington, Phoebe Rainey

William and Mary Rainey

Anne, 1/26/48, Nathanial Rainey, Anne Rainey, Mary Rainey
Wm., 1/26/50, none given
Danial, 4/3/53, Danial Knight, Nathanial Rainey, Eliz. Richardson
Peter, 9/1/54, Amos Love, Harwood Goodwynne, Mary Prichard
Peter, 4/13/56, Thomas Weathers, Joseph Richardson

William Rainey, aged 89 years. died 3/5/69, reported by George Randall
Mary Rainey, the wife of William, died 9/2/74, reported by Wm. Rainey

RAMSEY

Richard and Amy Ramsey

Booker, 8/26/64, John Winfield, Robert Winfield, Mary Love

RANDALL

Peter and Mary Randall

Peter, 5/29/40, Thomas Mitchell, Henry Mitchell, Susanna Cain

George and Betty Ruthford Randall

Peter, 11/22/50, Wm. Yarbrough, Wm. Woodlands, Phoebe Randall
Mary, 3/25/53, Robert Farington, Mildred Robertson, Angelica Cain
George, 8/12/56, Burwell Banks, John Winfield, Jane Green
Eliz., 12/23/58, Peter Randall, Olive Green Phoebe Green
Peyton, 1/4/69, Lawrence Gibbons Jr., Ro. Wynne Raines
Lucy, 2/9/67, Peter Green, Jane Rains, Eliz. Green
Betty Ruthford, 9/9/68, John Berryman, Jane Raines, Angelica Ingram

Peter and Olive Randall

John, 10/7/64, Fred Green, John Powell, Mary Tucker
Mary, 1/15/61, Wm. Yarbrough, Mary Yarbrough, B. Ruthford Randall
Eliz., 3/18/71, Nathanial Dunn, Eliz. Vaughn, Mary Hewett
Frances, 12/29/66, Peter Green, Eliz. Green, Lucy Harewell
Polly, 9/3/73, Isam Smith, Anne Gibbons, Eliz. Parham

RANDALL (Continued)
Peter and Frances Randall
Nancy, 1/1/74, Mathew Parham, Mary Jarrett, Prissilla Northington

RAWLINGS
John and Mary Rawlings
Gregory, 1/19/46, Gregory Rawlings, Mathew Hubbard, Hannah
Rawlings, Gregory Rawlings and Sarah

Gregroy Rawlings Jr. and Sarah
Jesse, 8/26/46, John Rawlings, Mathew Hubbard, Elizabeth
Roberts
James, 5/20/51, Samuel Harwood, Nathaniel Holt, Elizabeth
Holt
Sucky, 8/17/56, Thomas Moore Jr., Elizabeth Holt, Lucy Newsom
Gregory, 1/5/59, Lewis Johnson, Anslem Gilliam, Agnes Newsom
Rebecca, 6/10/62, Fred Holt, Lucy Moss, Elizabeth Newsom
Nancy, 1/20/65, none given
John, 5/18/67, none given

John and Mary Rawlings
Anne, 1/25/47, John Rawlings, Sarah Rawlings, Mosley Hogwood
Lucy, 12/15/49, Thomas Holt, Sarah Rawlings, Jane Gregg
Lydia, 6/5/54, John Pennington, Sarah Barrow, Mosley Hogwood
Molly, 3/7/57, Absolum Davis, Katherine Richardson, Hannah
Mannery
Elizabeth, 11/3/66, Beng. Phipps, Elizabeth --------, Mildred
Barker
Rebecca, 3/14/69, Isaac Ezell, Elizabeth Richardson, Anne Ezell
Richard, 9/15/71, John Land, Chas. Long, Anne Rawlings
Patty, 3/2/60, Joseph Armstrong, Sarah and Mary Long

Drury and Lydia Rawlings
James, 1/5/58, Joseph Harwood, Edward Shelton, Anne Harwood
Wm., 2/8/60, Richard Rawlings, Robert Armstrong, Anne Har-
wood
Salley, 11/22/61, Sampson Moseley, Rebecca Harwood, Mary
Pate

Richard and Anne Rawlings
Booker, 8/26/64, John Winfield, Robert Winfield, Mary Love

John and Lucretia Rawlings
Salley, 5/28/61, Isaac Rawlings, Rachael Prince, Olive Adams

Howell and Susanna Rawlings
Littleberry, 2/6/74, John and Eph. Hutchens, Susanna Rawlings
Miles, 2/3/75, Henry Rawlings, Charles Mabrey, Patty Mabrey

Isaac and Anne Rawlings
John, 1/26/69, Edward Whitehorn, Ambrose Grizzard, Elizabeth
Grizzard

John and Susanna Ray
Mary, 1/7/47, Richard Scoggin, Francis and Mary Crossland
Susanna, 10/25/49, John Moss, Eliz. Crossland, Sarah Porch
Eliz., 12/20/51, Edward Crossland, Mary Parsons, Margory
 Morrison
Anne, 9/21/53, Richard Scoggin, Susanna Hight, Anne Scoggin
Wm., 11/22/55, Wm. Ray, Jonas Crossland, Anne Porch
Salley, 11/20/58, John Wilkinson, Agnes Duncan, Mary Scoggin
Eliz., 2/5/61, John Crossland, Wilmouth Ray, Anne Lee
John, 2/5/63, Wm. Scoggin, Henry Porch Jr., Jane Scoggin
Frances, 11/7/65, Peter Jennings, Betty Cotton, Eliz. Wilkinson

William and Mary Ray
John, 1/9/50, John Ray, Edward Crossland, Eliz. Crossland
David, 5/13/53, Nathan Northington, Richard Scoggin, Sarah
 Moss
Sylvia, 6/12/56, Wm. Willie, Anne Ezell, Mary Meacum
Wm., 2/11/61, Jonas Crossland, Thos. Adkins, Susanna Ray
Amy, 5/1/63, Peter Jennings, Amy Tomlinson, Rebbecca Lee

Howell and Milly Ray
Molly, 2/2/72, Miles Duncan, Nancy Ray, Amy Duncan
Boyce, 7/23/74, Thos. Tomlinson, Agnes Duncan, Susanna
 Painter

REDDING
John and Sarah Redding
Mary, 1/15/53, Wm. Weathers, Mary Weathers, Amy Bailey

REED
Wm. and Martha Reed
Ann, 10/16/39, Wm. Reed Jr., Mary Eccles, Lucy Jackson

REIS
John and Mary Reis
Wm., 3/2/40, Patrick Smith, Christian Tatum, Eliz. Smith

RICHARDSON
Ben'g. and Mary Richardson
Martha, 8/14/39, John Richardson, Sarah Ezell, Eliz. Cooper
Eliz., 9/23/41, John Richardson, Eliz. Atkinson, Eliz. Grantham

Arthur and Mary Richardson
Thomas, 2/15/41, John Andrews Jr., Wm. Davidson, Prissilla
 Davidson
Rebbecca, 9/8/53, Arthur Smith, Hannah Atkinson, Eliz. Rich-
 ardson
Lucy, 12/23/44, John Alsobrook, Rebbecca Figures, Eliz. Bell
Fortune, 10/20/46, Richard Andrews, Sarah Carlisle, Katherine
 Velverton
Archer, 10/24/48, John Smith, Robert Carlisle, Eliz. Pepper

Arthur and Mary Richardson (Continued)

Zilpah, 12/10/52, Robert Pryor, Mary Walker, Olive Mangum
Mary, 9/30/53, Wm. Smith, Mary Burgess, Judieth Pepper
Sarah, 11/20/55, Wm. Ellis, Mary Wallace, Sarah Grizzard
Randolph, 12/22/59, Thos. Broadrib, Edward Wright, Rebbecca
   Wright

Wm. and Eliz. Richardson

Patty, 12/10/42, Chas. Delahay, Mary Randall, Amy Rainey
Eliz., 2/5/45, Wm. Richardson, Martha Richardson, Anne
   Rainey
Anna, 9/7/46, Edward Farington, Mary Rainey, Eliz. Farington
Wm., 4/28/48, Wm. Rainey, Thomas Wynne, Mary Cox
Mary, 1/13/50, Seymour Mahaney, Susanna Richardson, Mary
   Hutchens
Nathanial, 4/1/53, Peter Green, Wm. Knight, Sarah Wellborn
Salley, 12/20/55, Wm. Wellborn, Mildred Hill, B. Ruthford
   Randall

Wm. and Amy Richardson

Jordan, 1/15/50, John Richardson, Wm. Knight, Agnes Battle

Wm. and Martha Richardson

Patty, 11/2/41, John Farrington, Rebbecca Epps, Hannah Bell

William Richardson died 12/11/46, reported by Robert Farrington

Wm. and Laorel (Laura) Richardson

George, 6/24/52, John Rachael, Robert Bulloch, Martha Ezell

Joseph and Mary Richardson

Eliz., 2/13/61, none given
Wm., 10/17/65, Wm. Willie, John Curtis, Anne Curtis
Patty, 10/13/67, Wm. Winfield, Phoebe Rainey, Patty Wynne
Beckey, 5/22/72, Nath'l. Rainey, Francis Ingram, Rachael
   Sturdivant

Jordan and Sylvia Richardson

John Thorp, 8/24/72, John Cargil, Wm. Richardson, Amy
   Richardson

Jordan and Eliz. Richardson

Polly, 12/8/73, David Mason, Rebbecca Stewart, Lydia Battle

Arthur and Dolly Richardson

Wm., 12/20/70, Andrew Ramsey, Miles Birdsong, Salley Richardson
John, 3/15/73, Andrew Ramsey, Miles Birdsong, Salley Richardson

Thomas and Lucy Richardson

Salley, 7/10/69, Thos. Smith, Mary Capp, Selah Smith

RICHARDSON (Continued)
Thomas and Lucy Richardson (Continued)
Samuel, 8/20/66, Henry Underhill, Wm. Ellis, Lydia Smith
Susanna, 4/21/71, Anderson Ramsey, Suckey Andrews, Mary
White
Arthur, 9/1/73, Fred Andrews, Henry Ellis, Sarah Richardson
Rebbecca, 12/13/75, Wm. Velvin, Mary Velvin, Anne Carrell

RIX - RICKS
George and Frances Ricks
Christopher, 12/20/39, Chris. Tatum, Charles Lee, Bridget
Tatum
Timothy, 1/2/42, Peter Rives, Josh. Tatum, Bathia Tatum

RISBY
Thomas and Sarah Risby
Lucy, 9/25/57, Edward Shelton, Sarah Judkins, Tabitha Rolland

RIVERS
John and Martha Rivers
Hulda, 8/4/63, Abra. Winfield, Salley and Goodwynne Tucker
Harper, 5/17/65, John and Churchill Curtis, Patty Kelly

Wm. and Anna Rivers
Smith, 9/22/72, Peter Randall, John Washer, Anne Washer

John and Eliz. Rivers
Charles, born 7/28/69

RIVES
George and Frances Rives
Timothy, 1/21/42, Peter Rives, Josh. Tatum, Bathia Tatum
Frances, 4/2/45, Wm. Rives, Prissilla Rives, Ussle Leigh

John and Sarah Rives
Rebbecca, 3/7/49, Josh. Tatum, Charles Gee, Judieth Rives
John, 3/7/49, Thomas Mitchell, Eliz. Tatum, Amy Goodwynne

George and Sarah Rives
Martha, 2/22/67, Nich. Massenberg, Martha and Lucy Binns

John and Eliz. Rives
Winney, 1/4/47, Chris. Tatum, Frances Moore, Bathia Tatum

William and Frances Rives
Molly, 9/20/43, Peter Rives, Mary Rives, Frances Briggs
Frances, 12/27/45, Nath'l. Hood, Martha and Susanna Moore
Wm., 7/1/48, Thos. Atkinson, Wm. Weathers, Eliz. Atkinson

Peter and Eliz. Rives
Ruth, 9/14/45, Richard Rives, Dorothy Rives, Mary Marriable
Richard, 3/17/49, Richard and John Rives, Frances Rives
Mary, 1/25/55, Mathew Whitehead, Sarah Whitehead, Elenor
Rives

Peter and Eliz. Rives (Continued)

Selah, 2/9/58, Thos. Atkinson, Sarah Lee, Ruth Rives
Robert, 2/1/61, James Hern, Bruin Rives, Eliz. Hern

Wm. and Elenor Rives

Winney, 10/31/52, Wm. Green, Eliz. Cain, Mary Robertson
Frederick. 3/15/56, Nath'l. Whitehead, James Hern, Eliz.White-
head
Anne, 3/11/59, none given
Richard, 4/26/61, John Moss, Bruin Rives, Eliz. Hern
Eliz. Bridges, 5/29/63, Thomas Hern, Francis Rives, Susanna
Hern
Peter, 4/7/66, James Hern, Robert Whitehead, Jane Hern

Christopher Jr. and Eliz. Rives

Wm., 2/9/60, none given
Eliz., 2/25/61, John Mason, Eliz. Mason, Frances Rives
John, 5/26/65, none given
Nathanial, 5/23/63, none given
Frances, 7/12/72, none given
Christopher, 8/14/67, Wm. Dunn, Timothy Rives, Jane Mason
George, 7/12/72, David Mason, John Cargil, Winney Rives
Gabrial, 11/2/73, Eph. Moss, none others

George and Sarah Rives

Judieth, 10/29/65, Chris. Rives, Jacobina Willie, Rebbecca
Mason
Thos. Eldridge, 12/15/64, Wm. Willie, Timothy Rives, Eliz.
Willie
Martha, 2/2/67, Nich. Massenburg, Martha and Lucy Binns
George, 1/10/69, Wm. Eldridge, John Cargil, Martha Belches
Frances, 8/2/74, Timothy Rives, Martha Rives, Lucy Massen-
berg
Eldridge, 5/6/76, none given
Pamelia, 5/31/78, none given

Timothy and Martha Rives

Archibald, 6/9/75, John Cargil, Lewis Dunn Jr., Eliz. Massen-
burg
Chas. Binns, 2/14/74, John Jones, Wm. Willie, Eliz. Jones,
Mary Hay

William Rives Jr. and Anne

Beckey, 7/4/72, Thomas Hern, Elenor Richques, Sarah Hood

John and Amy Rives

Lucretia, 8/15/61, none given

Ben'g. and ------- Rives

Jesse, 1/2/62, none given

RIVES (Continued)
Timothy Rives Jr. and Eliz.
Betty Atkins, 3/21/69, John Adkins, Amy Adkins, Eliz. Chambliss
Judieth, 7/11/74, John Bonner, Selah Rives, Rebbecca Cotton

William Rives Jr. and Lucy
Charles, 8/25/66, Thos. Rosser, Chris. Rives, Isabel Bedingfield
Henry, 5/12/68, Isam Hawthorn, Mary Moss Jr., Eliz. Shands
Lavina, 2/21/70, John Lessenberry, Patty Peebles
Hartwell, 10/28/72, Timothy Rives, Chappell Gee, Winney Rives
Phoebe, 12/22/74, Ben'g. Bird, Susanna Epps, Jane Sykes

ROBERTS
Willett and Faith Roberts
Wm., 6/15/39, John Rachael, Jerimiah Ellis, Sarah Andrews
Sarah, 7/17/43, John Irby, Anne Ruffin, Mary Meacum
Mary. 3/8/41, Andrew Lester, Eliz. Ellis, Phoebe Johnson
Willett, 5/15/46, Nathanial Briggs, Thos. Bryan, Anne Gilliam

Willet (Willis) and Sarah Roberts
Susanna Bosseau, 4/29/72, John Jones, Rebbecca and Susanna Jones
Archibald, 1/15/75, Holmes Jones, Wm. Tomlinson, Katherine and Rebbecca Jones

ROBERTSON
Isacc Robertson
Isacc, 1/17/44, John Freeman, Jr., Charles Delahay, Rebbecca Gilliam
Mary, 8/7/52, Samuel Barlow, Elenor and Eliz. Cain
Eliz., 3/6/56, Samuel Wright, Martha Harper, Jeany Sykes

George and Mary Robertson
Rebbecca, 3/24/50, Edward Powell, Phoebe Parham, Mildred Parham

Nathanial and Winny Robertson
Sucky, 12/12/59, Arthur Delahay, Lucy and Betty Cain
Angelica, 5/9/62, Thos. Wade, Eliz. Woodland, Angelica Cain

RODGERS
William and Frances Rodgers
Martha, 5/26/51, Ben'g. Rodgers, Eliz. Land, Eliz. Smith
Joseph, 11/4/43, Joseph Rodgers, Jonathan Ellis, Selah Mangum
John, 1/12/49, Ben'g. Rodgers, Wm. Judkins, Mary Proctor

William and Catherine Rodgers
Frederick, 8/26/41, none given
William, 11/20/43, Ben'g. Ellis, Wm. Rodgers, Sarah Andrews
Levi, 1/11/45, Richard Proctor, John Berryman, Mary Judkins
Agnes, 5/16/48, Nich. Maggett, Lydia Proctor, Lucy Jordan
Sterling, 10/15/52, Robert Rodgers, Joshuah Proctor, Lydia Smith

RODGERS (Continued)

Joseph and Mary Rodgers
Faithey, 8/20/40, John Blow, Sarah Dowdning, Eliz. Vassor

------ and Eliz. Rodgers
Selah, 9/4/44, Wm. Rodgers, Francis Rodgers, Jane Bane

David and Janet Rodgers
Anne, 6/17/61, George Keer, Eliz. Briggs, Judieth Smith
John, 6/17/63, John Keer, Wm. Willie, Jacobina Willie

Nathan and Eliz. Rodgers
Randolph, 6/13/59, none given
Anne, 8/12/62, Wm. Hams, Lucy Hams, Mary Felts

Richard and Betty Rodgers
Burwell, 3/20/72, Wm. Rodgers, Jesse Jordan, Mary Rodgers

Thomas and Rebbecca Rodgers
Charlotte, 4/2/69, Jesse Turner, Mary Owen, Mary Hix

Jesse and Faith Rodgers
Langstron, 10/23/62, Wm. Rodgers, Peter Knight, Mary Rodgers
Richard, 8/6/68, Joseph Wrenn, John Ezell Jr., Prissilla Gilliam
John, 6/28/70, Rubin Rodgers, Jesse Jordan, Patty Roe

Rubin and Eliz. Rodgers
Lucy, 10/17/58, Emanuel James, Eliz. Rodgers
Thomas, 8/16/62, none given
Molly, 6/17/75, Joseph Rodgers, Mary and Eliz. Rodgers

ROE

Cannon and Sarah Roe
Eliz., 9/15/39, none given
Sarah, 9/10/44, John Jones, Susanna Burgess, Lucy Jones
William, 6/24/47, Robert Sandefour, Wm. Jones, Lucy Sill
(Ezell)
Amy (twin), 6/24/47, David Malone, Amy Jones, Frances Moss

Wm. and Patty Roe
Drury, 5/23/70, John Gilliam, John Land Jr., Eliz. Rodgers

ROLLAND

Joshuah and Eliz. Rolland
John, 12/29/40, Wm. Green, John Pitman, Eliz. Rolland
Sarah, 1/12/41, John Rolland, Eliz. Rolland, Tabitha Rolland
Rebbecca, 2/4/49, John Farington, Anne Felts, Mary Carlisle

Wm. and Eliz. Rolland
Lucy, 12/18/40, Wm. Judkins, Eliz. Bell, Anne Rose
Martha, 1/23/41, Thomas Weathers Jr., Mary Atkinson, Anne
Jordan
Jean, 3/14/44, Joseph Rolland, Sarah Moore, Eliz. Grantham

ROLLAND (Continued)

Wm. and Eliz. Rolland (Continued)

Wm., 5/26/48, Wm. Rose, Jesse Rolland, Agnes Seat
Jordan, 1/6/49, Edward Powell, Samuel Harwood, Mary Rolland
Mely, 11/13/52, Nath'l. Felts, Eliz. and Mary Rolland
Susanna, 8/23/46, John Farington, Edward Delaney, Eliz. Rolland

Joseph and Tabitha Rolland

John, 10/22/41, Josh. Rolland, Thos. Weathers, Eliz. Bell
Joseph, 2/11/61, John Rolland, Wm. Hill, Phoebe Rolland
Joseph, 11/22/43, Josh. Rolland, Wm. Rolland, Eliz. Rolland
Tabitha, 1/5/50, David Stokes, Mary Harwood, Anne Seat

Jesse and Martha Rolland

Jesse, 12/8/54, John Owen, Wm. Hill, Mary Rolland
Frederick, 7/5/53, Wm. Green, Nath'l. Felts, Eliz. Rolland

John and Mary Rolland

Webb, 9/27/46, Robert Webb, Wm. Rolland, Eliz. Rolland

Webb and Phoebe Rolland

Betsy, 11/26/65, John Owen, Tabitha Rolland, Frances Adams
John, 4/1/67, Boyce Owen, Wm. Spane, Sarah Stokes
Randolph, ?/?/?, Andrew Felts, Mary Owen, Wm. Rolland

Wm. and Mary Rolland

Lucy, 6/25/63, David Owen, Sarah Rolland, Anne Ezell
Fanny, 6/19/65, Young Stokes, Sarah Threewits, Lydia Owen
Sucky, 12/12/67, James Bell, Mildred Bell, Susanna Ezell
Joshuah, 10/21/70, Abel Mabrey, John Owen, Eliz. Rolland

John and Agnes Rolland

James, 12/12/66, Thos. Felts, Young Stokes, Sarah Woodland
Charlotte, 9/6/68, John Owen, Rebbecca Rowland, Susanna Felts
Nancy, 1/28/71, James Rodgers, Betty Owen, Eliz. Woodland
Herbert, 5/28/72, none given
John, 9/3/73, Isam Whitehead, John Atkinson, Eliz. Spane

Burwell and Sucky Rolland

Thomas, 2/21/74, Burwell Felts, Fred Freeman, Tabitha Rolland
Nathanial, 8/16/72, none given

ROSE
Richard and Martha Rose

Charles, 8/28/62, Bryan Fanning, Thos. Mumford, Eliz. Whitehead

William and Mary Rose

Richard, 3/8/57, Thomas Ezell, Michajah Petway, Eliz. Land
William, 2/2/59, Abel Mabrey, Wm. Harris, Susanna Mabrey
Mary, 7/30/54, Wm. Rolland, Mary Rose, Hannah Seat

ROSE (Continued)

William and Mary Rose (Continued)

Phoebe, 4/9/62, John Ezell Jr., Jesse Rodgers, Amy Threewit

Elijah, 3/19/65, Thomas Ezell, Jesse Rodgers, Amy Threewit

Fanny, twin, 3/19/65, Young Stokes, Sarah Threewits, Lydia
Owen

Frederick, 6/27/71, Edward Powell, Timothy Ezell, Sucky
Oliver

Fanny, 11/15/73, Robert Thompson, Amy Sledge, Molly Whitehead

Timothy Ezell, 7/21/74, Nathanial Felts, Nicholis Weathers,
Faith Weathers

Joseph and Hannah Rose

Ede., 3/19/63, Edmund Pate, Ede. Stacey, Patty Graves

ROSSER

John and Eliz. Rosser

James, 3/15/40, John Tatum, Richard Carter, Sarah Chappell

Sarah, 1/5/42, John Peebles, Anne Wren, Mary Moss

Mary, 3/17/43, Abraham Heeth, Mary Chappell, Eliz. Peebles

Thomas, 1/17/45, Edward Weaver, Thos. Chappell, Amelia
Chappell

ROTTENBERRY

John and Susan Rottenberry

Susanna, 3/19/37, Edward Eccles, Mary Ellis, Anne Ezell

Mary, 4/25/43, John Ellis, Mary Ellis, Katherine Threewits

RUFFIN

Edmund and Anne Ruffin

Mary, 12/24/39, none given

James, 7/23/41, Wm. Willie, John Irby, Eliz. Kinchen, Eliz.
Irby

Eliz., 9/22/42, Fred Bryan, Eliz. Kinchen, Eliz. Irby

Edmund, 1/2/44, Ben'g. Ruffin, Anne Brown, Rebbecca Morris

SAMMONS

John and Lucy Sammons

Jane, 3/4/59, none given

Robert, 2/3/64, Beng. Adams, Geo. Long, Mary Felts

James Sammons Jr. and Betty

Groves, 4/16/69, Geo. Long Jr., Edward Whitehall, Winney
Sammons

James and Anne Sammons

Timothy, 5/7/62, Wm. Seaborn, Wm. Kellum, Mary Pully

Ben'g., 12/15/56, Ben'g. Seaborn, John Sammons, Mary Rawlings

William and Rebecca Sammons

Beckey, 4/10/62, Chas. Long, Anne and Hannah Sammons

SANDEFOUR
Robert and Anne Sandafour
John, 3/18/33, none given
Sarah, 5/18/37, none given
Robert, 6/11/39, none given
A------, dgh., 12/11/41, Wm. Freeman, Susanna Freeman, Eliz. Denton
Eliz., 7/11/44, Peter Hawthorn, Sarah Hawthorn, Mary Stewart
Mary, 10/5/46, Wm. Stewart, Eliz. Willie, Rebbecca Barlow
Wm., 7/31/52, John Sandefour, Eliz. Wynne

John and Eliz. Sandefour
Lucretia, 9/26/55, Nath'l. Johnson, Lucy Whitehead, Anne Smith

SANDERS

Hulda Sanders born 1728, bab. 11/13/48, when 20 years old

William Sanders, born 1726, was bab. 11/13/74, when 48 years old

John and Mary Sanders
Mary, 11/3/56, John Ray, Eliz. Wilkerson, Agnes Duncan
Wm., 8/15/58, Robert Parsons, Wm. Parsons, Mary Tomlinson
Amy, 7/7/62, Burwell Tomlinson, Katherine Barker, Amy Parsons
Jeany, 12/22/65, Ben'g. Figg, Betty Tomlinson
Patty, 11/23/67, Fred Andrews, Lydia Andrews, Mely Duncan

Thos. and Anne Sanders
Hubbard, 9/3/66, Thos. Hunt, Robert Tucker, Dorothy Hunt
Betsy, 12/22/68, none given
Nancy, 4/9/71, none given
Thomas, 10/10/73, none given

John and Lucy Sanders
Mary, 4/20/72, John Avent, Mary Burras, Lucy Jarrett

SANSENICK
James and Margarett Sansenick
Lucretia, 9/22/40, Wm. Knight, Hannah Felts, Rebbecca Harris
James, 3/4/42, John Bulloch, Beng. Adams, Anne Bulloch
John, 2/17/44, John Ellis, Edmund Pate, Sarah Roberts
Wm., twin, 2/17/44, John Ellis, Edmund Pate, Anne Pate

SANTEE
Timothy and Martha Santee
Mary, 9/1/45, Jonathan Ellis, Eliz. Davis, Mary Judkins
Mary, 4/25/52, John Jeffreys, Prissilla Booth, Anne Jeffreys

SAWRY
William and Eliz. Sawry
Mary, 12/6/1739, Henry Sawry, Sarah Dowdning, Christian Hix

SAWRY (Continued)
Henry and Jean Sawry
Mildred, 8/22/38, John Brittle, Jean Bane, Anne Bane
Jean, 5/20/40, Danial Guthrie, Eliz. Brittle
Henry, 8/17/42, Simon Murphey, Thos. Grosse, Christian Hicks
Lucy, 1/17/44, Wm. Carrell, Anne Crosswit, Mary Hix
Edward, 10/25/46, James Bane, Wm. Hix, Eliz. Dowdning
Anne, 11/24/50, John Wallace, Eliz. and Mary Sawry

SAYERS
Francis and Eliz. Sayers
Asa, 10/4/50, Wm. Longbottom, James Carter, Ava Curry

SCOGGIN
Richard and Anne Scoggin
Sucky, 11/4/34, Henry Porch, Eliz. Crossland, Elenor Smith

Richard and Betty Scoggin
Jonas, 12/16/59, Jonas Scoggin, Jones Crossland, Roland Lucas
Willis, 5/24/61, Joseph Warwick, John Pate, Eliz. Ivey

Richard Scoggin Jr. and Jane
Rebbecca, 12/27/56, Richard Scoggin, Mary Scoggin, Amy Ivy
Eph., 3/26/59, Jones Crossland, Wm. Scoggin, Sarah Jennings
John, 6/29/61, none given
Eliz., 12/29/63, John Ray, Katherine McInnish, Susanna Scoggin
Albrighton Jones, 11/11/72, Nich. Weathers, John Underhill,
    Rebbecca Hogan

SEABORN
Ben'g. and Martha Seaborn
Phoebe, 8/12/58, none given
Chris, 5/8/60, Thomas Moore Jr., Anslem Gilliam, Lucy Dowdy
Martha, 3/13/62, none given
Josias, 8/5/64, John Ezell Jr., Geo. Long, Sucky Seat
Frances, 9/29/66, Wm. Seaborn, Frances Rand, Anna Shands
Howell, 6/2/69, Ben'g. Adams, Philip Harwood, Mary Mason.
Ben'g., 5/13/72, Danial Harwood, Isacc Rawlings, Anne Battle
Wm., 11/23/74, Wm. Seaborn, John Pate, Anna McLamore

Wm. and Frances Seaborn
Frederick, 8/28/66, Ben'g. Seaborn, Thos. Dowdy, Mason Bird
Betsy, 3/13/71, Philip Harwood, Rebbecca Avent.
Franky Bird, 7/20/74, Thomas Pate

SEAT
Robert and Mary Seat
Rebbecca, 12/14/39, Wm. Bell, Eliz. Rolland, Eliz. Bell·
Sarah, 8/24/42, Wm. Grantham, Katherine Grantham, Katherine
    Judkins

Robert and Anne Seat
Winney, 8/20/44, John Felts Jr., Mary and Kesiah Bulloch

SEAT (Continued)

Robert and Anne Seat (Continued)

Sucky, 11/9/47, Nath'l. Felts, John Bulloch, Jean Felts
Phoebe, 2/6/45, Nathanial Felts, Winefred Felts, Sarah Roberts
Robert, 8/11/49, Thomas Felts, John Bulloch, Jean Felts
Hartwell, 3/6/50, Lewis Adkins, Nath'l. Felts, Jane Seat
Nathanial, 12/8/55, John Sammons, Wm. Richardson, Anne
  Felts
Betty, 5/26/57, Thomas Felts Jr., Mary and Kesiah Bulloch
Lydia, 5/5/59, Wm. Hill, Rebbecca Seat, Agnes Felts

SEAWARD

Samuel and Sarah Seaward

Tabitha, 11/22/63, Wm. Rives, Susanna Exum (Epps)?, Mary
  Seaward
Polly Dixon, 5/2/74, Robert Hancock, Patty Epps, Martha Epps

SHACKLEFORD

Bannister and Lucy Shackleford

Lucy, 1/28/71, John Walker, Sarah Harewell, Mary Walker

SHANDS

Wm. Shands Jr. and Prissilla

Lucy, 1/8/39, Thomas Moore, Mary Moore, Phoebe Shands
Mary, 9/17/41, Christopher Golightly, Eliz. Moss, Eliz. Petway
Phoebe, 1/23/42, James Mason, Mary Moss, Eliz. Shands
Amy, 9/8/47, Chris. Golightly, Amy Dunn, Frances Golightly
Thomas, 8/26/52, Thomas Young, Thos. Shands, Sarah Tatum
Wm., 9/5/57, Edward Petway, Nath'l. Northington, Eliz. Petway
Wm., 10/22/55, John Shands, Thos. Rosser

Wm. and Mary Shands

John, 2/23/49, John Shands, Edward Shelton, Eliz. Shands

John and Eliz. Shands

Frances, 4/20/39, John Avent, Anne Warden, Mary Warden
John, 9/27/41, Wm. Shands, Wm. Shands Jr., Nazareth Shands
Mary, 6/8/49, Wm. Stewart, Mary Stewart, Phylis Simmons

John and Phoebe Shands

Viensa, 1/4/66, Aug. Shands, Prissilla and Eliz. Shands
Littleton, 5/29/67, Wm. Chamberless, Wm. Golightly, Aug.
  Shands

Aug. and Amy Shands

John, 11/5/70, John Adkins, Wm. Golightly, Mary Adkins
Thomas, 1/9/73, Wm. Shands, Thos. Peebles, Prissilla Shands
Prissilla, 12/26/74, Thomas Moss, Sarah Moss, Mary Underhill

SHELL

Lemon and Ruth Shell

Wm., 12/28/68, John Harrisson, Giles Underhill, Susanna
  Harrisson

SHELTON
Edward and Elizabeth Shelton
Sylvanus, 3/3/50, James Carter, Joseph Roberts, Sarah Roberts
Sterling, 1/18/53, John Moss, Henry Holt, Lucy Dunn
Salley, 8/9/54, Samuel Harwood, Mary Rawlings, Mary Land
Sucky, 6/5/56, James Bell, Mary Bell, Agnes Adams
Cyrill, 2/25/58, Robert Seat, Wm. Hutchens, Salley Risby

SIMMS
Millington and Joyce Simms
Howell, 12/22/65, Henry Jarrett, Thos. Adkins, Sarah Jones

-------- and -------- Simms
--------, 6/23/71, Thomas Vaughn, Mary Harewell

SINGLETON
Titus and Mary Singleton
Eliz., 6/2/51, Thomas Chappell, Eliz. Partridge, Anne Chappell

SLATE
Robert and Sarah Slate
John, 6/11/69, Arthur Delahay, John Hill, Anne Hill

Edward and Sarah Slate
Molly, 12/1/62, Abner Sturdivant, Nanny Jones, Amy Cocks

Wm. and Eliz. Slate
Martha, 3/10/63, James Turner, Sarah Wallace, Joyce Slate

SLEDGE
Chas. and Eliz. Sledge
John, 1/1/47, John Sledge, Martha Peebles, Sarah Sledge
Thos., 5/18/51, Thos. Peebles, Jas. Tomlinson, Mary Sledge
Susanna, 12/14/53, Wm. Peebles, Sarah Peebles, Eliz. Tomlinson
Austin, 5/15/56, Wm. Sanders, John Sledge, Anne Harrisson
Charles, 9/25/58, Wm. Evans, Henry Peebles, Susanna Weaver
Noah, 5/22/67, Ben'g. Hill, Sarah Hill
Salley, 8/10/70, James Adams, Mary Peebles, Eliz. Tomlinson

Amos and Sarah Sledge
Martha, 4/7/61, none given
Robert, 1/27/59, none given

John Sledge Jr. and Salley
Sterling, 10/4/66, John Hill, Curtis Lynn (Land?), Eliz. Lynn
Winney, 9/4/70, Levi Mason, Mildred Ivy, Lydia Hutchens
John, 1/26/72, Lewis Turner, James Adkins, Susanna Sledge
Danial, 7/31/74, Thomas Pate, Curtis Land, Susanna Sledge

John and Amy Sledge
Nathanial, 2/22/61, Amos North, Wm. Chambers, Anne Griffith
Hartwell, 1/8/65, John Ray, John Underhill, Wilmouth Porch

SLEDGE (Continued)

John and Amy Sledge (Continued)
Minns, 1/7/68, Thos. Adkins, Amos Sledge, Eliz. Wilkerson
Lucy, 2/26/70, Thos. Whitefield, Lucy Blaton, Jane Whitehead
Rebbecca, 4/16/75, Wm. Rives, Nancy and Eliz. Moss

SMITH

John and Mary Smith
John, 9/15/35, James Price, John Nuns, Nancy Price

John and Frances Smith
Rebbecca, 1/6/44, Henry Moss, Sarah Heath, Sarah Tatum

John and Agnes Smith
Joshuah, 12/22/67, none given

Arthur and Lydia Smith
Lucy, 10/20/41, Wm. Carrell, Hannah Carrell, Eliz. Smith
Lawrence, 8/24/44, Wm. Brown, Robert Carrell, Anne Crosswit
Frederick, 3/18/46, Robert Nicholson, John Smith, Sarah Brown
Arthur, 4/18/49, Richard Andrews, Wm. Owen, Mary Andrews
John, 12/2/51, Wm. Smith, John Andrews, Eliz. Birdsong
Ben'g., 8/18/56, Benjiman Smith, Harry Faison, Hannah Owen
Michael, 5/18/54, Thos. Broadrib, Andrew Lester, Eliz. Broadrib
Mely, 7/15/59, none given

Peter and Elenor Smith
Joshua, 3/1/39, Cannon Roe, Wm. Jones, Sarah Roe
Prissilla, 6/27/50, Peter Doby, Sarah Magget

Jones and Eliz. Smith
Isaac, 6/17/56, Isaac Collier, David Owen, Susanna Banks

Josiah and Eliz. Smith
Sarah, 11/14/60, Thos. Kirkland, Anne Wilkerson, Rebbecca Parker
Charles, 9/20/62, Charles Collier, Thomas Butler, Susanna Collier

Josiah and Rebbecca Smith
Wm., 6/23/67, Ben'g. Smith, Arthur Smith Jr., Judieth Smith

Joseph and Hannah Smith
Thomas, 3/6/63, Sarah Rose, Nathan Rodgers, Prissilla Jones

Ben'g. and Judieth Smith
Lucy, 11/19/58, none given
Eliz., 11/61/60, Wm. Ellis, Eliz. Ellis, Mary Stacey

Edward and Judieth Smith
Frances, 6/2/56, Daniel Epps, Eliz. Lee, Mary Cotton

Littleberry and Amy Smith
Anna, 3/23/62, Aaron Smith, Mary Powell, Judieth Green

SMITH (Continued)
Joseph and Rebbecca Smith
Anne, 9/5/62, Steven Pepper, Sarah Smith, Sarah Wallace
Cherry, 3/11/69, Arthur Smith, Eliz. Turner, Martha Massen-
gale
Mary, 2/22/73, Jones Glover, Mary Glover, Parmelia Field
Eliz., 7/5/75, none given

Lawrence and Mary Smith
Peggy, 11/28/67, Ben'g. Hill, Lucy Gilbert, Salley Andrews
Robert, 2/22/70, John Irby, Henry Cook, Eliz. Hill, Amy Cook

Josiah and Agnes Smith
Dolly, 2/14/70, Jacob Warwick, Lucy Dunn
Patty, 10/2/71, Wm. Smith, Sarah Smith

John and Rebbecca Smith
Mary, 2/2/73, Jones Glover, Mary Glover, Parmelia Field
Eliz., 7/5/75, none given

Isam and Patience Smith
Williamson, 8/3/63, Ben'g. Lanier, Burwell Banks, Eliz. Smith
Prissilla, 6/28/66, Wm. Parham, Frances Parham, Lucy Ma-
haney
Sarah, 1/29/68, Thomas Hunt, Eliz. Gibbons, Mary Bonner
Lucy, 2/9/72, Wm. Loyd, Martha Powell, Rebbecca Robertson

William and Mary Smith
John, 1/13/69, James Turner Jr., Joseph Stacey, Sarah Kennybrough
Eliz., 4/22/70, Averis Wilkerson, Mary Butler, Rebbecca Carrell

William and Salley Smith
Natty, 3/26/69, Lewis Hern, Jacob Warwick, Aggy Smith
Becky, 11/12/72, Thomas Tate, John Jones, Mary Grizzard
John, 11/28/74, Josh. Smith, Agnes Smith, Jean Bane

SOLOMAN
Lewis Solloman Jr. and Betty
John, 9/20/40, Lewis Soloman Sr., Richard Hay, Martha Solo-
man
Mary, 9/6/52, Peter Soloman, Mary Crossland, Ruth Soloman
James, ?/?/?, Wm. Soloman, Richard Barlow

William and Ruth Soloman
Judieth, 10/2/37, none given
Wm., 12/22/38, none given
Ussle, 7/30/40, none given
Isam, 7/6/41, Lewis Soloman Jr., Richard Hay, Martha Soloman
Sucky, 2/22/50, John Dennis, Mary Prince, Ester Hay

SOUTHALL
Holmes and Eliz. Southall
Farneau, 8/29/61, Robert Glover, Henry Ivy, Mary Dansey

SOUTHWORTH
-------- and Mary Southworth
Charles, 2/22/65, Wm. Lofting Jr., Lewis Dunn, Mary Gilliam

SOWERSBERRY - SOWSBY
Beng. and Eliz. Sowsberry
Selah, 2/8/45, Lemuel Zill (Ezell)?, Martha Pare, Anne King
Allen, 11/10/51, John Pennington, Jesse Gilliam
Ben'g., 10/28/54, Wm. Rodgers, Lewis Tyus, Mary Rodgers
Henry, 12/18/62, Jesse Rodgers, Howell Cooper, Fortune
   Gilliam
Hartwell, 2/29/61, Isam Ezell, David Ederlista, Eliz. Ezell

SPANE
William and Judieth Spane
Wm., 10/8/40, Nicholis Kellerman, Wm. Winfield, Thany
   Whitehead
Obedience, 3/14/43, Wm. Jones, Eliz. Hern, Sarah Woodlief
John, 12/20/53, John and William Owen, Sarah Wellborn
James, 9/18/62, Wm. and Littleberry Spane
J------, Robert Whitehead, John King, Lucy Evans

James and Mary Spane
Absolum, 2/17/49, Peter Rives, Mathew Whitehead, Jane Hern
Eliz., 4/9/53, James Hern, Eliz. Whitehead, Mary Rolland

Drury and Mildred Spane
Epps, 7/15/58, Ed. Whittington, Edward Powell, Eliz. Vines
Thomas, 7/12/60, Ben'g. Owen, Edward Slate, Agnes Oliver
Augustine, 4/30/53, John Owen, Jesse Rolland, Mary Spane

John and Judieth Spane
Littleberry, 3/23/43, none given
Miles, 4/17/51, Thos. Spane, Jesse Rolland, Lucy Bailey
Eliz., ?/?/?., Burwell Green, Susanna Green, Thany Spane

James and Thany Spane
Sucky, 4/22/58, Thos. Whitehead, Eliz. Rodgers, Mary Rawlings

Thos. and Sarah Spane
Charles, 3/21/69, Wm. and Jesse Rodgers, Mary Mannery

John and Sarah Spane
Clairbourne, 4/14/63, John Owen, Edward Davis, Susanna Davis
Hezekiah, 12/26/70, Anderson Sturdivant, Abra. Bolton, Eliz.
   Porch
Nancy, 7/7/73, Wm. Cocke, Sucky Oliver, Betty Hill

SPANE (Continued)
William and Mary Spane
John, 1/29/69, Anderson and Jesse Sturdivant, Biddy Spane
Eliz., 3/12/71, James Spane, Betty Spane, Winefred Adkins
Hartwell, 9/8/73, Robert and John Wynne, Milly Wynne
Danial, 4/26/75, Sampson Mosley, Richard Woodruff, Vina Pare

Absolum and Margaret Spane
Margarett, 12/22/71, Gabrial Barr, Anne Barr, Eliz. Spane
Wm. Thomas, 4/26/70, Jesse Rodgers, James Cook, Thany
    Spane
Beckey, 2/17/74, Timothy Ezell, Salley Reis, Phoebe Harrisson

SPEED
James and Helen Speed
John, 12/2/70, John Speed, Wm. Stewart, Susanna Hunt
Henry, 10/24/73, Henry Jarrett, Fred Hines, Hannah Howell

SPIERS
John and Sarah Spiers
Henry, 6/12/75, Wm. Willie, Richard Woodruff, Mary Woodruff

STACEY
Simon and Catherine Stacey
Mary, 9/9/45, Jonathan Ellis, Eliz. Davis, Mary Judkins
Joseph, 4/27/48, John Stacey, Joseph Stacey, Eliz. Wright
Martha, 9/24/51, Wm. Ellis, Mary Pleasant, Sarah Simms
Simon, 12/8/54, John Gibbons, Ben'g. Smith, Lydia Proctor
Edmund, 11/23/66, Edward Wright, Simon Stacey Jr., Martha
    Stacey

Simon Stacey Jr. and Sarah
Katherine, 11/4/68, Fred Andrews, Lydia Andrews, Martha
    Stacey
Ben'g., 4/2/70, Steven Andrews, Wm. Lamb, Mary Andrews
Wm. Andrews, 8/2/72, Richard Andrews, Lawrence Stacey,
    Susanna Andrews

Simon and Eliz. Stacey
Jenny, 7/22/60, Edward Wright, Rebbecca Wright, Sarah An-
    drews
Steven, 7/31/61, Joseph Stacey, Steven Pepper, Rebbecca Pepper

Simon and Mary Stacey
Katherine, 10/4/69, Franklin Clark, Janet and Eliz. Rodgers

Simon Stacey and Eliz. Morris
Magalone, 3/15/68, Wm. Warburton, Alice Warburton, Lucy
    Myers

Joseph and Faith Stacey
Kinchen, 1/18/63, Simon Stacey, Mary and Martha Stacey
Eliz., ?/?/56, none given

134

STACEY (Continued)
John and Anne Stacey
Robert, 5/25/57, Simon Stacey, Edward Wright, Sarah James
John, 2/5/62, none given
Sarah, 1/3/59, Joseph Stacey, Mary Stacey, Faith Bradley

Simon and Mary Stacey
Hannah, 10/4/69, Edward Wooten, Lucy Gilbert, Jean Bane
Katherine, twin, Franklin Clark, Janert and Eliz. Rodgers
Bengaman, 4/2/70, Steven Andrews, Wm. Lamb, Mary Andrews
Wm. Andrews, 8/2/72, Richard Andrews, Lawrence Stacey,
   Susanna Andrews
Nicholis, 3/28/74, Lawrence Stacey, John Freeman, Hulda
   Wooten

STAFFORD
Cudworth and Martha Stafford
James, 6/23/50, Thos. Stafford, Chris. Tatum, Agnes Moss
Jordan, 9/26/54, Giles Underhill, John Crossland, Mary Under-
   hill
Joshuah, 10/3/57, John Ray, Clement Hancock Jr., Mary Han-
   cock
David, 1/19/60, none given
Molly, 8/9/62, John Tatum, Susanna Moss, Eliz. Cotton
Mary, 6/11/68, John Underhill, Sarah Underhill, Lucy Blaton
Sterling, 9/18/70, Nathanial Northington, John Cock, Anna -----

STEAGAL
John and Winefred Steagal
John, 12/12/39, none given
Agnes, 2/3/40, none given
Anne, 2/3/40, none given

STEVENS
John and Anne Stevens
John, 2/16/33, none given
Mary, 10/13/37, none given
Thomas, 7/25/39, John Gilliam, Richard Barker, Anne Gilliam
Eliz., 10/13/43, none given

Thomas and Anne Stevens
John Washington, 2/7/64, Robert Newsom, Wm. Cock, Hannah
   Cock

STEWART
John and Lucretia Stewart
Wm., 5/3/75, Wm. Stewart, Thos. Ogburn, Selah Stewart

Wm. and Mary Stewart
James, 11/3/43, Wm. Shands, Wm. Shands, Jr., Eliz. Shands
Thomas, 6/18/52, Mathew Wynne, James Williams, Mary
   Marriable
Charles, 1/18/57, Isacc Mason, Wm. Willie, Anne McGee

STEWART (Continued)
Wm. and Mary Stewart (Continued)
Eliz., 3/7/62, Wm. Weathers, Anne Stewart, Frances Stewart
Charlotte, 9/29/63, Henry Mitchell, Sally Ogburn, Amy Shands

STOKES
Sylvanus and Cecelia Stokes
Eliz., 8/20/40, Joseph Rolland, Tabitha Morris, Eliz. Rolland
Lucy, 5/13/42, Marcus Stokes, Eliz. Shelton, Hannah Bell
Lydia, 1/27/47, John Bell, Martha Johnson, Mary Bell

Sylvanus Stokes died February 6, 1747-8.

James and Anne Stokes
James, 2/10/43, Wm. Ezell, Wm. Rolland, Cecelia Stokes

Jones and Anne Stokes
Sylvanus, 2/18/37, Wm. Knight, Vaughn Wellborn, Rebbecca
Harwood
James, 2/10/43, Wm. Ezell, Wm. Rolland, Cecelia Stokes

John and Sarah Stokes
John, 8/20/43, Frances Hutchens, Samuel Stokes, John Hutchens
Phoebe, 11/17/45, Wm. Ezell, Eliz. Rolland, Eliz. Bell
Rebbecca, 3/27/52, James Carter, Eliz. and Agnes Carter
Tabitha, 8/25/55, Ben'g. Richardson, Agnes and Hannah Mannery
Nath'l., 3/23/59, none given
Sarah, 11/9/61, Nath'l. Holt, Mary Ezell, Eliz. Stokes
Mourning, 11/14/64, James Williams Jr., Eliz. Ezell, Mary
Stokes

The above John Stokes died during the year of 1764

Young and Sarah Stokes
Zadock, 7/14/69, Nath'l. Felts, David Owen, Sarah Threewits

Samuel and Mary Stokes
Rebbecca, 10/14/59, none given
Samuel, 3/3/62, Ben'g. Adams, Wm. Hill, Mary Crossland

Thomas and Anne Stokes
Richard, 4/17/71, Wm. Stewart Jr., Jesse Sturdivant, Lucy
Gilliam
Anne, 3/13/73, Moses Knight, Susanna Newsom, Frances Wood-
ruff
Polly, 6/19/75, Wm. Hardy, Frances Sturdivant, Anna Williams

STURDIVANT
William and Frances Sturdivant
Margarett, 2/25/57, John Sturdivant, Prissilla Wynne, Lucretia
Parham
Hannah, 6/22/59, Thos. Wrenn, Lucretia and Martha Parham
Robert, 3/16/51, John Wellborn Jr., Charles Sturdivant, Anne
Sturdivant

STURDIVANT (Continued)

William and Frances Sturdivant (Continued)

William, 12/28/63, Wm. Wynne, Robert Parham, Lucretia
    Sturdivant
James, 5/14/67, Hollum Sturdivant, Jr., John Eccles, Mary
    Wynne
Frances, 9/8/69, Thos. Parham, Sarah and Anne Wynne
Mary, 11/28/65, John Wynne, Agnes Wynne, Eliz. Sturdivant
Eliz., 3/20/71, James Cock, Amy Cocke, Anne Hood
Prissilla, 9/10/73, Charles Sturdivant, Lucretia Wynne, Anna
    Sturdivant
Peter, 4/13/75, Charles Sturdivant, Lucretia Wynne, Anne
    Sturdivant

Charles and Anne Sturdivant

Charles Williams, 12/20/61, John Sturdivant, Wm. Wynne, Anne
    Sturdivant
Robert, 8/10/63, Mathew and Thos. Sturdivant, Tabitha Sturdi-
    vant
Mathew, 4/22/66, Steth Wynne, Robert Parham, Patty Wynne
Lucy, 8/14/68, Isacc Bendall, Sarah Bendall, Sarah Wynne
Danial, 2/13/71, Thos. Parham, John Wynne Jr., Eliz. Wynne
Anthony, 6/8/73, Henry and Seth Moss, Eliz. Marriable

Abner and Rachael Sturdivant

Charles, 1/18/62, Edward Slate, John Sturdivant

John and Martha Sturdivant

Betsy, 9/13/69, Wm. Wynne, Sarah Wilborn, Susanna Sturdivant
John, 3/6/72, Fred Freeman, Wm. Wynne, Frances Sturdivant
Hamlin, 11/11/73, Wm. Sturdivant, Steth Wynne, Anne Wynne
Lewis, 5/23/75, Thos. Sturdivant, Thos. Adkins, Lucretia Stur-
    divant
Wm., 12/12/76, Robert Wynne, Wm. Sturdivant, Milly Wynne

Anderson and Jemimma Sturdivant

Joel, 1/13/73, Fred Owen, Thos. Horn, Eliz. Hill
Nancy, 8/12/75, Joel Threewits, Sarah Sturdivant, Amy Three-
    wits

Mathew and Rachael Sturdivant

Ede., 9/26/70, Richard Massenberg, Mary Moore, Selah Hight

John and Rachael Sturdivant

Sarah, 5/16/41, Bengerman Wheeles (Wheeler), Eliz. Pare,
    Eliz. Hatley
John, 4/3/43, John Housman, Thos. Weathers Jr., Eliz.
    Wheeless
Jesse, 2/24/44, Wm. Parham, Wm. Weathers, Anne Threadgale
Anderson, 3/11/46, John Tatum, Susanna Weathers

Henry and Margarett Sturdivant

Thomas, 3/4/40, John Spane, Robert Rives Jones, Lucretia
    Stokes

STURDIVANT (Continued)
   Henry and Margarett Sturdivant (Continued)
Anne, 11/13/44, Hollum Sturdivant, Amy Booth, Eliz. ------?

   Hollum Sturdivant Jr.(56) and Mary
John, 4/30/48, Peter Threewits, Martha Sturdivant, Eliz. Sturdivant
Susanna, 11/2/50, Thos. Bobbett, Eliz. Rotenberry, Judieth Cook
Wm., 1/8/53, Robert Newsom, Richard Rives Jr., Sarah Rotenberry
Lucretia, 5/3/56, John Wellborn, Martha Sturdivant, Frances Sturdivant
Hollum, 1/4/63, Robert Wynne, Wm. Winfield, Phoebe Wynne
Frances, 2/7/67, John Wynne Jr., Mary Wynne, Anne Wynne

   Eliz. Sturdivant
John Threewits, 12/14/49

   Mathew and Sarah Sturdivant
Oliver, 1/26/40, Thomas Oliver, Thos. Taddoch, Agnes Oliver
Christobel, 2/1/42, Wm. Oliver, Rachael Sturdivant, Eliz.Ezell
Susanna, 5/14/46, Wm. Partan, Johanna Partan, Eliz. Oliver

   Mathew and Tabitha Sturdivant
Edward, 2/8/50, Wm. Sturdivant, Edward Threewits, Eliz.Wynne

   Nathanial and Tabitha Sturdivant
Henry, 4/3/49, Wm. Stewart, James Mason, Mary Stewart

   James and Mary Sturdivant
John, 3/3/63, Hollum Sturdivant Jr., John Winfield, Mary Sturdivant
Jemima, 3/21/65, Robert Winfield, Frances Winfield, Anne Hill

   John and Eliz. Sturdivant
Henry, 4/11/53, Wm. Wynne, John Sturdivant, Eliz. Longbottom
Wm., 10/4/48, Wm. Weathers, Warwick Gilliam, Agnes Malone
John, 8/22/57, Wm. Sturdivant, Bryan Fanning, Frances Threewits
Thomas, 11/7/66, Peter Winfield, Robert Parham, Anne Sturdivant
Joel, 11/1/67, Robert Wynne, Fred Freeman, Lucy Wynne

   Thomas and Anne Sturdivant
Ben'g., 12/8/69, Abra. Winfield, Burwell Weelborn, Anne Freeman
Henry, 12/24/67, Steth Wynne, John Sturdivant, Mary Epps
Anne, 1/22/72, Robert Wynne, Mary Parham, Rachael Sturdivant
Rebbecca, 5/25/75, Charles Sturdivant, Martha Sturdivant, Anne Wynne

STURDIVANT (Continued)
William and Mary Sturdivant
Hartwell, 9/8/73, Robert and John Wynne, Milly Wynne

SULLIVAN
Samuel and Hannah Sullivan
Hartley, 2/20/73, Wm. Lamb, Peter Johnson, Rebbecca Jones

A TRANSCRIPT OF AN ORIGINAL REGISTER PAGE

TEMPERENCE
Thomas and Hannah Peters
Temperence, 12/20/61, James Miller, Betty Hunt

J. Gray Edmunds and Eliz.
Tempe., 11/12/65, Fred Hines, Frances Briggs, Prissilla
Edmunds

Jesse and Mary Williamson
Temperence, 7/30/67, Ben'g. Lewis, Mary Rachael, Betty
Clancy

David and Lydia Pennington
Tempe., 3/27/69, Isam Gilliam, Patty Clanton, Peggy Newsom

John and Mary Gilliam
Tempe., 4/14/71, Wm. Andrews, Anne and Eliz. Andrews

Charles and Mary Kight (Knight)
Temperence, 10/6/73, Joel Bulloch, Mary Bulloch, Anne Capel

TABITHA
John and Eliza Mitchell
Tabitha, 10/11/38, none given

Joseph and Tabitha Rolland
Tabitha, 1/5/50, David Stokes, Mary Harwood, Anne Seat

Thomas and Anne Mitchell
Tabitha, 10/31/51, Wm. Dunn, Sarah and Judieth Rives

John and Sarah Stokes
Tabitha, 8/25/56, Ben'g. Richardson, Agnes and Hannah Mannery

John and Mildred Hill
Tabitha, 10/17/56, Wm. Wellborn, Mary Rolland, Eliz. Curtis

David and Lydia Pennington
Tabitha, 10/8/58, none given

Henry and Prissilla Mitchell
Tabitha, 1/22/67, Wm. Dunn, Eliz. Weeks, Angelica Mabrey

TABITHA (Continued)
John and Judieth Crouch
Tabitha, 4/16/68, none given

TACKETT
Ben'g. and Lydia Tackett
Barthowlemew, 5/8/70, none given

TATUM
Christopher and Eliz. Tatum
Agnes, 4/1/40, Chaney Tatum, Francis Rives, Rebbecca Roberts
Chris., 6/10/43, Henry and Joshuah Tatum, Bathia Tatum

John and Eliz. Tatum
Mary, 8/28/41, James Price, Eliz. Weaver, Eliz. Lee

Peter and Sarah Tatum
Edward, 7/16/41, John Tatum, Robert Hix, Bathia Tatum
Sarah, 10/9/44, Chris. Tatum Jr., Mary Moss, Rebbecca Heeth
Winney, 12/9/49, Josh. and Boyce Tatum, Mary Tatum

Thomas and Eliz. Tatum
Mary Williams, 9/22/69, Wm. Heeth Jr., Anne Mitchell, Eliz.
   Andrews
Peter, 10/27/73, Edward Smith, Eph. Onie, Mary Painter

TEMPLE
Henry and Eliz. Temple
Henry, 4/24/58, none given
Lucretia, 7/6/61, Henry Mitchell, Prissilla and Eliz. Mitchell
Jesse, 11/13/63, none given
Martha, 8/28/64, Henry Mitchell, Prissilla and Eliz. Mitchell

THREADGALE
John and Anne Threadgale
Mary, 9/24/43, none given
Eliz., 8/25/46, Thomas Morris, Lucy Dunn
Wm., 2/6/48, Wm. Cathcart, Isacc Edwards, Anne Edwards
John, 1/17/50, Nicholis Partridge, John Andrews, Eliz. Pepper

THREEWITS - THWAITES
Peter and Amy Threewits
Sarah, 2/4/46, Eliz. Threewits, Mary Crossland, Hollum Stur-
   divant
John, 5/9/49, Thomas Bobbett, Thos. Nunn, Eliz. Winn
Joel, 12/2/51, Wm. Sturdivant, John Cocke, Judieth Cocke
Frances, 11/14/58, none given
Frederick, 2/24/61, Soloman Graves, Wm. Rolland Jr., Sarah
   Threewits

Thomas and Jane Threewits
Rebbecca, 2/10/59, Nath'l. Parham, Frances Parham, Mary
   Threewits.

THOMPSON

Wm. and Hannah Thompson

John, 6/24/44, John Bell Jr., Samuel Northington, Sarah Judkins
Wm., 8/10/47, Wm. Thompson, Henry Gee, Mary Bell
Susanna, 11/16/49, Baalam Bell, Lucy Dunn, Eliz. Bell

William and Jensey Thompson

Nancy, 2/7/74, Robert Thompson, Amy Sledge, Molly Whitehead

THROWER

Thomas and Phoebe Thrower

John, 1/10/45, Soloman Wynne, Thos. Moore, Mary Moore

TOMLINSON

John and Mary Tomlinson

Eliz., 11/25/39, Jehu Barker, Eliz. Danial, Rebbecca Heeth

Richard and Mary Tomlinson

Thomas, 8/21/47, Thomas Adkins Jr., Mathew Tomlinson,
Susan Moore
Richard, 1/12/48, Thos. Hobbs, John Adkins Jr., Eliz. Adkins

Thomas and Mary Tomlinson

Wm., 8/17/49, Wm. Tomlinson, Charles Barker
John, 12/28/54, Ben'g. Tomlinson, Robert Jordan, Eliz. Jordan
Robert, 2/9/57, Robert Judkins, John Gibbons, Eliz. Bane
Eliz., 3/15/60, Robert Carlisle, Rebbecca Hyde, Mary Stacey

Thomas and Sarah Tomlinson

Herbert, 4/21/57, David Jackson, James Fawn, Katherine Mc-
Innish
Edward, 3/27/60, John and Jesse Moss, Anne Epps
Thomas, 11/15/62, Burwell Banks, Geo. Ezell, Eliz. Willie
James Epps, 2/4/69, David and Wm. Darden, Mary Darden
Archibald, 1/12/72, Wm. Wyche, James Epps, Mary Watson

Ben'g. and Jane Tomlinson

Harris, 10/12/52, Joseph Carter, Henry Bonner, Phoebe Bonner

William and Mary Tomlinson

Wm., 1/14/58, Henry Weaver, Nath'l. Dunn, Susanna Weaver
Molly, 12/15/66, Joseph Denton, Mary Mason, Rebbecca Denton
Henry, 11/20/55, none given
Jane, 10/20/56, Mich'l. Jarrett, Jane Jarrett, Betty Stokes
Hardy, 2/12/63, James Tomlinson, Travis Weaver, Amy Weaver
Betty, 9/14/68, Geo. Rives, Isacc Wright, Mely Duncan
Richard, 8/17/64, John Adkins, Geo. Ezell, Eliz. Adkins

James and Amy Tomlinson

Mary, 9/3/66, Travis Weaver, Susanna Tatum, Patty Hulin
Burwell, 7/25/65, Richard Cotton, Edward Weaver Jr., Eliz.
Cotton

TOMLINSON (Continued)
Thomas and Olive Tomlinson
Eliz., 10/1/72, Giles Underhill, Mary and Sarah Partridge
Mary, 9/9/74, John Potts, Patty Hunter, Jane Tomlinson

Richard and Anne Tomlinson
Martha, 4/19/70, Thomas Tomlinson, Mary Harper, Sarah Hobbs

Alex and Sarah Tomlinson
Littleberry, 3/18/61, Nath'l. Tomlinson, Sarah Tomlinson,
    Eliz. Weeks
Eliz., 12/11/62, Wm. Gilbert, Fanny Biggons, Sarah Mason
Frankey, 3/11/65, Geo. Rives, Nath'l. Bedingfield, Eliz.Dunn
James, 8/1/67, James Glover, John Walker, Frances Glover

John Tomlinson Jr. and Susanna
Lucas, 4/11/46, John Adkins, Christopher Tatum Jr., Bathia
    Tatum

TROUGHTON
Andrew and Molly Troughton
Swan, 10/20/57, James Cotton, Jesse Jones, Alice Stagg

TROTTER
James and Anne Trotter
Wm., 3/10/52, Richard Bird, Ben'g. Moss, Eliz. Weaver

TUDOR
Henry and Eliz. Tudor
Mathew, 10/20/52, Wm. Hix, Samuel Harwood, Mary Hix
Bridget, 5/7/57, Philip Harwood, Mary Pate, Rebbecca Harwood
Hannah, 7/30/58, Ben'g. Adams, Eliz. Ezell, Ester Anderson

Owen and Lucy Tudor
Phoebe, 7/8/64, Nathan Rodgers, Lucy Harris, Eliz. Rodgers
Fanny, 3/19/66, Henry Tudor Jr., Anne Wellborn, Sarah Slate
Harris, 4/26/68, Jesse Rodgers, Edward Slate, Letty Waller
Lucy, 10/20/71, Joshuah Smith, Hannah Hix, Sarah Pate

Henry Tudor Jr. and Sarah
Jesse, 8/8/62, Burwell Wellborn, Wm. Hill, Martha Graves
Henry, 8/5/63, Henry Gee, Thos. Dowdning, Amy Moss
Lavina, 3/14/67, Richard Hay Jr., Eliz. Bulloch, Mary Jenks
Salley, 1/30/72, Nath'l. Newsom, Lucy Fort, Rebbecca Toddy
    (Tudor)

TUCKER
Robert and Diana Tucker
Sarah, 9/4/30, none given
Samuel, 1/13/33, none given
Winefred, 3/1/35, none given
Robert, 8/22/37, none given

TUCKER (Continued)
Joel and Judieth Tucker
Patty, 2/8/56, none given
Joseph, 10/26/60, Ben'g. Tucker, David Threewits, Mary Tucker
Eliz., 4/16/64, John Wynne, Anne Sturdivant, Drusilla Tyus

David and Athalia Tucker
Patty Colson, 11/22/66, Mason Harewell, Mary Goodwynne,
  Patty Tucker
Hartwell, 10/17/64, Thomas Hunt, Lawrence Gibbons, Jr.,
  Mary Morris
David, 12/31/68, Robert Evans, Wood Tucker, Prudence and
  Martha Evans

Robert and Mary Tucker
Lucretia, 12/23/59, John Winfield, Mary Prichard, Olive Green
Colson, 2/15/62, Ben'g. Tucker, Peter Green, Amy Freeman
Hannah, 2/15/69, Joseph Tucker Jr., Amy Tucker, Agnes Har-
  risson
Steth, 6/14/71, Ro. Wynne Raines, Thos. Shands, Jane Raines

Joseph Tucker Jr. and Amy
Mary, 8/9/71, Wood Tucker, Lucretia Winfield, John Raines

TURNER
James and Anne Turner
Arthur, 9/6/43, Arthur Richardson, Wm. Davidson, Mary Rich-
  ardson
James, 4/3/45, Wm. Carrell, Wm. Davidson, Eliz. Dowdning
  (Dowdny)
Jesse, 6/30/47, John Smith Jr., James Bane, Martha Smith
Sarah, 1/26/49, James Turner Jr., Sarah Smith, Anne Crosswit

John and Rebbecca Turner
Winney, 3/30/51, David Turner, Eliz. Mabrey, Jane Jarrett
Elias, 10/28/52, none given
Sarah, 9/10/54, Burwell Gilliam, Agnes Battle, Amy Felts

James and Eliz. Turner
Wm., 8/26/54, David Jones, James Wallace, Sarah Briggs
Edmunds, 2/12/59, Jarrett Wallace, Robert Carlisle, Eliz.
  Bryant
Nancy, 8/8/64, none given
Hines, 11/13/66, James Turner, Henry Hines, Selah Edmunds
Betsy, 3/28/73, Richard Christian, Sarah Wallace, Sarah Jones

James and Jean Turner
Peggy Douglas, 1/25/71, none given
Miles, 1/19/72, none given
Ben'g., 2/4/75, John Bane Jr., Danial Turner, Sarah Turner

TYUS
Thomas and Eliz. Tyus
John, 1/18/58, none given

TYUS (Continued)

Thomas and Eliz. Tyus (Continued)

Thomas, 1/14/63, Richard Hill, Francis Drinkard, Eliz. Smith

Absolum and Sylvia Tyus

Rebbecca, 2/2/65, Absolum Williamson, Eliz. Gibbons, Rachael
Flowers

Absolum Tyus was deceased in 1765

Richard and Eliz. Tyus

Susanna, bab. 4/13/60, none given

Lewis and Amy Tyus

Lewis, 5/16/65, Richard Hill, Eph. Parham, Margery Hill

Ben'g. and Eliz. Tyus

Williamson, 11/15/63, James Greenway, Wm. Parham, Eliz.
Tyus

Parmelia, 11/15/65, Thomas Lane, Rebbecca Wright

Edwain, 8/3/70, Jesse Williamson, Nath'l. Parham, Sylvia
Bonner

J. Williamson, 12/?/73, Drury Stokes, Lewis Johnson, ------
Williamson

UNDERHILL

John and Amelia Underhill

John, 11/21/40, John Thompson, John Moss, Mary Moss (?)

John Underhill Jr. and Eliz.

Henry, 4/23/64, Thomas and Joshuah Moss, Mary Adkins

Lucy, 2/1/67, Aug. Shands, Sarah Moss, Sarah Underhill

Patty, 8/29/69, Giles Underhill, Mary Adkins, Amy Shands

Rebbecca, 1/2/72, Thos. Whitefield, Lydia Andrews

Giles and Sarah Underhill

Salley, 1/7/57, Davis Moss, Eliz. Mason, Mely Edmunds

Mely, 2/2/59, none given

Wm., 3/5/61, David and Thos. Moss, Mary Hancock

Betsy, 3/1/63, John Underhill, Eliz. Moss, Salley Jones

Mary, 3/3/65, Isam Underhill, Eliz. Moss, Prissilla Shands

James, 10/14/65, Jesse Rodgers, Rubin Hicks, Wynefred Mason

Henry and Mary Underhill

Howell, 3/6/57, none given

Rebbecca, 8/7/60, Giles Underhill, Abigail Proctor, Martha
Bennett

Mary, 2/7/64, Henry Moss Jr., Eliz. Underhill, Mary Adkins

Susanna, 3/15/67, John Underhill Jr., Sarah Edmunds, Mildred
Duncan

Eliz., 6/14/69, Steven Andrews, Eliz. Jarrett, Sarah Jones

John, 8/19/75, James Underhill, Abraham Jones, Nancy Lucas

144

UNDERWOOD
Thomas and Rosamund Underwood
Mary, 11/22/40, Mathew Hubbard, Anne Main (?), Anne Hay

Beadles and Rachael Underwood
Mark, 8/11/48, John Avent, Richard Underwood, Margarett
Avent
Anne, 3/24/32, Samson Huson, Sarah Roberts, Anne Sammons

Mark and Ester Underwood
Betsy, 8/7/71, Lewis Underwood, Sarah Hay, Milly Whitehorn

Lewis and Gilly Underwood
Margarett, 10/3/65, Ben'g. Phipps, Prissilla Jones, Eliz.Graves
Hubert, 1/19/71, John Rowland, Nathan Rodgers, Martha Sea-
born

Lewis and Eliz. Underwood
Hamlet, 8/20/58, Edward Pate, Wm. Longbottom, Jane Mabrey

VAUGHN
Thomas and Dorothy Vaughn
Thomas, 9/20/51, none given
Eliz., 1/12/54, none given
Martha, 6/7/56, none given
Anne, 1/7/57, Vines Collier, Anne Gibbons, Tabitha Mitchell
Judieth, 6/16/62, Henry Broadnax, Anne Broadnax, Sarah
Harewell

Peirce and Faith Vaughn
Louisa, 12/7/60, James Williams Jr., Eliz. Williams, Eliz.
Ezell

VERRELL
John and Susanna Verrell
Wm., 12/24/55, Wm. Moore, Epps Moore, Anne Moore
James, 2/24/64, Robert Petway, Epps Moore, Martha Moore
Eliz., 2/18/59, John Mason, Eliz. Gee, Eliz. Dansey
Martha, 3/27/65, Aug. Clairbourne, Sarah Rives, Rebbecca
Mason
John, 8/4/57, Edward and John Petway, Eliz. Petway

VINES
Thos. and Eliz. Vines
John, 5/10/48, Lawrence Gibbons, Geo. Robertson, Dorothy
Vaughn
Isacc Willis, 3/19/45, none given
Lucas, 1/22/49, Thomas Vaughn, John Mitchell, Anne Hill
Herbert, 7/58, none given

Thomas and Mary Vines
Wm., 5/20/60, Ro. Wynne Raines, Mathew Parham Jr., Anne
Mitchell

VINES (Continued)
Thomas and Mary Vines (Continued)
Thomas, 10/5/61, Isam Smith, Burwell Banks, Mary Banks
Isacc Willis, 1/21/66, Thos. Booth, Wm. Malone, Lucretia
    Butler
John, 4/19/68, John Petway, Wood Tucker, Rebbecca Parham
Eliz., 4/19/70, Miles Collier, Eliz. Kirkland, Eliz. Vines
Mary, 1/26/73, Wm. Dabney, Eliz. Gibbons, Eliz. Vaughn
Martha, 1/19/75, Edward Powell Jr., Martha and Eliz. Powell

WADE
Thomas and Susanna Wade
James, 12/29/44, James Cain, James Cain Jr., Eliz. Cain
Susanna, 6/2/49, none given
Eliz., 10/4/53, James Moss, Anne and Eliz. Cain
Patty, 9/31/56, George Randall, Patty Underwood, Mary Green
Thomas, 3/27/50, Wm. Yarbrough, Peter Green, Lucy Cain
Mary, 1/24/63, Nathanial Robertson, Mary Rowland, Olive
    Randall

Robert Farington reported the death of James Wade 11/16/48

WALDEN
John and Sarah Walden
James, 9/16/47, Thos. Wrenn, Thos. Wrenn Jr., Hannah Wrenn
Jonathan, 3/26/51, James and Nathan Northington, Hulda Wrenn

WALKER
Francis and Faith Walker
Francis, 2/16/33, none given
Rowland, 6/23/41, none given
Anne, 3/7/37, none given

Freeman and ------ Walker
Frances, 5/9/62, Henry Broadnax, Anne Gibbons, Sarah Jones

Bengiman and Lucy Walker
Eliz., 4/9/66, David Walker, Elenor Hobbs, Anne Wrenn

John and Amy Walker
Eliz., 9/2/73, Ben'g. Mathews, Rebbecca Robertson, Frances
    Davis

John and Hannah Walker
Robert, 10/1/71, Robert Owen, Jesse Sturdivant, Eliz. Owen

John Walker and Jane Land
John Bruton, 10/10/69, John Land Jr., Wm. Hern, Sarah Hern

WALL
Samuel and Eliz. Wall
Susanna, 4/15/72, Lawrence Stacey, Mary Stacey

WALL (Continued)

Aaron and Eliz. Wall

Thomas, 10/3/49, Chas. Hill, Ben'g. Clark, Jane Petway

WALLACE

Thomas and Rebbecca Wallace

Jesse, 2/20/43, Robert Jones, John Turner, Mary Hix

Thomas and Sarah Wallace

Lucy, 9/20/44, Henry Gerrard, Sarah Jones, Mary Turner
Selah, 2/5/47, Edmund Almond, Eliz. Jarrett, Sarah Turner

James and Mary Wallace

Rebbecca, 2/18/53, Arthur Murphey, Margarett and Martha
Jarrett

Jesse and Prissilla Wallace

Rebbecca, 3/2/68, Wm. Hines Jr., Howell Jones, Mary Jones,
Rebbecca Mason
Jarrett, 2/4/70, Thos. Hargrave, John Barker, Selah Wallace
Sarah, 11/15/72, Nath'l. Felts, Eliz. Jarrett, Mary Boyce

Thos. and Unity Wallace

Ben'g., 4/26/61, Joseph Armstrong, Wm. Willie, Alice Newsom

Wm. and Jane Wallace

Rebbecca, 11/27/49, John Smith, Mary Wallace, Lucy Nicholson
Charity, 5/6/52, Joseph Bell, Jane Jarrett, Judieth Pepper

Wm. and Sarah Wallace

Selah, 10/12/42, Wm. Willie, Amy Winkle, Eliz. Smith
Sarah, twin, Wm. Willie, Mary Briggs, Martha Roberts

WALLER

Samuel and Mary Waller

Sarah, 11/12/55, Josh. Cotton, Betty Cotton, Susanna Hight

WARBURTON

Wm. and Alice Warburton

Frances, 10/14/70, John Broadrib, Mart Stacey, Eliz. Ellis

WARDEN

John and Sarah Warden

John, 9/25/44, Thomas Wrenn, Robert Pully, Anne Seaborn

WARWICK

Jacob and Eliz. Warwick

Wyatt, 1/29/69, Thomas Pate, John Irby, Anne Whitehill

WEATHERS

Wm. and Mary Weathers

Thomas, 11/29/45, Thos. Weathers, Sloman Wynne, Susanna
Weathers

WEATHERS (Continued)
Wm. and Mary Weathers (Continued)
Sarah, 12/1/47, Richard Rives, Dorothy Rives, Lydia Weathers
Wm., 2/26/50, Wm. Rives, John Bradley, Frances Rives
John, 2/25/52, Peter and John Rives, Frances Rives
Jesse, 1/12/54, Richard Rives Jr., Ben'g. Weathers, Mary Nun
Willie, 3/29/58, Ben'g. Tomlinson, Edward Smith, Sarah Bradley
Isam, 8/22/60, Nathanial Dobie, James Denton, Eliz. White

Michael and Faith Weathers
Mary, 12/13/56, Thos. Weathers, Mary Rose, Susanna Harris
John, 5/21/58, Micajah Petway, Nathan Rodgers, Eliz. Woodland
Hartwell, 8/6/55, Wm. Rose, Wm. Woodland, Agnes Woodland
Howell, 6/22/60, Peter Rives, Thos. Felts Jr., Sarah Adams
Wm., 6/9/62, John Owen, Danial Horton, Eliz. Woodland
Betsy, 3/29/68, Danial McInnish, Mary Weathers, Sarah McInnish
Edmund, 12/26/72, Womack Gilliam, Timothy Ezell, Frances Gilliam

Ben'g. and Mary Weathers
Edmund, 1/23/58, Wm. Weathers, Wm. Petway Jr., Eliz. Dansey

Thos. and Susanna Weathers
Ben'g., 1/12/66, Edward Slate, Robert Slate, Amy Atkinson
Sucky, 12/19/68, Thos. Ezell Jr., Anne Wellborn, Selah Hines

Isacc and Unity Weathers
Lucy, 10/31/61, Wm. Parsons, Mart Weathers, Lucy Blaton

WEAVER
Edward and Mary Weaver
Edward, 2/7/38, John Rosser, Edward Weaver, Eliz. Weaver
Susanna, 6/23/41, John Griffith, Susanna Emery, Eliz. Griffith
Travis, 3/18/43, Thos. Griffith, Travis Griffith, Betty Weaver
Amy, 9/17/46, John Adkins, Jane Weaver, Amelia Underhill
Lucy, 9/22/49, Robert Jones Jr., Amy Chappell, Mary Weaver
Wm., 11/16/52, Wm. Tomlinson, Wm. Cotton, Martha Ivey
Winney, 10/12/55, Henry Weaver, Betty Prince, Jane Griffith
John, 2/26/60, Edward Weaver Jr., John Rives, Susanna Weaver

Steven and Elenor Weaver
Isam, 3/21/38, Peter Hawthorn, John Weaver, Eliz. Kellerman
Frances, 8/30/39, Nath'l. Hawthorn, Josh. Hawthorn, Eliz. Kellerman
Steven, 10/18/42, John Hawthorn, Nath'l. Tatum, Frances Denton

John and Eliz. Weaver
Amy, 4/15/41, John Vincent, Mary Shelton, Bridget Tatum

Gilbert and Eliz. Weaver
Aaron, 2/8/39, Robert Hix, John Thompson, Mary Epps

WEAVER (Continued)
Travis and Sarah Weaver
Micajah, 1/13/63, Peter Rosser, Mary Weaver, Sarah Rosser

Travis and Anne Weaver
Eliz., 3/31/66, Richard Cotton, Sarah Partridge, Mary Adkins

Henry and Mary Weaver
Lucy, 12/22/60, none given
Peter, 1/18/63, John Adkins, Edward Weaver Jr., Amy Adkins

WEBB
Chas. and Eliz. Webb
Micajah, 14/11/41, Charles Gilliam, Henry Freeman Jr., Eliz.
Webb

John and Lucy Webb
Salley, 12/19/67, none given

Robert and Eliz. Webb
Nathanial, 10/30/40, Robert Land, Edward Shelton, Mary Webb
Herman, 9/23/52, Chas. Judkins, James Carter, Mary Judkins
Sarah, 3/10/54, Levei Gilliam, Mary Judkins, Mary Lofting
Frances, 12/2/57, Richard Johnson, Lucy Newsom, Lydia Pennington
Susanna, 8/27/59, Thos. Moore Jr., Anne Moore, ----- Carter
Robert, 11/8/61, John Judkins, Lewis Johnson, Martha Gilliam
Eliz., 4/2/63, Gray Dunn, Ruth Dunn, Lucy Moss

WEEDAN
Edward and Eliz. Weeden
Mary, 5/2/41, Moses Fitzpatrick, Mary Taylor, Sarah Wallace

WELLBORN - WILBORN - WELBURN
John and Judieth Welborn
Frances, 1/3/39, Wm. Yarbrough, Susannah Parham, Anne
Yarbrough

John and Anne Welborn
Henry, 6/2/39, Wm. Richardson, Thos. Wynne, Mary Richardson

John and Temperence Welborn
Wm., 8/6/49, Richard Geary, Wm. Welborn, Anne Patterson
Eliz., 10/6/55, James Carter, Amy Hill, Amy Freeman
Sarah, 1/26/61, Edward Powell, Lucretia Hill, Lucy Mahaney
Frances, 1/10/64, Wm. Winfield, Frances Oliver, Phoebe Freeman

Wm. and Eliz. Welborn
Mary, 1/28/49, none given
Joel, 3/30/55, Wm. Richardson, Edward Powell, Mary Hill
Wm., 8/7/60, John Rolland, Bryan Fanning, Mary Hill

WELLBORN - WILBORN - WELBURN (Continued)

Wm. and Sarah Welborn
Wm., 2/20/64, James Hern, Michael Weathers, Rebbecca Seat

Henry and Mary Welborn
John, 3/11/64, Robert Winfield, Edward Slate, Eliz. Delahay
Betty, 2/14/66, Jesse Sturdivant, Sarah Sturdivant, Anne Ezell

Burwell and Sarah Welborn
Thomas, 8/28/65, Thomas and Wm. Hern
Mary, 9/12/67, Arthur Delahay, Mary Hill, Sucky Delahay
Henry, 9/7/69, Thos. Sturdivant, John Sturdivant, Anne Welborn
Fanny, 7/14/73, Wm. Parham, says he forgot the others

Benjiman and Betty Welborn
Betty, 2/29/72, John Malone, Winefred Robertson, Mary Mangum
Beckey, 2/22/67, Wm. Spane, Anne Welborn, Susanna Delahay
Ben'g., 4/18/70, Chas. Delahay, James Cain Jr., Lucretia Cain
Richard (twin), Seth Price, Chas. Delahay, Rebbecca Dunn
Polly, 3/11/75, Robert Slate, Mary Hewett, Eliz. Hill

Henry Welborn died 9/9/66, reported by John Welborn

WHEELER
Joseph and Mary Wheeler
Joseph, 8/14/33, none given
John, 12/11/34, none given
Eliz., 12/27/37, none given
James, 2/2/39, Thomas Oliver, Wm. Abbott, Mary Bobbett
Christopher, 3/23/41, Edward Jackson, Mary Parsons, Eliz.
   Passmore

Ben'g. and Eliz. Wheeler
Isam, 9/8/41, Philipp Bailey, James Wilbourne, Susanna Simmons
Wm., 4/15/?, Nath'l. and John Hood, Susanna Howell

WHITE
Ben'g. and Lucy White
John, 4/2/52, Nath'l. Lewis, Joseph Bell, Susanna Bane
Hannah, 1/6/57, Joseph Smith, Sarah Alsobrook, Eliz. Broadrib

James and Patty White
Warren, 9/9/67, John Warren, John Wesson, Sarah Kennybrough
Peggy, 11/30/76, Nic'h. Presson, Salley Hicks, Rebbecca White

WHITEFIELD
Robert and Mary Whitefield
Jeanny, 4/10/53, Peter Hawthorn, Rebbecca Hawthorn, Sarah
   Bird
Wm., 1/16/57, Edward Walker, Frances Niblett, Fanny Hawthorn
Mary, 10/21/60, none given

WHITEFIELD (Continued)
Thomas and Winney Whitefield
Mary, 9/21/60, none given
Franky, 2/14/65, John and Mary Lessenberry, Anne Whitefield
Patty, 3/16/67, Donald McInnish, Eliz. Gilbert, Amy Sledge
Wm., 8/6/72, John Underhill Jr., James Glover Jr., Mason
Hobbs
Betty, 10/10/74, John Shands, Selah Hobbs, Sarah McInnish

WHITEHEAD
Robert Whitehead Jr. and Mary Thany
Eliz. Cole, 3/19/53, James Spain, Thany Spane, Frances Hood
Mathew Cole, 7/16/37, Edward Wright, Wm. Willie, Mary Briggs
Nanny, 2/20/60, James Horn, Mely Rives, Nath'l. Rainey
Mely, 1/6/63, John Hood, Anne Barr, Amy Moss
Williams, 1/28/70, Wm. Rodgers; James Cocke, Eliz. King
Mathew, 2/6/71, Wm. Hardy, Fred Owen, Eliz. Spain
James, twin, John Owen, David Woodruff, Sarah Hardy

Robert Whitehead Jr., and Amy
Lorana, 7/29/75, Charles Williams, Vina Pare, Mary Woodruff

Thomas and Lucy Whitehead
James, 8/20/59, James Spain, John Owen, Lucy Evans
Salley, 1/26/62, Richard Rose, Winney Newman, Eliz. Wynne

Mathew and Sarah Whitehead
Mathew, 3/22/39, Wm. Richardson, James Hall, Mary Spain
Robert, 10/21/44, John King Jr., Alex. Dickens, Sarah King
Isam, 8/21/47, James Spain, Robert Whitehead, Judieth Spain
John, 10/17/53, Peter Rives, Abner Sturdivant, Eliz. Rives

Isam and Sylvia Whitehead
Salley, 10/5/69, David Woodruff, Biddy Spain, Eliz. Spain
Judieth, 10/5/72, Wm. Spain, Anne Atkinson, Eliz. Spain
Wm., 1/25/74, John and Wm. Rowland, Mary Spain

Mathew Whitehead died 12/30/69, reported by Robert Newsom

WHITETHORN
Philipp and Mary Whithorn
John, ?/?/?, none given

Philipp and Mely Whithorn
Nancy, 3/16/72, John Whitehorn, Molly Whitehorn, Sarah Hay

WHITTINGTON
Edward and Penelope Whittington
Jane, 4/13/47, Nath'l. Hood, Sarah Hood, Eliz. Johnson
Penelope, 3/12/54, Wm. Green, Mary Farrington, Mary Green
Burwell Green, 1/26/57, John Wellborn Jr., Joseph Richardson,
Mary Rollins

WHITTINGTON (Continued)
John and Eliz. Whittington
Owen, 12/13/47, John Owen, Richard King Jr., Eliz. Sowersberry
Sarah, 12/22/50, Edward Whittington, Mary Enson, Jane Hern

John and Sarah Whittington
Eph., 3/29/58, John and Wm. King, Eliz. Hood
Cornelius, 4/24/49, Burwell Gilliam, Thos. Battle, Winefred
  Woodruff
Richard, 1/16/53, Fred Green, James Williams Sr., Alice
  Knight

William and Mary Whittington
Sarah, 6/4/54, Nic'h. Jarrett, Jane Jarrett, Mary Green
Lucy, 10/10/57, Micajah Stokes, Aggy Stokes, Eliz. Adams
Robert, 10/8/75, Edward Whittington, Peter Threewits, Pene-
  lope Whittington

WIGGENS
Richard and Tabitha Wiggens
Judieth, 3/5/47, Lucy Norris, Anne Seat
Richard and Judieth Wiggens
------, dgh., 7/28/41, Geo. Ezell, Sarah Ezell, Sarah Robets
Wm. and Agnes Wiggens
Richard, 4/18/49, Richard Wiggens, Thos. Northcross, Tabitha
Wiggens
David and Eliz. Wiggens
Jemima, 6/24/50, Timothy Ezell Jr., Elenor Smith, Eliz. Clifton
Betty, 10/8/54, Wm. Weathers, Anne Ezell, Mary Denton
Richard and Sarah Wiggens
Phoebe, 12/8/49, Joseph Harwood, Sarah and Eliz. Harwood
Lewis, 5/7/51, Edward Shelton, Joseph Land, Eliz. Shelton
Lydia, 6/20/62, Sampson Moseley, Mary and Sarah Pate

James and Sarah Wiggens
Thomas, 11/2/60, Thos. Cullam, Thos. Cooper, Eliz. Cullam
Lucretia, 10/18/62, Henry Underhill, Betty and Anne Cullam
James, 7/2/66, Petway Johnson, Simon Stacey, Anne Cullam
Mary, ?/?/68, Wm. Cullam (torn)
Frederick, 8/6/70, James Cooper, Josh. Johnson, Anne Cullam
Salley, 11/2/72, Thos. Cullam Jr., Eliz. and Lucy Cooper

WILCOX
Wm. and Anne Wilcox
John, 10/28/71, Richard Cock, Thos. Presson, Mary Wilcox
Samuel, 1/31/74, John Mason Jr., Thos. Adams, Mary Partridge

WILKINSON
John and Sarah Wilkinson
Lucy, 8/24/50, Chris. Tatum, Francis Tatum, Mary Wilkinson
Hubbard, 12/17/53, Thos. Adkins Jr., Richard Wilkinson, Eliz.
  Cotton

WILKINSON (Continued)
John and Anne Wilkinson
John Sykes, 1/20/53, Thos. Huson Jr., Wm. Elliatt, Eliz. Cain
Wyatt, 10/12/55, Thos. Wade, Peter Green, Susanna Banks
Wm., 11/22/60, Burwell Banks, Wm. Kirkland, Milly Wilkerson
Anne, 4/24/63, Wm. Yarbrough, Eliz. Smith, Eliz. Gibbons

Wm. and Eliz. Wilkinson
Wm., 12/1/56, John Underhill Jr., Alex Hay, Amy Sledge
John, 2/8/61, James Crossland, Wm. Cotton, Eliz. Cotton
Winny, 11/14/58, Thos. Stafford, Mary Tomlinson, Joyce Adkins
James, 5/20/63, Thos. Adkins, Jr., Nath'l. Duncan, Mary Adkins

Thos. and Sarah Wilkinson
Wager, 6/4/57, Lewis Adkins, Nath'l. Duncan, Joyce Atkins
Thomas, 8/11/59, Wm. Hewett, Lewis Brown, Martha Brown
Elisha, 9/19/62, James Adams, Thos. Wynne, Mary Wilkinson
Mary, 3/4/66, Joel Knight, Hannah Knight, Rebbecca Rowland

Richard and Betty Wilkinson
Burwell, 2/11/60, Thos. Adkins, Henry Cotton, Agnes Duncan
Henry, 11/11/64, Thos. Adams, Henry Underhill, Fanny Petway
John, 5/13/67, Beng. Barker, Joseph Denton, Mary Adkins
Richard, 11/13/69, John Petway, Giles Underhill, Fanny Petway
Wm., 9/18/72, John Adkins, Danial McInnish, Elenor Hobbs

WILLIAMS
John and Eliz. Williams
Meryday, 7/6/43, John Jones, Shore Hatley, Eliz. Grantham
Frederick, 5/20/46, John Weaver, James Price, Mary Price
Amy, 9/11/47, Francis Redding, Mary Epps, Sarah Williams
Margarett, 7/6/48, Wm. Willie, Eliz. Willie, Sarah Bird
Eliz., 10/5/52, John Weaver, Sarah Williams, Rebbecca Hawthorn

James and Eliz. Williams
Chany, 9/28/42, Richard Woodruff Jr., Sarah Sykes, Anne Ryals
Charles, 9/16/40, Joseph Mason, Wm. Clark, Ruth Tatum

James Williams Jr. and Eliz.
Rebbecca, 3/31/62, Samuel Harwood, Amy Harwood, Anthony Williams
Philipp, 1/7/64, Charles Williams, Howell Pennington, Agnes Harwood

Charles and Eliz. Williams
John, 8/8/66, Wm. Moore, Wm. Cocke, Thany Williams
Thomas, 6/10/68, James Williams Jr., Robert Whitehead, Lucy Gilliam
Mary, 3/21/70, John Cock, Eliz. and Prissilla Gilliam
James, 7/27/71, John Cock, Ben'g. Adams, Eliz. Williams

WILLIAMSON
John and Martha Williamson
Patty, 6/28/40, Robert Tucker, Mary Wynne, Eliz. Lilly

Thos. and Mary Williamson
Jemima, 11/18/69, none given

Jesse and Mary Williamson
Henry, 1/15/65, Josh. Pennington, Drury Clanton, Mely Clanton
Temperence, 7/30/67, Ben'g. Lewis, Mary Rachael, Betty
    Clanton
Rebbecca, 2/21/69, Isam Gilliam, Sarah Graves, Mary Rachael
    Jr.
James, 2/27/72, James Williams, Wm. Lofting Jr., Eliz. Wil-
    liams
Joseph, 11/26/75, Thos. Stokes, Wm. White, Prissilla Gilliam

WILLIE
Wm. and Eliz. Willie
Margarett, 1/8/44, Rev. John Betty, Robert Jones Jr., Martha
    Eldridge, Sarah Jones

WINFIELD
William and Sarah Winfield
Abraham, 10/19/39, Abra. Winfield, Edward Eccles, Martha
    Winfield

Abraham and Susanna Winfield
Clairbourne, 4/12/69, Joseph Carter, Arthur Delahay, Susanna
    Carter
Thomas, 3/26/71, Peter and Robert Winfield, Judieth Winfield
Kesiah, 1/19/73, John Malone, Frances Winfield, Mary Malone

Robert and Frances Winfield
Beckey, 1/31/62, John Winfield, Mary Farrington, Anne Sturdi-
    vant
Henry, 3/15/64, Peter Winfield, James Sturdivant, Mary Sturdi-
    vant
Harris Gilliam, 10/19/60, Abra. Winfield, Thos. Tyus, Susanna
    Sturdivant
Eliz., 9/29/71, John Winfield, Patty and Sucky Winfield

John and Lucy Winfield
Wm., 11/6/61, James Greenway, Thos. Tyus, Mary Rottenberry
Hannah, 11/20/63, Abra. Winfield, Lucy Hill, Lucy Mahaney

William Winfield Jr. and Eliz.
Wm., 4/29/62, John Wynne, James Sturdivant, Sucky Winfield
John, 3/7/67, John Malone, Joseph Richardson, Patty Winfield
Eph., 10/24/69, Peter Green, Joseph Richardson, Agnes Free-
    man

WINFIELD (Continued)
Peter and Lucretia Winfield
Robert, 4/18/62, Seth Pettypool, Anne Pettypool, Sucky Freeman
Sarah, 2/7/71, Wood Tucker, Eliz. Tucker, Mary Jones

William and Eliz. Winfield
James, 10/7/55, John Curtis, Soloman Graves, Lucia Curtis
John, 3/7/67, John Malone, Joseph Richardson, Patty Winfield
Eph., 10/24/69, Peter Green, Joseph Richardson, Patty Winfield

William Winfield Jr. and Eliz.
Fanny, 8/20/64, Abra. Winfield, Mary Wilkerson, Anne Wilkerson

WILSON
John and Katherine Wilson
Wm., 7/6/72, Nic'h. Wilson, Thos. Hargrave, Mary Gibbons

WOOD
Charles and Dorothy Wood
Sarah, 11/13/51, Joseph Rolland, Mary Stokes, Hannah Northcross

WOODHAM
Thos. and Eliz. Woodham
Mary Anne, 9/5/50, Samuel Griffin, Francis Smith, Mary Griffin

WOODLAND
Wm. and Judieth Woodland
Agnes, 9/6/40, John Bell, Mary Mannery, Anne Rose
Sarah, 6/31/56, Thos. Weathers, Sarah Woodland, Susanna Craig

Wm. and Eliz. Woodland
Faithy, 4/26/59, Edward Pate, Faithy Weathers, Mary Rosser
Phoebe, 2/26/58, John Stokes, Agnes Woodland, Kesiah Ezell

WOODRUFF
David and Frances Woodruff
James, 1/3/53, James Williams Jr., Joel Woodruff, Sarah Williams
Richard, 5/19/54, Mathew Wynne, Wm. Rodgers, Rebbecca Longbottom
David, 3/3/60, Wm. Longbottom, Wm. Rodgers, Rebbecca Longbottom
Frances, 3/1/61, Thos. Whitefield, Rebbecca Longbottom, Mary Williams
Williams, 8/2/62, Sloman Wynne, Moss Williams, Mary Wynne
Charles, 12/27/65, Charles Williams, James Rodgers, Lydia Stokes
Patty, 7/21/66, John Cock, Eliz. and Mary Hill
Winny, 1/7/68, Robert Whitehead, Eliz. Hood, Jane Northcross
John, 1/13/70, Isam Whitehead, Jordan Knight, Mary Spane

WOODWARD

John and Susanna Woodward
Goodwynne, 11/25/66, John Woodward, Thos. Wade, Angelica Cain
Nanny, ?/?/?, Wm. Wade, Anne Wilkerson, Amy Woodward
Mary, 2/5/72, Micajah Cain, Bathia Cain, Mary Wade

John and Eliz. Woodward
Kesiah, 4/27/57, James Cain Jr., Anne Wilkerson, Susanna Banks

WOOTEN

Edward and Hulda Wooten
Edward, 12/4/66, none given
Thomas, 1/23/61, Lawrence Smith, Thos. Presson, Lucy Smith
Sylvia, 4/22/62, John Brown, Sarah Presson, Mary Stacey
Salley, 10/16/68, Wm. Wooten, Mary Stacey, Janet Rodgers
Wm., 3/15/67, Wm. Brittle, Abner James, Mary Hix

WRENN

Thomas Wrenn Jr. and Hannah
Sarah, 6/26/47, John Pennington, Mary Heeth, Amy Dunn
Anna, 10/22/50, Wm. Dansey, Mary Dansey, Sarah Wrenn
Nath'l., 4/1/52, Hartwell Marriable, Robert Hancock, Mary Marriable
Hulda, 5/10/55, James Wrenn, Anthony Hancock, Anne Dansey
Mary, 3/24/58, Wm. Stewart, Mary Stewart, Eliz. Dansey
Jesse, 4/24/63, Moses Pennington, Steven Lee, Lucretia Pennington

Thomas and Eliz. Wrenn
Fortune, 2/25/52, Agnes Atkinson, Hulda Hargrave

Joseph and Anne Wrenn
David, 1/14/61, Wm. Wrenn, Wm. Lofting Jr., Sarah Johnson
James, 6/22/62, Thomas Moore Jr., Ben'g. Seaborn, Eliz. Webb
Joseph, 7/6/67, Burwell Lofting, Barham Moore, Eliz. Moore
Wm., 2/29/69, Moses Lofting, Sylvanus Bell, Jemima Johnson
Henry, twin, John Crossland, Thos. Whitefield, Molly Crossland
Jemmy, 7/8/71, Nath'l. Newsom, Levi Gilliam, Jemima Rachael
Thomas, 9/2/72, Curtis Land, Wm. Moore, ------ Freeman

Thomas and Rebbecca Wrenn
Salley, 8/7/74, Henry Underhill, Mary Underhill, Salley Moss

Joseph and Sarah Wrenn
Howell, 4/27/50, James and Joseph Wrenn, Winefred Woodruff
Joseph, 12/20/52, Moses Pennington, Ben'g. Seaborn, Hulda Wrenn
Moses, 9/11/53, Moses Pennington, Isacc Mason, Mary Dobie
Elias, 9/10/55, Nath'l. Northington, John Pennington, Lucy Dunn

156
WRENN (Continued)
                Joseph and Sarah Wrenn (Continued)
Howell, 12/26/57, Ben'g. Hunt, Clement Hancock Jr., Eliz.
    Bedingfield

WRIGHT
                Edward and Rebbecca Wright
John, 11/4/56, Simon Stacey, Wm. Ellis, Katherine Stacey
Eliz., 2/2/69, Archer Richardson, Eliz. Ellis, Martha Stacey
Edward, 6/2/64, Arthur Richardson, Simon Stacey Jr., Mary
    Stacey
James, 4/8/67, Petway Johnson, Wm. Warburton, Eliz. Morris

WYCHE
                James and Winefred Wyche
James, 2/18/53, Wm. Johnson, Lewis Johnson, Eliz. Avery

                Ben'g. and Eliz. Wyche
George, 3/7/59, Wm. Johnson, Thos. Peters Jr., Hannah Howell
Wm., 2/28/62, Samuel Pete, Edward Clanton, Mary Pete
Peggy, 8/10/63, Thos. Pete, Martha Pete, Martha Avery

WYNNE
                John Wynne Jr. and Eliz.
Peter, 3/18/53, Thos. Wynne, Thos. Wynne Jr., Susanna Rich-
    ardson
Mary, 8/23/57, Joseph Richardson, Martha Richardson, Mary
    Green
Eliz., 3/15/59, Wm. Richardson, Susanna Curtis, Margarett
    King
Phoebe, 3/14/61, John Winfield, Martha Kelly, Mary Richardson
Peggy, 2/9/66, Clairbourne Curtis, Anne Booth, Patty Freeman
Susanna, 3/8/68, Wm. Malone, Drusilla Mitchell, Anne Rainey
Anne, 7/28/71, Robert Winfield, Mildred Wynne, Martha Rainey

                John and Agnes Wynne
Thomas, 11/4/65, John Sturdivant, Steth Wynne, Eliz. Wynne
Green, 11/4/65, Mathew Wynne, John Wellborn Jr., Lucy Ma-
    haney
Frances, 4/24/69, Steth Parham, Lucy Parham, Prissilla Wynne

                Wm. Wynne Jr. and Nancy
Hartwell, 12/6/74, Mathew and Steth Wynne, Anne Wynne

                William and Mary Wynne
Thomas, 2/19/41, Thos. Wynne, Wm. Yarbrough, Frances
    Robertson
Mary, 2/22/43, Wm. Richardson, Martha Richardson, Martha
    Ezell
Wm. Richardson, 9/28/46, Henry Holt, Wm. Green, Eliz. Green

                Mathew and Sarah Wynne
Martha, 1/11/43, Mathew Parham, Martha Parham, Eliz. Shands

WYNNE (Continued)
Mathew and Sarah Wynne (Continued)
Anne, 2/20/47, Robert Sandefour, Francis Wynne, Charity Clifton
Sloman, 5/24/50, Sloman Wynne, Henry Sturdivant, Prissilla Parham
Mathew, 5/7/54, Mathew Sturdivant, David Woodruff, Eliz. Parham
Bolling, 10/23/57, Wm. Stewart, Thos. Wynne, Eliz. Wynne
Salley, 12/8/58, Steth Parham, Anne Gilliam, Lucretia Nunn
John, 12/25/60, Sloman Wynne, John Wynne Jr., Mary Stewart

Sloman Wynne Jr. and Mary
Steth, 6/12/41, Thos. Thrower, Ben'g. Moss, Phoebe Thrower
John, 6/6/46, none given

Steth and Sarah Wynne
John, 10/4/62, Steth Parham, John Moss, Frances Moss
Gray, 6/23/67, Robert Wynne, Charles Sturdivant, Martha Wynne
Hamlin, 10/12/70, Eph. and Seth Moss, Jemima Hancock
Eliz., 2/12/74, John Sturdivant, Martha Sturdivant, Susanna Moss

Martha Wynne died 12/3/59, reported by Thomas Wynne

John and Frances Wynne
Lucy, 1/13/41, Chas. Partan, Anne Partan, Lucy Wynne
Aggy, 12/5/47, Mathew Wynne, Sarah and Betty Wynne

Wm. and Prissilla Wynne
Mathew, 3/15/59, Steth Wynne, Jesse Moss, Lucretia Parham

Eliz. Wynne and ----------
Robert, 7/16/59, none given
William, 12/17/62, Wm. and Charles Sturdivant, Fanny Sturdivant

John and Agnes Wynne
Thomas, 4/8/63, Mathew Wynne, John Wellborn Jr., Lucy Mahaney
Green, 11/4/65, John Sturdivant, Steth Wynne, Eliz. Wynne
Frances, 4/24/69, Steth Parham, Lucy Parham, Prissilla Wynne

Robert and Lucy Wynne
Buckner, 1/21/60, none given
Nancy, 5/7/75, Mose Knight, Mary Sturdivant, Mildred Wynne
Betty, 2/26/61, Steth Parham, Frances and Susanna Moss
Lucy, 12/18/62, Wm. Stewart, Mary Stewart, Judieth Tucker
Robert, 5/20/64, Peter Threewits, Wm. Sturdivant, Amy Threewits
Mathew, 7/3/65, Mathew Wynne, Wm. Wynne, Elenor Hobbs

WYNNE (Continued)

Robert and Lucy Wynne (Continued)

Peter, 10/11/69, Thos. Parham, Hollum Sturdivant, Sarah Wynne
Threewits, 1/8/71, John Sturdivant, Lucy Parker
Steth, 4/25/73, Drury Parton, Fred Freeman, Eliz. Sturdivant

John Wynne Jr. and Eliz.

Peter, 3/18/53, Thos. Wynne, Thos. Wynne Jr., Susanna Richardson
Mary, 8/23/57, Joseph Richardson, Martha Richardson, Mary Green

YARBROUGH

Lazarus and Anne Yarbrough

Mary, 1/14/42, Wm. Yarbrough, Mary Hix, Mary Dickens

Wm. and Mary Yarbrough

Mary, 6/21/46, Wm. Wynne, Eliz. Woodland, Winefred Smith

Wm. and Hannah Yarbrough

Patty, babt. 1768, none given
Wm., 3/15/75, Seymour Robertson, Chamberlain Jones, Susanna Jones
Rhoda, 9/18/73, Peter Cain, Rhoda Harewell, Mary Mitchell

Samuel and Mary Yarbrough

Mary, 10/19/73, Ambrose Brown, Mary Mitchell, Sarah Winfield

YEAROUT

John and Catherine Yearout

Robert, 5/9/52, Soloman Graves, Walter Beer, Sarah Graves

YOUNG

Thomas Young Jr. and Mary

Frederick, 7/11/52, John Tatum, Edward Epps, Mary Epps
Drury, 4/11/54, Nathan Beddingfield, Wm. Aldridge, Katherine McInnish
Joshuah, 9/10/56, Chris Tatum, Thos. Mitchell, Agnes Tatum
Rebbecca, 10/13/59, Wm. Shands, Rebbecca Denton, Anne Epps
Eppes, 4/8/62, Geo. Rives, Henry Dunn, Frances Temple

INDEX

DIGBIE, Judieth 89.
DIGGS, Wm. 11.
DILLARD, Thos. 102.
DINKINS, 36.
DIXON, Anne 48; Patty 65; Wellington 48.
DOBIE, DOBY, 36; Elenor 12-56-69; Eliz. 12-34-60-69; Hannah 36-108-Joseph 104; Mary 38-56-83-86-94-104-155; Nath. 94-147; Peter 130.
DOONE, 36.
DOWDEN, 37.
DOWDNING, DOWDNY, Amelius 106; Eliz. 127-142; Sarah 123-126; Thos. 141.
DRAKE, 37; Sarah 66.
DOWDY, 37, Eliz. 66; Lucy 66-71-127; Thos. 101-127.
DRINKARD, Francis 143,
DRIVER, Thos. 6.
DUFF, 37, Wm. 106.
DUNBARRE, John 100.
DUNCAN, 37; Agnes 118-126-152; Amy 113-118; Anne 104; Boyce 37; Danial 37-77; David 61-63; Eliz. 61; John 63; Joseph 31; Mely 126-140; Mild. 143; Miles 104-118; Nath. 2-14-25-36-7-63-152.
DUNN, 37-8; Agnes 67; Amy 2-14-37-86-94-107-128-155; Eliz. 12-35-87-93-141; Gray 4-105-148; Henry 158; John 2-27; Lavinia 38; Lewis 27-33-4-38-45-89-99-121-132; Lucy 2-14-38-45-50-47-79-87-101-129-131-139-140-155; Mary 38-87-101-89; Nath. 41-140; Rebb. 49-105-116-149; Ruth 148; Thos. 24-37-78-113; Vina 105; Wm. 3-25-37-8-80-86-7-92-95-121-138.

-E-

EATON, John 6-11-31-42-83; Rosanna 83.
ECCLES, ECHOLDS, 38; Betty 38; Ed. 125-153; Eliz. 48-52-105; John 136; Mary 41-96-118; Robt. 38; Susa. 38; Thos. 48.
ECKMAN, 39, Adam 37.
EDLESDISTA, 39, David 132.
EDMONDS, EDMUNDS, David 66-110; Eliz. 29-41-58; Gray 29-39-72-101; John 15-29-39-53-66-110; Judieth 9; Mary 39-58; Mely 143; Phylis 9-39-53-66; Prissilla 39-100-138; Rebb. 64-73; Sarah 143; Selah 142; Susa. 72-100.
EDWARDS, 39; Anne 139; Eliz. 38-93-97; Isaac 139; Mary 12.
ELDRIDGE, 39-40; Anne 39; Eliz. 39; John 40; Judieth 39-40; Martha 39-40-52-153; Mary 40-52; Thos. 40-52-75-77-111; Wm. 27-40-61-2-76.
ELLIOTT, Wm. 152.
ELLIS, 40-41; Anne 62; Beng. 4-15-40-41-81-100-122; Edmund 41; Ed. 60; Eliz. 4-15-6-74-115-122-130-146-156; Hannah 4-105; Henry 120; Jerimiah 122; John 40-42-43-50-67-125-126; Mary 125; Sarah 35-85-112; Susa. 85-100; Wm. 21-40-44-45-74-85-112-119-120-130-133-156.
EMERY, 41; Mary 103; Sarah 44.
ENSON, Mary 151.
EPPS, 41, Amy 25-49; Anne 36-92-95-97-103-140-158; Danl..36-90-130; Ed. 24-41-49-60-79-86-97-158; Eliz. 130; Francis 19-105-115; Jas. 98-140; Joseph 90; Mary 24-49-50-83-94-108-137-147-152-158; Phoebe 29-78-105; Reb. 53-119; Susa. 109-122; Wm. 39-55.
ESKRIDGE, 41.
EVANS, 42; Anne 11-63-83-85-89;

Elenor 31; Lucy 132-150; Martha 142; Prudence 142; Robt. 142; Sarah 83; Wm. 7-25-80-100-129.
EZELL, 42-3, Agnes 43-83-84; Amy 43; Anne 35-40-42-43-50-69-75-93-97-99-106-112-113-117-118-124-125-149-151; Eliz. 42-43-66-94-96-99-132-135-137-144; Geo. 20-41-43-86-101-106-140-151; Isam 99-101-103-109-132; James 11; Jane 46; John 29-40-42-45-47-58-66-86-112-125-127; Kesiah 154; Lemuel 47; Lucy 27-47; Martha 85-115-119-156; Mary 24-42-43-109-135; Moly 55; Sarah 58-118-151; Susa. 43-124; Tabitha 7-12-43-113; Thos. 3-43-45-58-101-124-125; Timothy 8-11-35-40-41-42-51-69-75-86-90-93-109-125-133-151; Wm. 43-83-84-96-109-113-135.
EXUM, 44, Beng. 44; Martha 128; Patty 128; Susa. 128.

-F-

FAISON, 44, Harry 130; Lucy 18.
FANNING, 44, Bryan, 96-124-137-148.
FARRINGTON, Ed. 12-35-44-119; Eliz. 35-119; John 53-119-123-4; Mary 16-42-44-54-116-150-153; Mrs. 54-55; Robert 44-48-55-116-119-145.
FAWN, 44, Anne 115; Jas. 70-140.
FELTS, 44-5-6; Agnes 19-45-128-Amy 45-142; Andrew 43-101-124; Anne 41-44-45-58-63-123-128; Betty 20; Burwell 124; Drury 108; Elinor 45-67; Eliz. 2-11-45-64; Frances 19-44-46; Fred. 45; Hannah 5-33-45-66-68-73-82-126; Helen 45; Isam 45; Jean 44-58-128; John 2-45-58-127; Kath. 76; Mary 20-43-45-58-64-107-123-125; Nath. 2-19-20-33-43-45-51-56-58-64-67-80-86-124-5-128-135-146; Rich. 2-34-89; Sarah 17-44-68; Suck 45-89; Susa. 42-47-124; Tabitha 45; Thos. 19-42-44-45-64-73-124-128-147; Wm. 10; Winefred 128.
FIELD, 46; Anne 48-58-100; Bathia 53; Bartholemew 46; Mary 44-48; Mild. 75; Milly 75; Parmelia 131; Rich. 58; Sarah 92; Theophilas 111.
FIGG, 46; Beng. 126.
FIGURES, 46, Bart. 102; Mary 9-14-23-72; Rebb. 72-102-118.
FIRE, FIER, FEAR, 46.
FISHER, Chas. 26; Eliz. 26; Hannah 83; Mary 26-30; Susa. 26.
FITCHET, Dedimus 46; Wm. 46.
FITZGERALD, Eliz. 72; Wm. 72.
FITZHUGH, Eliz. 77, Thos. 77.
FITZPATRICK, 46; Moses 148.
FLOOD, 47; Sarah 85.
FLOWERS, Rachael 143.
FLOYD, Maurice 52.
FLUELLEN, Wm. 77.
FONNEL, Rachael 63.
FORT, 47, Fred 8-20-84-85-99; John 5-87-99; Lucy 8-141; Mary 10-99.
FREEMAN, 47-8-9; Agnes 54-78-81-105-153; Amy 5-43-48-63-88-90-102-115-142-148; Anne 137; Arthur 47; Betty 63; Charlotte 22-48; Elenor 47; Eliz. 32-47-8-86; Frances 102; Fred. 96-124-136-7-158; Henry 35-48-49-148; Jemimah 38; Joel 20; John 44-56-115-122-134; Jones 41-47; Josiah 47-54-83; Kesiah 38; Lucy 19-41; Martha 21-38-75-88-96-115; Molly 47; Nath. 21-38; Patty 63-99-115-156; Phoebe 54-83-148; Prudence 63; Sally 5; Sarah 62-110; Sucky 154; Susa. 28-47-126; Thos. 47-56; Wm. 48-126.

-G-

GALE, Simon 11-90.
GARLAND, 49, Patty 3.
GARY, 49; Wm. 32.
GEARY, Eliz. 7; Rich. 148.
GEE, 49, Amy 3-49; Anne 13-98; Boyce 62; Bridgit 76; Capt. 49; Chas. 24-36-49-61-93-104-120-122; Eliz. 16-28-49-94-144; Henry 5-16-49-52-88-95-110-140-141; Mary 16-38-93; Sarah 61-62-92-93; Wm. 49.
GERRARD, Eliz. 108; Henry 77-146; Mary 77.
GIBBONS, 49-50; Anne 29-50-79-116-144-145; Capt. 8; Edmunds 111; Eliz. 50-78-105-131-153-145-152; John 81-133-140; Lawrence 26-41-49-50-78-82-91-111-116-142-149; Lucy 41-78-88; Mary 100-154; Rebb. 74-81; Thos. 97.
GIBBS, 50; Anna 58-69; Eliz. 49; Martha 14; Mathew 86-105; Parnel 103; Permillia 95.
GILBERT, 50; Anne 30-75-76-94; Eliz. 41-60-150; Ellis 43; Hannah 75; Jas. 76-80-95; John 10-75-76; Lucy 10-11-33-67-76-95-131-134; Martha 41-46-65-75-76-95-97-106-112; Wm. 45-50-72-75-83-141.
GILKS, 50.
GILLIAM, 50-1; Aggie 71-89; Agnes 45-88-89-113; Amy 10-47-85-87; Anne 4-10-11-106-115-122-134-157; Anslem 87-89-110-117-127; Betty 24-87; Burwell 11-47-85-86-87-89-115-142-151; Chas. 8-27-148; Drury 87; Edmund 45-89; Eliz. 23-47-75-102-112-113-115-152; Frances 147; Fortune 132; Hinchy 27-47-115; Isam 12-27-43-47-50-76-87-96-110-138-153; James 98; Jane 68; Jesse 68-83-109-132; John 27-34-48-57-81-89-95-96-106-110-115-123-134; Levi 47-68-75-76-81-83-115-148-155; Lucretia 84; Lucy 52-87-135-152; Lydia 55; Martha 93-148; Mary 10-48-65-71-75-85-87-90-96-110-115-132; Mely 53-71; Mild. 47-105; Patty 43; Phoebe 89; Prissilla 13-30-34-68-87-108-109-152-153; Rebb. 48-122; Ruth 60; Salley 96; Saml. 90; Sarah 45-70; Tabitha 47-66; Thos. 76-81-115-Warwick 36-63-69-137; Wm. 13-52-65-115; Womack 147.
GLOVER, 51; Frances 75-141; Jas. 19-92-97-141-150; Jones 47-131; Joseph 23-51; Mary 51-131; Robt. 12-38-132; Thos. 92.
GOLIGHTLY, 51-52; Amy 60; Chris. 128; Frances 128; John 51; Mary 95; Wm. 102-128.
GOOD, 52.
GOODWYNNE, 52, Amy 120; Hannah 52; Harwood 116; Jesse 49; Joseph 29; Mary 142; Thos. 52-76; Wm. 52; Winefred 49.
GORDAN, 52.
GOWAN, Jas. 100.
GRAIN, Soloman 53-65.
GRANTHAM, 52; Eliz. 12-19-62-81-85-118-123-152; Hannah 25; Wm. 127.
GRAY, Beng. 51; Jas. 51; Mary 12; Mild. 4-77; Susa. 74-77.
GRAVES, GROVES, 52; Beng. 108; David 28-76-110; Eliz. 67-144; Martha 47-141; Patty 125; Rachael 114; Rebb. 52; Sarah 153-158; Soloman 78-139-154-158; Wm. 52-510.
GREEN, 53-4-5; Burwell 42-49-88-132; Chas. 62; Eliz. 48-53-80-106-116-156; Fred. 18-9-41-48-54-56-63-70-72-115-116-151; Jane 20-70-72-88-116; Judieth 21-88-104-130; Jody 54; Letitia 70-105; Lucy 48-

70-91; Mary 13-54-72-88-103-145-
150-151-156-158; Nath. 35-41-44-
58-78-83; Olive 105-115-116-142;
Patty 36; Penelope 42-106; Peter
16-34-54-55-57-58-70-72-88-105-
115-116-119-142-145-154-154;
Wm. 48-53-90-105-121-123-124-
150-152-156.
GREENWAY, Jas. 153.
GREGG, Jane 117.
GRIFFIN, 55; Martha 83; Mary 86-
154; Olive 23; Saml. 154; Thos. 23.
GRIFFITH, GRIFFIS, 55; Anne 23-
63-129; Eliz. 81; Fanny 102; Mary
61; Saml. 61; Travis 33; Wm. 17.
GRIZZARD, Ambrose 73-101-102-
117; Eliz. 117; Mary 7-131; Pen-
rose 96; Sarah 99-102-119; Wm. 88.
GROSSE, Thos. 127.
GROSWIT, ,55; Anne 55; Thos. 55.
GRUSSETT, Anne 17-18; Marma-
duke 17; Thos. 67.
GRUB, Mary 96.
GUTHRIDGE, Anne 17.

-H-

HADDEN, 55; Guthridge 105.
HAGOOD, John 31; Mary 31.
HALE, HALES Beng. 9-31; John
45-67.
HALL, 55; Eliz. 24-31; Jas. 150;
Susa. 73-105; Thos. 51; Willis 24.
HALLEY, Eliz. 17.
HALSEY, Joseph 86-110.
HAMILTON, 56; Anne 38-60; Susa.
24.
HAMLIN, 56; Rich. 110; Sarah 14;
Steven 17-58.
HAMS, Eliz. 105; Lucy 50-123;
Mary 71; Sarah 66; Wm. 123.
HANCOCK, 56-7; Anthony 34-36-
56-155; Clement 2-56-134-156;
Eliz. 37; Hannah 67; Jemimma 49-
113-157; Lucy 48-56; Mary 2-48-54-
97-134-143; Rebb. 48; Robt. 47-76-
109-128-155.
HARDY, 57; Sarah 150; Wm. 63-
135-150.
HAREWELL, 57; Eliz. 80; Jas. 95;
Lucy 57-116; Mark 43-57-80; Mar-
tha 8; Mary 129; Mason 57-142;
Rhoda 158; Rich. 5; Saml. 108;
Sarah 57-128-144; Sterling 70.
HARGRAVE, 57, Anne 16; Aughus-
tine 56; Eliz. 33; Hulda 155; John
19-43-70-98-99; Thos. 102-112-
146-164.
HARLEY, Rivena 37.
HARNE, HARNES, Joseph 90; Lew-
is 102.
HARPER, 57; Anne 18-54-70-71;
Ed. 18-70; Martha 122; Mary 141;
Mely 57; Wm. 55-65; Wyatt 10-
71-105.
HARRARD, 58.
HARRIS, 58; John 11, Lewis 58;
Lucy 46-89-102-141; Mary 24; Patience 111; Rebb. 126; Wm. 20-45-
124.
HARRISON, HARRISSON, 58-59;
Agnes 142; Anne 27-58-75-106-129;
Beng. 27-34-86; Betty 2-56; Chas.
27; Cole 109; Eliz. 101; Henry 12-
52; Jas. 91; Jemima 68; John 2-
39-53-56-58-76-128; Joseph 99-
100; Lucy 66; Mary 28-58; Phoebe
133; Susa. 2-56-68-106-108.
HARWOOD, 59; Aggy 88; Agnes 88;
Amy 9-47-152; Anne 8-117; Danl.
9-59-87-88-99-127; Eliz. 5-22-43-
59-84-85-151; John 69; Joseph 117-
151; Kath. 34; Mary 30-51-88-90-
124-138; Phil. 14-87-88-99-127-
141; Rebb. 46-117-135-141; Saml.
9-84-88-103-111-117-124-129-141-

152; Sarah 5-40-108-151.
HATLEY, Eliz. 136; Hannah 81;
Shore 152.
HATTON, 59.
HAWTHORNE, 60; Eliz. 61; Fanny
60-100-149; Frances 60; Isaac 36;
Isam 84-90-122; John 60-147; Jo-
seph 36; Josh 14-35-36-60-69-147;
Nath. 40-147; Peter 14-37-60-83-
86-97-112-126-147-149; Rachael
14; Rebb. 14-18-37-60-93-97-149-
152; Sarah 60-86-97-126; Susa. 40.
HAY, 61; Alex 152; Anne 144; Dr.
93; Eliz. 23-86-114; Ester 131;
John 40-76; Judieth 13; Lucy 19;
Marg. 19-22-40-95-109; Mary 110;
Patience 31; Rich. 19-65-96-131;
Ruth 61; Sarah 31-114-144-150.
HEATH, HEETH, 61-62; Abraham
61-62-125; Anne 62; David 107;
Eliz. 61; Jas. 61-2; Jemima 62;
John 62; Joseph 61-62; Josiah 62;
Mary 61-62-155; Rebb. 24-61-62-
139-140; Rich. 61; Sarah 104-130;
Susa. 61-Thos. 62; Wm. 32-49-
61-62-139.
HERN, HORNE, 62-63; Eliz. 17-
62-66-75-83-85-121-132; Eph. 63;
James 7-35-62-108-121-132-149;
Jane 121-132-151; Jesse 63; John
63-75-145; Lewis 131; Lucy 51-63-
84; Lydia 63; Mary 7-63; Sarah 48-
89; 96-145; Susa. 28-62-71-121;
Thos. 63-108-121; Wm. 43-51-63-
80-85-99-113.
HEWETT, 63; Betty 13; Eliz. 13-
35; Mary 2-21-100-116-152.
HICKS, Christian 127; Eliz. 44;
Rubin 143; Salley 149; William 19-
44.
HIGHT, 63; Anne 31-58; Howell 22-
31-64; Johannah 10; John 33-60-64;
Julius 64; Sarah 63-75; Selah 31-
54-64-136; Susa. 63-118-146; Thos.
63; Wm. 31-58.
HILL, 64; Amy 65-70-102-148;
Anne 91-102-129-131-144; Beng. 7-
30-129-131; Betty 132; Burwell 35;
Chas. 146; Eliz. 19-30-83-136-149-
154; Eph. 64-107; Frances 90;
Green 94; Hannah 16-33; Jas. 43;
John 35-36-64-129; Judieth 31; Lucretia 65-148; Lucy 65-102-128;
Lydia 18; Marjorie 52-63-84-143;
Martha 65; Mary 13-20-30-32-42-
65-102-108-148-154; Mely 115;
Michael 42-65-90-102; Mild. 4-
21-35-54-102-108-119; Rich. 16-
50-52-64-65-143; Sarah 50-89-92-
129; Temperance 26; Wm. 2-19-
42-45-50-90-101-124-128-135-141.
HINES, 66; Anne 26; Christian 37-
66; David 37-66; Eliz. 26-66-98-
106; Fred. 8-26-39-66-106-138;
Hartwell 26; Henry 26-142; John
78-98-133; Mary 66-110; Olive 26-
39; Rebb. 66-74-109; Rich. 110;
Salley 66; Sarah 26-39; Susa. 66;
Thos. 66; Wm. 26-66-75-108-146.
HIX, 66-67; Anne 80; Christian 126;
Eliz. 86; Faith 62; Hannah 108-141.
Jas. 66; Jenny 67; John 60; Joseph
32-66; Mary 8-9-31-52-65-67-86-
99-108-123-127-141-146-153-158;
Robt. 20-60-67-86-139-147; Priss.
67; Tubal 45; Wm. 7-17-45-53-62-
68-87-108-127-141.
HOBBS, 67-68; Elinor 44-145-152-
157; Eliz. 67; Fred. 44; Joseph 67;
Kath. 9; Katy 2; Mason 150; Sarah
2-67-75-141; Selah 150; Thos. 38-
140.
HOGAN, Beng. 74; Rebbecca 127.
HOGWOOD, 68; Geo. 5-67; Moseley
117.
HOLLAND, Eliz. 71.
HOLLOM, Guthridge 105.

HOLLOMAN, Joseph 85; Martha
85.
HOLLOWAY, 68; Eliz. 115; Sarah
12.
HOLT, 68; Abby 13; Anne 5-71-86-
113; Chas. 12-71-101-117; Fred.
86-117; Henry 129-156; Nath. 4-
108-110-117-135; Thos. 5-27-38-
117.
HOOD, 68-69; Anne 84-136; Eliz.
151-154; Frances 150; John 36-102-
149-150; Lucretia 69-104; Lucy 83;
Nath. 34-35-62-82-104-108-120-
149-150; Pamelia 56; Ruth 63; Sally
28; Sarah 12-35-62-90-104-121-
150.
HOOPER, Jas. 98.
HORN, 69; Eliz. 68; James 68-
99-150; Jane 84; Lucy 84; Mary
51; Sarah 75; Thos. 136; Wm. 11-
63-108.
HORNSBY, Thos. 112.
HORTON, 69; Amos 69; Danial 147.
Eliz. 69; Martha 73; Sarah 69.
HOUSE, John 105; Thos. 100.
HOWELL, 69; Hannah 133; 156;
Susa. 149; Wm. 66.
HUBBARD, 69; Mary 10-73-109;
Math. 6-10-61-109-117-144; Rebb.
84; Sarah 90; Thos. 6.
HUFF, 69.
HULIN, 69; Eliz. 55; Martha 44;
Olive 81; Patty 140.
HUMPHREY, Chas. 112.
HUNT, 70; Beng. 156; Betty 110-
138-Dorothy 8-126; Eliz. 70; John
70; Mary 70; Nancy 70; Sarah 70-
106-111; Susa. 133; Thos. 20-21-
54-82-126-131-142; Wm. 54.
HUNTER, 70; David 4-18-39-100;
Hartwell 32-75; Patty 141; Sarah
33; Wm. 32-37-84-107.
HUSKINS, Mary 75.
HUSON, 71; Fanny 84; Lucy 27;
Mary 17; Samson 144; Selah 102;
Tapenns 27; Thos. 13-57-82-105-
152.
HUTCHENS, 71; Anne 68-71; Eph.
43-89-93-117; Frances 35-67-8-
71-109-135; Howell 39; Jane 27;
John 71-117-135; Lewis 45-53;
Lydia 129; Martha 39-41-69; Mary
119; Sarah 35; Wm. 22-31-62-68-71-
83-85-97-115-129; Winefred 37;
Winney 28.
HUTTON, Goodrich 86.
HYDE, 72; Beng. 87; Mary 12;
Rebb. 16-140.

-I-

INGRAM, 72; Angelica 116; Frances 54-119; Francina 54-115; Joseph 54-108-116; Mary 16-72-88.
IRBY, 72; Eliz. 125; Hugh 72; John
15-17-74-79-100-108-113-122-125-
146; Mary 15-39; Thos. 72; Wm. 4
IVY, IVEY, 72-73, Amy 61-63-72-
73-75-127; Anne 45-72-73-112;
Christian 80; Dan;. 30-67; Ede 73;
Eliz. 32-72-73-74-76-7; Henry 73-
132; Jas. 3; John 47-72-3; Lucy 73;
Mely 80; Prissilla 73; Rebb. 67-73;
Sarah 33; Thos. 33-72-75-76; Winney 36.

-J-

JACKSON, 73; Chas. 38; David 140;
Edward 149; Henry 13-54-68; Lucy
118; Robt. 91; Susa. 68.
JAMES, 74; Abner 18; Anne 41;
Emanuel 40-102-123; Michael 18-
Nath. 74; Sarah 134.
JARRETT, 74; Cherry 9; Eliz. 10-
16-74-107-143-146; Fred. 55-74-
81; Henry 25-39-66-74-77-89-79-

164

MASON, 92; Anne 34-51-106;
Chris. 29-92-97; David 7-10-27-
34-37-8-51-56-61-67-70-78-88-
93-4-97-109-119-121; Davis 89;
Eliz. 25-34-80-88-92-3-101-108-
121-143; Frances 97; Henry 112;
Isaac 12-93-106; 111-134-155;
James 34-67-92-3-97-128-137;
Jane 49-121; John 2-12-16-25-34-
70-80-82-3-101-121-144-151; Joseph 29-31-34-36-49-67-83-87;
Levi 129; Littlebury 73-92; Lucretia 109; Mary 16-34-38-51-67-
88-92-3-102-109-127-140; Phoebe
29; Rebb. 92-3-101-121-144-146;
Rich. 73-96; Samson 68; Sarah 8-
110-141; Wm. 49-92-93-105; Wyn-
efred 143.
MASSENBURG, Col. 4; Eliz. 26-
46-121; John 23; Lucy 22-105-121;
Nich. 22-120; Rich. 130.
MASSENGALE, Danl. 46-67; Eliz.
46; Jas. 67; Lucy 59; Martha 8-
131; Nich. 59.
MATHEWS, Beng. 105-145; Eliz.
35; Jas. 8-35; Lucy 115.
MEACUM, 93-4; Anne 86-97;
Banks 38-94-98; Eliz. 43-49-86-
94; Frances 93; Henry 93-4-97-
112; John 2; Joshua 97-112; Mar-
tha 98; Mary 97-118-122.
MEANLEY, Wm. 19.
MEGGS, Eliz. 23.
MELTON, Israel 35.
MILNER, Jas. 91.
MILLER, Jas. 110-138.
MILTON, John 35.
MITCHELL, 93-4; Amy 52-95;
Anne 139-144; Branch 95; Cath. 8;
Chas. 78; Dorothy 22; Drusilla
156; Eliz. 94-97-139; Henry 95-116-
135-139; John 66-144; Mary 158;
Nath. 67-95; Prissilla 41-139;
Reaps 3; Robt. 21; Sarah 97; Tabitha 39-95-102-144; Thos. 38-56-
92-95-111-120-158; Wm. 16-41-
53-54-72-80-115.
MONTGOMERY, 95; Eliz. 49-76;
MOODY, Mary 78; Thos. 62.
MOORE, 95-6; Anne 12-13-27-
74-87-96-111-144-148; Barham
96-155; Betty 113; Eliz. 99-110-
155; Epps 12-41-50-61-86-97-
144; Francis 58-67-120; Lucy 61-
94; Martha 34-52-92-96-98-109-
110-120-144; Michael 74; Mary
14-41-71-76-83-110-128-136-140;
Phoebe 87-98; Rebb. 96; Sarah
110-115-123; Susa. 2-34-41-62-
92-120; Susan 140; Thos. 27-38-
43-49-52-66-75-84-87-95-110-
128-127-140-148-155; Wm. 96-
144-152-155.
MOORING, Lucy 23
MORELAND, Helen 86.
MORGAN, 96; Eliz. 28; Mary 31.
MORRIS, 96; Eliz. 156; Marjory
56; Mary 142; Tabitha 135; Thos.
139.
MORRISON, Marjory 118.
MOSELEY, Sampson 43-59-99-
117-133-151.
MOSS, 97-8; Agnes 134; Amos 34;
Amy 5-36-47-141-150; Beng. 14-
36-63-97-141-157; David 143; Eliz.
31-61-83-99-128-130-143; Eph.
2-44-97-113-121-157; Gabrial 97;
Hannah 50; Henry 2-83-94-97-8-
112-130-136-143; Jas. 97; Jesse
140-157; John 2-20-3p-36-64-5-
66-84-91-83-97-112-3-118-121-
129-140-143-157; Josh. 44-93-
143; Lucy 63-117-148; Martha 86-
58-96; Mary 25-38-41-97-112-
122-125-128-139-143; Nancy 130;
Ruth 83-95-98; Salley 155; Sarah
24-31-37-58-66-97-101-118-128-

143; Steth 90-136-157; Susa. 13-
94-97-134-157; Thos. 2-8-31-33-
75-77-102-128-143; Wm. 9-25-
29-47-63-86-7-97-107.
MULLINS, 98.
MUMFORD, Thos. 124; Wm. 80.
MURPHEY, 98; Arthur 146; Mary
57; Rich. 57-62-89; Simon 17-110-
127.
MURRY, Anne 39.
MUSSELWHITE, 98; Thos. 86.
MYERS, Lucy 133.
MYHAM, Terrance 7.
MYRICK, Anna 10; Eliz. 13-78;
John 53-81; Mrs. 10; Owen 10;
Wm. 10.

-N-

NANTS, Martha 16.
NASH, 98.
NATTY, Eliz. 109.
NELSON, 98.
NEWMAN, Winney 150.
NEWSOM, 98-9; Aggy 5-99; Agnes
117; Alice 9-80-99-146; Ede 68-
99; Eliz. 51-114-117; Fanny 99;
Jemima 93; Jesse 5; Lanier 84;
Lewis 76-96; Lucy 117-148; Mar-
tha 13-84; Mary 99; Mild. 9; Mil-
ly 5; Nath. 8-9-20-27-37-47-80-
84-88-90-93-96-141-155; Peggy
110-138; Polly 5; Robt. 64-5-134-
137-150; Sampson 112; Sucy 88;
Susa. 11-135; Thos. 55-87-93;
Wm. 47-83-103; Winefred 108.
NIBLET, 99-100; Eliz. 106; Fran-
cis 2-14-86-98-106-149.
NICHOLS, Lucy 102.
NICHOLSON, 100, Eliz. 4-33-77-
100; Flood 100-106; Floyd 100; Harris 15-56-100; Henry 25-73; John
4-15-30-50-100-106; Lucy 81;
Mark 85-100; Mary 39-73-106;
Rich. 56; Robt. 15-25-53-100-112-
130; Wm. 15-33-77-100-109.
NORRIS, Lucy 151; Mary 16.
NORTH, Amos 129; Hannah 6.
NORTHCROSS, NOTHCROSS, 100-
1; Abigail 101; Hannah 11-101-154;
Jas. 11-101; Jane 154; Peter 105;
Rich. 6; Tabitha 6; Thos. 75-88-
151.
NORTHINGTON, 101; Anne 52;
Cam'l. 12; Eliz. 13-101; Jabes
101; Jas. 145; Nathan 13-47-118-
128-145; Nath. 37-89-134-155;
Philis 6-13-15; Prissilla 117; Saml.
42-97-101-108-140; Sarah 68; Ster-
ling 12.
NORTON, Alice 114; Joseph 114.
NUBINS, Anne 43.
NUNN, NUNS, 101; Danl. 16; Eliz.
13-16; John 130; Lucretia 157;
Mary 11-16-28-38-105-147; Thos.
139.

-O-

OGBURN, 101-102; John 19-31-
32-72-102-111; Phoebe 111; Rich.
8-98; Sally 135; Sarah 4-102; Thos.
102-134.
OLIVER, 102; Agnes 60-114-132-
137; Anne 115; Drury 26; Eliz. 17-
21-137; Frances 26-91-112-148;
Isaac 105; John 90-105; Lucy 7-77-
102; Mild. 102; Sucky 125-132; Susa. 24-42; Thos. 137-149; Wm. 6-
26-42-137.
ONIE, Eph. 139.
OWEN, 102; Beng. 43-51-101-103-
115-132; Betty 124; Boyce 124; David 58-102-3-124-137-135; Eliz.
28-63-68-102-145; Fred. 63-102-
136-150; Hannah 23-68-130; Hulda
13; John 13-23-43-62-3-83-101-

103-124-132-147-150-1; Lydia 124-
5; Mary 63-123-4-Rebb. 101; Robt.
43-54-63-102-3-145; Sarah 63-102;
Wm. 68-130-132.

-P-

PAINTER, 103-4; John 2-11-14-
60-67-82-3-102; Mary 139; Rich.
64; Susa. 118.
PARE, 104; Aggie 104; Anne 80-
91-104; Eliz. 136; John 28-80-106;
Martha 132; R bb. 104; Thany 30;
Vina 133-150; Wm. 28.
PARHAM, 104-5; Abraham 39-104;
105; Anne 3-24-48-53-59-96-104;
Drury 99; Eliz. 71-86-104-5-115-
116-157; Eph. 73-104-5-143; Frances 65-105-131-139; Geo. 91; Hannah 13-84; James 106; Jane 2-105;
John 59; Lucretia 38-135-157; Lucy
48-156-7; Martha 105-135-156;
Mary 28-57-105-137; Math. 13-35-
54-5-105-117-144-156; Mild. 122;
Nath. 19-38-65-78-104-111-139-
143; Peter 100; Phoebe 48-78-105-
122; Prissilla 13-95-105; Rebb.
20-38-105-145; Sarah 97; Selah
20-38; Steth. 49-105-156-7; Susa.
148; Thos. 3-53-57-68-93-95-104-
105-136-158; Wm. 8-29-38-50-54-
71-78-104-5-131-136-143-149.
PARISH, Jas. 41.
PARKER, 106; Boyce 2; Drury 6-
9-17; Eliz. 111; Fred. 59; John 74;
Lucy 158; Mary 10-76-77-106-111;
Rebb. 130; Rich. 26; Sarah 77-79-
109-110; Susa. 111; Thos. 110; W
Wm. 111.
PARSONS, 106; Amy 126; Eliz.
106; Mary 99-118-149; Robt. 106-
126; Wm. 3-58-126-147.
PARTON, PARTAN, 106-107; Anne
82-157; Chas. 157; Drury 92-104-
158; Jesse 104; Johanna 106-137;
Mary 28-104; Mild. 92-104; Wm.
58-106-7-137.
PARTRIDGE, 107, Eliz. 2-7-8-9-
26-107-108-112-129; Jesse 7-9-
107; Mary 9-50-107-141-151; Nich.
2-10-14-32-107-112-139; Rich. 4-
7-9-101; Sarah 107-146-148; Thos.
33; Wells 2-3-111; Wm. 7.
PASSMORE, Eliz. 50-149; Geo.
50;
PATE, 107; Anne 11-21-30-107-
126; Edmund 38-65-73-99-107-125-
126; Ed. 73-107-144-154; Eliz. 21-
80-107; John 31-59-73-80-127;
Mary 55-59-61-65-66-90-117-141-
151; Mely 108; Mild. 108; Ruth
108; Saml. 108; Sarah 107-141-
151; Thos. 20-80-127-129-146.
PATRICK, 108.
PATTERSON, 108; Anne 90-148;
Geo. 72.
PEEBLES, 108-9; David 108; Eliz.
14-61-114-125; Henry 25-129;
Mary 92-129; Nath. 83; Patty 122;
Sarah 25-107-129; Thos. 101-128-
129; Wm. 107-8-129.
PEERMAN, Lucretia 42; Lucy 42.
PEET, PEETS, Mary 15-110;
Saml. 6; Thos. 106.
PIERSON, John 84.
PENNINGTON, 109-110; Anne 69;
Edmund 56; Eliz. 13-26-36-104-
110; Faith 43-96-109; Hannah 30-
56-109; Howell 69-152; John 87-
89-104-109-117-132-155; Joseph
13-34-104-109-149; Josuah 110-153;
Leah 87; Lucretia 155; Lucy 13-
71-110; Lydia 84-87-8-110-148;
Martha 28; Mary 109; Molly 86;
Moses 110-155; Moss 109; Rebb.
109; Salley 86-104-110; Sarah 47;
Thos. 69-81-109-115.